S Q U A D S   W R I T E !

"THE GIRL WE'RE ALL FIGHTING FOR," FROM THE DRAWING BY PRIVATE C. LEROY BALDRIDGE
IN THE STARS AND STRIPES FOR MAY 10, 1918

Squads Write!

A SELECTION OF THE BEST THINGS
IN PROSE, VERSE AND CARTOON
FROM

THE STARS AND STRIPES

OFFICIAL NEWSPAPER OF THE A. E. F.

Edited

and with not too Serious Comment

by

JOHN T. WINTERICH

Fully Illustrated

HARPER & BROTHERS PUBLISHERS
NEW YORK AND LONDON
1931

E000154021

101 062 142

940.497 WINT

Q940.49 WIN.

M31603

★

TO THE MEMORY OF

LIEUTENANT W. F. MILTENBERGER
SERGEANT FIRST CLASS DAVID R. BAWDEN
PRIVATE FIRST CLASS HOMER G. ROLAND
PRIVATE CARL D. McINTOSH

WHO DIED IN FRANCE WHILE SERVING ON THE STAFF OF
THE STARS AND STRIPES

CONTENTS

ILLUSTRATIONS

SQUADS WRITE!

CHAPTER ONE

A LABEL FOR AN ARMY

Three men—Private Hudson Hawley, Field Clerk James A. Britt, and Corporal John T. Winterich—were the founders of *The Stars and Stripes*. All three had had training in the making of newspapers—Winterich had been one of the editors of the *Springfield Republican*. At Neufchâteau one winter night early in 1918 these three foregathered to descant upon the growing American Expeditionary Forces and—like the fraternity of reporters the world over—to talk shop; and these men agreed that the chief need of the expedition was an agency that might put the various American military elements in France in touch with each other, tell every man what the expanding force was like and what it was trying to do, and build homogeneity and singleness of purpose within the expedition such as no other agency could evoke—in short, the A.E.F. needed a newspaper. The idea was communicated to General Pershing, who promptly approved it. Thus was *The Stars and Stripes* officially born.—
From "DEMOBILIZATION," *sixth and last volume in the series* "HOW AMERICA WENT TO WAR," *by Benedict Crowell, Assistant Secretary of War and Director of Munitions, and Robert Forrest Wilson, Formerly Captain, United States Army. New Haven: Yale University Press, 1921.*

I HAVE no right to speak for Hudson Hawley and James A. Britt (by whom is intended, beyond peradventure, George W. B. Britt), but for myself I can categorically affirm that I was never a corporal, have never been in Neufchâteau, had been "one of the editors of the *Springfield Republican*" only by the ultimate distention of that superelastic term, and had nothing whatsoever to do with the founding of *The Stars and Stripes*. The picture, however, even with me out of it, remains sufficiently engaging. Hawley and Britt, I make no doubt, foregathered on not one but many winter nights in Neufchâteau, and returned to quarters well after Taps roaring segments of Gilbert and Sullivan and trying to pronounce homogeneity.

The way of the historian of the contemporary or nearly contemporary scene is infinitely harder than that of the transgressor—one can say him nay *viva voce*, and how delighted any of us is to do it! And if a fragment of "How America Went to War" seems to have been singled out for special condemnation, let it be explained at once that the Crowell-Wilson chronicle offers a far more detailed and significant appraisal of the work of *The Stars and Stripes* than does any other important portrayal of America's war effort that has yet appeared. The present compilation of extracts from *The Stars and Stripes* is offered not as formal history, but as an *olla podrida* of informal quotation bulwarkedy and supplement the quotations them- principal excuse for inclusion is to amplif by notes of personal reminiscence whose selves.

The Stars and Stripes was the official newspaper of the American Expeditionary Forces. The first number appeared on February 8, 1918, and the seventy-first and last on June 13, 1919.

So much is demonstrable, incontestable, authentic. But *The Stars and Stripes* could obviously have never been established unless some one had had the idea of establishing it and then executed the idea. *The Stars and Stripes* was anybody's idea—an idea, certainly, that burgeoned in the brain of about every newspaperman in the A. E. F. and many outside it, burgeoned but did not blossom.

The first American officer to occupy the unenviable post of chief press censor of the A. E. F. was Lieutenant-Colonel Frederick Palmer. Grown wise in the ways of correspondents and of headquarters staffs alike through a generation of reporting in most of the troubled corners of the world, Colonel Palmer was alert to the advantages of expression and suppression alike. The more accurately he maintained himself at a fixed point centrally posited between the devil and the deep sea the better he was doing his job. He was heavily outnumbered on both flanks; he needed help and got it. His staff was gradually augmented, and among the earliest increments was Second-Lieutenant Guy T. Viskniskki, late of Camp Meade and the Seventy-ninth Division. Viskniskki (to be known hereinafter in these indentures as Visk) was able, like Palmer, to see both sides of the shield. He was an old soldier as military age was reckoned in 1917, having served as a sergeant of Engineers in Porto Rico during the Spanish-American War, and he was also a veteran newspaper syndicate executive.

Visk was one of the everybodies who thought it would be fine to have an army newspaper. Visk's title to immortality consists in the fact that he wound the idea up and made it tick. Aided by Palmer's good offices, Visk received from headquarters three not particularly rousing cheers and permission to go ahead—permission and not much else. Plant, paper supply, staff—these and related appurtenances he was left to provide through his own ingenuity. These assembled, he could toy with the problems of circulation and distribution. How he managed it is a story he alone has the right to tell, and I hope that some day he will tell it. It will be the story of a nebulous hunch that developed into one of the triumphs of publishing history.

The Stars and Stripes was two weeks old when I reported for duty in the publication offices in the Hôtel Ste.-Anne in Paris, close to the Palais Royale and the Louvre. Here, in a commandeered and converted bedroom, all but crowding each other out into the corridor, Visk and two other lieutenants, Charles Phelps Cushing of the Marines and William K. Michael of the Infantry, were laboring to produce a third, fourth, and, it was hoped, subsequent issues. The editorial enlisted personnel consisted, at the moment, of Private Hudson Hawley, a dismantled machine-gunner from the Twenty-sixth Division who had formerly contributed to the *joie de vivre* of the city room of the *Hartford Times* and the *New York Sun*. Private Abian A. Wallgren, a cartoonist who for years had shuttled back and forth from one Philadelphia newspaper to another, had reached Paris three days earlier

"A NEWLY MINTED CORP'RAL, COMIN' DOWN THE LINE," DRAWN BY PRIVATE WALLGREN TO
ACCOMPANY VERSES BY PRIVATE HAWLEY

from some remote warren of the Fifth Marines, paid a brief visit to the office, and forthwith been swallowed up in one of the twenty *arrondissements*.

Private Hawley, despite the scarcity of elbow room, was contriving to produce a prodigious quantity of material destined for publication. He had written most of the first two numbers of *The Stars and Stripes* and stood ready to write the next two hundred. Owing to the newsprint shortage, the newspapers of Paris were limited to four pages on five days a week and to two pages—a single sheet—on the remaining two. As long as Hawley was turning out copy, not so much the freedom as the very life of the Parisian press was at stake.

The first dozen and more issues of *The Stars and Stripes*, sent out from the clamor of the Hôtel Ste.-Anne to those groping, scattered units which comprised the infant

A. E. F., seem to me, when I now glance through them, rather unimpressive emanations. There is a faint scent of the college annual—sometimes even of the high-school annual—about them. (This statement is going to produce an indignant collect cable from Hawley, A.B., Yale, 1914, who at last accounts was in Rome.) There is the taint of the house organ, of the pep-punch-personality school—the odor, not exactly of sanctity, but of pedagogy.

Now, thirteen years later, the explanation is rather palpable. The war, so far as America was concerned (America in France perhaps even more than America at home), had not yet emerged from the lark stage. A single division had had a taste of the front line; a second was entering the line as the first number of *The Stars and Stripes* went to press. Blood had been shed—just enough blood so that, had the war ended that February, we of the earliest A. E. F. could have come back each wearing a vicarious red badge of courage. The only real peril lay in the passage of the Atlantic—that achieved, one set foot on French soil almost with hilarity, convinced that the worst was over. One would soon be home again after a pleasant and moderately exciting European excursion—something that in dull, normal times people paid money for. America had made good her threat to put men in France —that would be enough to bring Germany to her knees. We had called the Kaiser's bluff with a counter-bluff; he would soon be crying, "Peace! Peace!" and there would be peace. As a finale to the whole rather protracted episode there was to be a "spring offensive" under British and French auspices (with perhaps a few complimentary tickets issued to picked American units) which would end the war, worse luck, before we could catch up with it. A few of the singularly fortunate among us might hear the whine of a shell and have something to talk about, next summer and forever after, in Bridgeport or Peoria or Sacramento. Meanwhile, so far as the payroll permitted, we would eat, drink, and be merry, but tomorrow we should not die.

A discordant note had sounded with the explosion of the torpedo that sank the transport *Tuscania* on February 5th. Germany, somebody remarked, was playing for keeps. Here, for the first time, we suffered a loss in bulk. A corporal and two privates of the First Division had been killed in action in November and their names were blazoned to the world—they were headlines. Now, with two hundred and ten lost with the *Tuscania*, we had a casualty list, which was a little different.

Meanwhile, so far were we as yet from the full stature of an army that we did not even have a name for ourselves. *The Stars and Stripes* sought to remedy this defect in its second number. It printed a Signal Corps photograph of a smiling American private (I wonder who he was, and what became of him) with the caption: "A Picture Without a Title." Below it appeared half a column of text which summarily disposed of "Sammy" and "Amex" as suitable designations for the American soldier, but offered nothing in their place, preferring to have the A. E. F. speak for itself. (I regret to note that in the very next issue "Amex" got into a top head, and if I didn't write it Cushing must have.)

The A. E. F. was slow in speaking. It had not yet got into the habit of writing letters to the editor—subsequently it became one of the best composite letters-to-the-editor writers in American history. A solitary communication on the subject got into print in the fourth number:

> To the Editor of *The Stars and Stripes*:— Re "A Picture Without a Title" in today's *Stars and Stripes*. Call 'em "Glories," or, in singular, "Glory"; collectively, "Glory Boys," keeping in mind the chorus of "John Brown's Body," "Glory, Glory, Hallelujah."

Happily this suggestion did not budge an inch.

In the issue for March 29th appeared, under the title "Down With Sammie" (we seem never to have quite made up our minds whether it should be "Sammy" or "Sammie"), the following editorial:

> A Sammie may be defined as an American soldier as he appears in an English newspaper or a French cinema flash. It is a name he did not invent, does not like, never uses and will not recognize. When he sees it in the papers from home, it makes him sick. The American doughboy has had his baptism of fire, but he has not yet been christened.
>
> The name "Sammie" was ineffectually wished on our troops the day of their arrival in France. The French soldiers had been "poilus" and the British "Tommies" since long before 1914, but, like the Australians, the Americans arrived nameless in France. It was not long, to be sure, before the gallant band that sailed from under the Southern Cross had become known the world around as the "Anzacs," but this was used so fulsomely after Gallipoli that the boys themselves acquired a distaste for it, and of late have taken to describing themselves as "Aussies." "Aussie," then, is now the fashion, and some day the A. E. F. will, literally, make a name for itself. Some day it will find a substitute for the unsatisfactory, the really painful, "Sammie."
>
> When, in the fullness of time, the American army has been welded by shock and suffering into a single fighting force, with one mind, one heart and one spirit, the American soldier will find his name. It will be the inspiration of some ambulance-driver, perhaps, or the outburst of some eloquent cook. It will strike the fancy of a passing guard and be forwarded through military chan-

nels like a sentry's call. Wounded boys will carry it back to base hospitals and ammunition-train drivers will spread it to the base ports. Some reporter will hear it at some distant bar and put it into the story he has to write that night. It will be printed in America. Paragraphers and cartoonists and vaudeville comedians will use it. It will be caught up at home and in the training camps.

"A CROSS-COUNTRY EVENT," BY WALLGREN (BELIEVED TO BE AN AUTOBIOGRAPHICAL FRAGMENT)

The name will be fastened on. The American soldier will have been christened. He does not know now what that name will be. He simply knows it won't be "Sammie."

No inspired ambulance-driver or eloquent cook rose to the occasion. Neither did anyone trouble to point out that the reason why the Australian resented the application of "Anzac" to himself was that "Anzac" meant "Australia-New Zealand

Army Corps," and an Australian is not a New Zealander. Neither did anyone seem to resent the reference to American soldiers as "boys"—*The Stars and Stripes* of its own accord soon purged itself of this trace of paternalism.

The business was not resumed in print until three weeks later, having served meanwhile as a topic for involved debate in the editorial office. Visk was strong for "doughboy." "Doughboy" had long been the shining hallmark of the American infantryman. Its origin has never been satisfactorily explained, but it dates back certainly as far as the Civil War, and may have sprung from the fact that the Federal infantryman sometimes received a flour ration from which to construct his own bread. Custer used the expression, employing it clearly to define foot-soldiers as distinguished from mounted troops. It was gaining currency and probably losing some of its technical individuality in the World War army—Hawley, for no known reason, had instituted departments called "Etiquette Hints for Doughboys" and "A Doughboy's Dictionary" in early issues of *The Stars and Stripes*.

The staff indorsed Visk's views heartily—not every view, but this one, at all events. "Doughboy" was good American; it had tradition behind it; it was gaining a degree of somewhat confused acceptance. The campaign was launched in the issue for April 19th with an editorial called, "We're All Doughboys":

> A letter in the editor's mail signed "Subscriber"—we are too young to get letters from "Old Subscriber"—asks tartly if we are aware that there are other kinds of soldiers in this army besides doughboys. Answer: We are not. As we read the definition in the dictionary known as "General Usage," a doughboy is an American soldier—any American soldier.
>
> More and more in the training camps and in the trenches, over there and over here, the name "doughboy" is attaching itself to every living man who wears the olive drab. Time was when it was applied only to enlisted infantrymen. Time was when there was a suggestion of good-natured derision in it. But of late, with the original doughboys in the very vanguard of the A. E. F., the name appears insensibly to have taken on a new accent of respect. Infantrymen and artillerymen, medical department boys and signal corps sharks, officers and men alike, all of them are called doughboys and some of them are rather proud of it. Our cartoonist—leatherneck though he is—is a doughboy. So is General Pershing. So are we all of us.
>
> If "Subscriber" does not like the name, he need not cancel his subscription, because, after all, it was no doing of ours. If a better name—"Yanks," perhaps—gets into circulation, we shall use it. If, on the other hand, "doughboy" should

in time become the universal name for the American soldier, we cannot claim to
have invented it.

We have only one claim to fame. It is this. Never, so help us, have we nause-
ated and unnerved a doughboy by calling him a Sammie.

No loud and sustained applause greeted this inferentially epochal declaration. A
few Marines seemed somewhat sullenly resentful, but concluded that the announcement did not carry enough weight to merit the dignity of starting an argument
about it.

Two weeks later, in the May 3d issue, appeared on the editorial page a piece of
special correspondence from London under the heading "Yank." The correspond-
ence really was special; the correspondent was George T. Bye of the Reciprocal
News Service. For the earliest issue (Hawley, try as he might, simply could not
write the whole paper) Visk had made heavy drafts on the good will of numerous
American correspondents in France—Lincoln Eyre of the *New York World*, Junius
B. Wood of the *Chicago Daily News*, Frank P. Sibley of the *Boston Globe*, W. S.
Ball of the *Providence Journal*, W. J. Pegler of the United Press, C. C. Lyon of the
Newspaper Enterprise Association, Herbert Corey of the Associated Newspapers,
Norman P. Draper of the Associated Press, and Henry G. Wales of the Interna-
tional News Service—and Bye had been nominated to cover us in Great Britain.
He outlasted all the other civilian writers for *The Stars and Stripes*, for with the
growth of our own staff we were soon able to handle all France like a city news
department. Bye's contribution to the problem of nomenclature was this:

There is both rhyme and reason for calling Ay-Ee-Effers in Europe "Yanks,"
say those-who-twitch-their-noses-at-the-sound-of-"Sammy" who have been long
enough in this comfortable part of the Great Arena to make up their minds.

Any reliable thesaurus will show that Yank has a rhyming affinity with many
such words as

Bank	Hank	Sank
Crank	Lank	Swank
Dank	Rank	Tank

"And Yank is the name applied to us by England and France before the war,
though the French made it 'Yanqui,'" said Captain Q——. What is important
about Captain Q——'s opinion in the matter is that he had been over here, as
an American observer with General Haig, long before the first boat loaded
with American fighting men reached these shores.

"I'm from Virginia," continued Captain Q——, "and there was a time when a Virginian would have felt he was being called a foreigner if anyone applied 'Yank' to him. But I rather like Yank now, and when it comes to a choice between Yank and Sammy, there can be only one answer.

"Maybe a few battles will evolve something else, but I'm afraid we'll stay Yanks just as the British fighter has remained Tommy Atkins."

"Yank" is the unanimous vote at the base section here.

Bye's confusion of a thesaurus with a rhyming dictionary was deplorable and can be forgiven only if one consider the exigencies of war—equally deplorable was the spelling *theosaurus*, the work of Mr. Bye or another, which I have corrected in the

"THE YANKS ARE COMING!" FROM THE DRAWING BY CAPTAIN WALLACE MORGAN

transcription. (There will be no *sics*, by the way, in this book. The misprints of war days will uniformly be corrected, and anyone who requires them—they were few enough—will have to consult an original file of *The Stars and Stripes*.)

"Yanks" unquestionably was gaining ground, not by the conscious incubation of propaganda, but by usage. The very issue in which the "We're All Doughboys" editorial appeared had reproduced on the front page a smashing drawing by Captain Wallace Morgan labeled "The Yanks Are Coming!" and there had been an early editorial which had borne the same title. "Yankee" and "Yank" had appeared in numerous heads, in fact, throughout the entire discussion. The inconsistency was not at all apparent at the time. While *The Stars and Stripes* was conducting its campaign, a campaign in which the whole staff believed whole-heartedly, all unconsciously that very staff, along with the rest of the A. E. F., was innocently exploiting the name by which the A. E. F. would be known. In the issue for May 17th was printed a piece of verse of negligible literary value but of some historical significance. Signed "F. A. M., Jr.," it was called "From One of 'Em":

Dey're goin' to call me "Sammy"—
My Gawd, what have I did?
Why don't they make it "Ferdinand,"
Or "Cutie dear" or "Kid"?

I wonder for dat handle
Just who I got to t'ank?
Why don't they cut dat "Sammy" stuff,
And stick to good old "Yank"?

Now, dere's a name I fall for,
It's big and strong and frank,
Yo, dere's a sound dat's got some stuff,
A good, loud-bellowed "YANK!"

I'll bet some Sewin' Circle
Or some newspaper crank
Wished dat dere "Sammy" on me. Hell!
Why don't they call me "Yank"?

This poem produced the following reply from an unreconstructed Southerner:

To the Editor of *The Stars and Stripes*:

There seems to be a bit of discussion in *The Stars and Stripes* about the name Sammy being unsuitable and even disagreeable for the members of the A. E. F. In the issue of May 17th a poem eulogized the term Yank, and suggested its use instead of the trite and familiar term Sammy. I wonder if our poetic friend recalls the fact that that term once represented a stupendous strife in our own house and would not appeal very strongly to some of our loyal friends.

Sam is the familiar name which fittingly characterizes our beloved nation. It means the whole nation and not a part of it; it stands for everything big and noble. And out of respect for these loyal hearts, let us cut out some of our pride and be simply Sammies.

SERGEANT,—Aero Squadron.

The unnamed sergeant's strictures were deemed sufficiently important to call for the following editor's note, which was printed with his letter:

No name that ever ends with the diminutive "y" or "ie" will ever, in the opinion of *The Stars and Stripes*, be adopted as its own by the personnel of the A. E. F. A nickname, to become universally popular, must at least have a rugged, man-size sound. Sammy lacks this primal requisite, and, hence, as far as the great majority of the A. E. F. is concerned, has long since been kicked out of doors.

The Stars and Stripes, as emotional pacemaker to the A. E. F., came, I think, to a full realization of the acceptance of "Yanks" before the army itself did. In its issue of August 2d, by which date the A. E. F. had become an army indeed, the paper capitulated triumphantly in an editorial called "Yanks It Is":

Nicknames are not manufactured. When they are, the "nick" doesn't stick. Ten thousand of the world's greatest thinkers working ten hours a day for ten years couldn't plaster a nickname on the American Army that would stick ten minutes.

For the American Army has already received its nickname over here that nothing can shake loose. That nickname is Yanks. Nothing more, nothing less, nothing else.

It wasn't manufactured for the American Army, it wasn't carefully thought out by any prearranged mental drive. It was just the nickname every one over here took for granted.

Yanks, as applied over here, has lost its old American turn. It no longer means a soldier of the North. It means a soldier from the United States, North, South, East, or West, so long as he wears the khaki of Uncle Sam and battles or works under the old flag. It means Dixie and Yankee Doodle rolled into one. It is the symbol of a united country pointing in mass formation towards the Rhine and on beyond. It means that 1861 to 1865 is forgotten, demolished, blotted out against the mighty epoch of 1917—to a finish.

"Sammy" was a joke, and a painful one. "Buddy" failed to land. The others hit the soapy chute with equal éclat. One nickname alone has withstood the shell fire of discussion. It is Yanks—Yanks, representing North and South, East and West, anything wholly American.

You can't manufacture a nickname in a century, but one can be hooked to you in a day. Yanks it is.

And Yanks it stayed, despite an occcasional protest which brought an immediate rejoinder, until the Flag was lowered from Ehrenbreitstein.

CHAPTER TWO

OFFICERS AND SOLDIERS

PRIVATE HAROLD WALLACE ROSS of the Eighteenth Engineers (Railway) reported for duty at the Ste.-Anne bearing an encased Corona as the sign-manual of his calling. Now a portable typewriter does not make a reporter any more than a box of water-colors makes a painter, but Ross, it appeared, had worked on most of the newspapers listed in Ayer's Directory. He had enlisted in San Francisco in the first week of the war, succumbing, despite the sophistication with which his knocking about should have endowed him, to the bait that his promotion to a corporalship would be only a matter of hours. Arriving in France well within the first hundred thousand, he had manifested hallucinations regarding a military career and had wangled the privilege of attending the officers' training school at Langres. That redoubtable stronghold in the foothills of the Vosges is fifteen hundred feet above sea level and, like most of the rest of France, is unheated. Ross shivered there a few wintry weeks, caught the scent of the flesh-pots of Paris and the paste-pots of the city desk, and took his field marshal's baton out of his knapsack and flung it into the Marne.

A day or two after Ross's and my arrival Visk told us that a man named Woollcott was expected and we began to wonder whether *The Stars and Stripes* was going to be made into a depot brigade for the A. E. F. Hawley had met Woollcott in the States and said that we mustn't mind him—he had been a dramatic critic on the *New York Times* and had probably got into the Army by a clerical error. What in blazes, Ross wanted to know, were we supposed to do with a dramatic critic? Hawley said he himself would scorn the obvious allusion to the theatre of operations but that he had rather expected such a crack from one of us.

Our disdain soared to fresh heights when we came face to face with Woollcott and found that he wore sergeant's chevrons on his sleeves, and Ross's personal disdain went a notch higher when he learned that Woollcott was a college man. So were Hawley and I but we were at least privates. Woollcott came from a base hospital at Savenay, near St. Nazaire, and the splendid health record subsequently established by the A. E. F. was probably due in no small measure to his early departure for Paris. Eventually he became the paper's mainstay at the front—a fact that makes me recall with pride that I accompanied him on his first journey to those parts of France in which the war ceased to be an academic entity. We slept, I remember, in a thick wood in which a reserve battalion of the Twenty-third Infan-

A PRIMITIVE WALLGREN ESSAY IN THE FIELD OF STRAINED INTERNATIONAL RELATIONS. THE SPELLING IS UNUSUALLY ACCURATE FOR A STARS AND STRIPES CARTOONIST

try rested from its labors in the famous and sanguine sector northwest of Château-Thierry. Far off to the left, toward dawn, three guns, friendly or hostile (or one gun firing three times), went pop . . . pop . . . pop, with intervals of perhaps five seconds between the pops. A hand nudged me in the darkness and a courteous voice inquired, "Is that a barrage?"

The earliest issues of *The Stars and Stripes* possessed at least the virtues of reflecting their public. They could hardly help it. It was Visk's conviction that the paper ought to be written as far as might be by enlisted men. During the whole span of *The Stars and Stripes'* existence there was a steady concourse of commissioned applicants for places on the staff. They were uniformly wished godspeed after being told that the paper was already officered up to the hilt.

It was matter for perpetual delight among us, as among all of related station in the A. E. F., to note that the phrase "officers and soldiers" was the creation not of a plodding guardhouse humorist but of the higher Army powers themselves. "Officers and soldiers," ran sundry general orders, will do thus and so or will not do this and that. There was a colonel at G. H. Q. who was wont to rave futilely at this invidious distinction. "Damnation!" he would declaim. "What's all this about 'officers and soldiers'? I'm a soldier even if I am a colonel!" And he was.

Now we of the staff were not anti-officer. Some of our best friends were officers. But there was a commissioned viewpoint and there was an uncommissioned viewpoint, and as enlisted men in the A. E. F. outnumbered officers perhaps twenty to one, it was plainly our duty, as a morale-fostering agency, to have regard for the greater good we might do the greater number. We were exhortatory enough ourselves in those early issues, but an officer staff would have been many times more so; our own sermonizing may have had little enough effect, but commissioned sermonizing would have had less.

I cannot convince myself that this editorial, called "Can You Fill His Shoes?", performed the slightest service except to get itself read and thereby consume two minutes of ennui:

> The man who wears a uniform in war times never knows what duty he may be called upon to perform. He is a private today, but tomorrow morning he may be a corporal; and if he hasn't learned how to lead a squad, he will bitterly repent that he failed to prepare for the emergency.
>
> Do you know what a guide does? If you don't, now is the time to be learning —you may be the man picked for that job tomorrow morning.
>
> Something may happen to your platoon sergeant. Whoever steps out to fill his place had better be all set for it.
>
> Somebody in your shack is going up from the ranks pretty quick to a warrant or a commission. If the non-com who draws those gold bars hasn't watched what a second lieutenant's work is like, he is going to be the joke of the company until he learns it.

Are you already a second lieutenant? You are content, perhaps, to know how to handle a platoon. But tomorrow morning every officer in the company but yourself may be packed off to a corps school and then you'll find yourself *pro tem* with 250 men on your hands—a whole company to drill and discipline and ration and a baffling lot of "paper work" to tackle.

So all up and down the line. You who now are captains may, before spring sets in, be wearing gold or silver leaves. You who are majors may be leading regiments—either your own, or organizing new outfits of National Army men overseas.

So don't let your evenings all slip by in pleasant gossip around the Q. M. stove. Wake up to what you may have to face tomorrow morning—the chance to make good in new and bigger jobs. How about it? Can you climb, or are you a hopeless fixture?

Everything a man can learn about the Army game will come in handy. Don't lose any more time about it. Get busy!

We seemed to be somewhat uncertain about our own position in the matter, for a month later we committed the glaring inconsistency (though it glared at none of us at the time) of urging "Don't 'Better Yourself' ":

One of the saddest figures in Army life is the high-spirited youngster who, with beating heart and head erect, makes for the nearest recruiting station, offers his all to his country, and then 24 hours after reaching camp hears the whisper, "Better yourself," and starts on a career of self-seeking sycophancy.

He has been infected, and it is an infection that spreads. Probably it spreads the more rapidly in our Army just because advancement in America has been so splendidly open to the humblest citizen, because we have all heard the get-ahead gospel since childhood, because each and every one of us started out with the notion that he stood a fair chance of being President some fine day.

The Kaiser has no great cause to fear the major who, on the first day of his majority, says to himself, "Now, how soon can I become a lieutenant colonel?" instead of "O Lord, help me to shoulder this new responsibility."

A real soldier has no time to think about promotion. He does his job for all he is worth and takes what ranks come along.

The young lieutenant who, instead of bending all his wits to see how much work he can get done every 24 hours, spends all his time scheming for a captaincy, is a pretty poor lieutenant and would make a pretty poor captain. He is like the doughboy whose rifle is never clean except for inspection. He does everything for show, and there is no health in him. He really belongs on kitchen police, although that would be hard on the cooks.

Don't "better yourself." Better the Army.

Such vague generalizing as characterizes the two extracts just given typifies perhaps the nadir of editorial comment. As we got to know more about our Army, as there got to be more Army for us to know about, we could and did improve by process of becoming specific. By the end of May we could print "The Right to Write":

It has been reported to us that in one camp the harassed lieutenants, swamped with the job of censoring mail, took it upon themselves to forbid their men writing more than one short letter a week. If this be true, they not only exceeded their authority in a high-handed manner, but flagrantly violated the letter and spirit of a general order.

So important as a factor in *morale* does G. H. Q. consider the exchange of letters between the A. E. F. and home that part of a general order was devoted to the subject in such terms as these:

"To write home frequently and regularly, to keep in constant touch with family and friends, is one of the soldier's most important duties. . . . All officers should realize this fact, and both by encouraging their men and providing them with the proper facilities, do everything in their power to interest them in the vital question of writing home."

What the aforesaid lieutenants did in their bailiwick, through what they considered over pressure of work, other officers may have attempted for reasons of their own, in theirs. We can imagine nothing less enviable than the plight of such officers if the news of their ruling were to reach G. H. Q.

Exactly how many officers were reading general orders and, having read them, were taking them to heart is beyond the reach of the statistician. But it is safe to say that more officers read that editorial than had read the general order which it quoted, and, having read it, paid due heed. In affairs like this *The Stars and Stripes* could perform a service whose value even the stupidest G. H. Q. (which the A. E. F.'s was not) would have been able to appraise. And I think that an editorial of the pattern of "Two Soldiers", while keyed on no general order and despite its didacticism, was also effective:

The other day permission was asked of an officer in charge of the baggage and packages carried by a train which runs betwen two important American centers in France, to place aboard some bundles which it was important should be delivered quickly in the various towns through which the train passed. He objected. He "wasn't supposed to haul them," it seemed, and it "made a lot of extra work and trouble for the baggageman."

Appeal and argument finally gained the concession that "if the baggageman wanted to take them it was all right."

The baggageman was a private, and he was sweating at his job of hustling trucks aboard.

"Sure, I'll take 'em," he said. "I don't mind."

On the battle front the United States gives the Medal of Honor to the man who "performs a deed so clearly above and beyond the call of duty that no one could justly blame him for leaving it undone." There isn't any medal for a man in the S. O. S. who performs a job "so clearly above and beyond the call of duty that no one could justly blame him for leaving it undone"; but just the same he is doing a great service for his country.

The perspiring private who took the packages was helping to win the war. The officer who was afraid it would be too much trouble wasn't.

War is about nine-tenths work and one-tenth fighting. If some task helps to win the war—if it just helps to keep things running smoothly in the A. E. F.—it is as noble to perform it as it is to fight. We ought to be glad of the opportunity to do an extra job and proud of its fulfillment. It is for our country.

There were plenty of officers who could take this rebuke, entitled "According to the Man," to heart:

An enlisted man was walking along the street. Two American officers, a lieutenant and a major, passed him, and he snapped up to a salute. The major returned it absently, mechanically, without looking at the man and without halting his conversation. The lieutenant ducked his head to meet his hand, so that it was impossible for the enlisted man to tell whether the lieutenant was looking at him or not.

The enlisted man walked on. Towards him was coming an American captain. He carried his left arm in a sling and leaned upon a cane. He walked slowly, almost painfully, and his arm was in a sling because a Boche bullet had smashed it.

Again the enlisted man saluted. The convalescing officer crooked his cane over his temporarily useless left wrist, looked the enlisted man square in the eye, and returned the salute.

This time the enlisted man was proud of his Army.

The captain happens to have been Archie Roosevelt.

The irony of "Discouraging" was applied with all the deftness of a cart-horse stepping a minuet, but it must have made at least one officer blush and numerous others pensive:

> "It is more or less discouraging to the reserve officers," writes an officer to this paper, "to see no advancement as a reward for conscientious effort when provisional second lieutenants who completed the same course ——"
> Etc., etc., etc.
> It is more or less discouraging—or would be for some people—to be a private, spend a tolerably uncomfortable winter in a dugout or an Adrian barracks, neither of them steam-heated, and then, when spring comes, hike a hundred and fifty kilometers along a dusty road into battle and die there.
> It will be more or less discouraging for most of the reserve officers to find that there is one among them who thinks and feels as we have quoted him above.
> For there are a whole lot of old-fashioned people in the Army, both officers and men, who have come into the war to serve their country.
> Of course, there's nothing to be said for them. It's such a terribly old-fashioned idea.

This comment, I am sure, was read with many an appreciative chuckle from enlisted throats all the way from Bordeaux to Bar-le-Duc. Such occasional lambasting of an officer served an added purpose—a purpose, it should be added, not deliberately evolved by *The Stars and Stripes* staff in all its wisdom. It made it possible for the editorial page to commit itself occasionally to downright preachment to the enlisted man himself, as in "How to Lengthen the War":

> A private in a truck train went to a reserve tank the other day, opened the faucet, and drew off a liberal quantity of gasoline in a bucket.
> "I guess," he remarked, "the old man would raise hell if he saw this, but I've got to wash my pants."
> Yes, the "old man" probably would have raised hell. If he is the right kind of an "old man," he would have raised seven or eight different kinds of it.
> Millions of schoolboys are selling war savings stamps in the States to keep us going over here and millions are stinting to buy them. There were three gallons of gasoline in that bucket and, what with the money it cost to make it and to build and run the ships to get it over here, we shouldn't be surprised if it represented a whole week's work for some bright-eyed, enthusiastic, patriotic schoolboy.
> The private in question would probably fight if you accused him of betraying his friends in the trenches. Yet gasoline means airplanes, and airplanes

mean dead Germans, and dead Germans mean live Americans. It's the same with every commodity we handle. Conservation and care mean lives and a shorter war.

The effectiveness of "A Letter Home" was not marred by its high percentage of readability—it might be explained that the soldier's name, duly given in the original editorial, was not James Jones:

James Jones, late of Salem, Mass., and more recently of Battery D in a certain regiment of Field Artillery, A. E. F., wrote a nice long piece about the war in the form of a letter to his mother. As Mrs. Jones showed it to someone on the home town paper, and as the home town paper immediately printed it with a picture of James taken by the best photographer in Salem, we are privileged to reproduce some of its choicer passages. *Les voilà:*

We are not eating beef for the present. It costs too much and roast turkey is the substitute. We get it every day. . . . We are the first Americans in the trenches. The regulars are doing guard duty in the big French cities. . . . The Germans started to run back. Battery D of Salem started to fire in front of them so they could not run away, and when they started to surrender we would not think of it. About six or seven out of 500 Germans got back.

Dear, dear—a gross flattery of the Army mess, an entirely false claim for James' division, a baseless slur on the regulars, and a witless libel on the American Army, all in one well-meaning letter home.

What are we to think of the mental powers of James and his like who pen such rubbish?

What are we to think of the mental powers and sense of responsibility of the censor who passes such rubbish and so transmits it to gullible Salem?

And what, oh, what are we to think of the mental powers and sense of responsibility and general right to remain in the newspaper business of whatever editor of the *Salem Evening News* scatters such rubbish through the homes of a New England town that has not been queer in its head since the days of the Salem witchcraft?

Any one with a decent minimum of knowledge about the A. E. F. could have told that James was writing rot. Such a decent minimum is expected of every editor back home. Great expectations—disappointed almost every time we pick up a home town paper!

CHAPTER THREE

WAYS AND MEANS

A T THIS distance in time and space and emotional subsidence the inner processes of getting out *The Stars and Stripes* take on a more romantic coloring than they are entitled to. The business of producing a newspaper has always been looked upon by the lay eye (civilian or military) as one of the more abstruse mysteries. It was Woollcott's view at the time that one of the reasons why we suffered no interference from G. H. Q. was that G. H. Q. regarded *The Stars and Stripes* as a manifestation of the black arts which had somehow insinuated itself into the military establishment, and felt that the insertion of so much as a finger into this incomprehensible mechanism might produce a weird and unpleasant discombobulation. This view was perhaps unjust to G. H. Q. It is quite possible that G. H. Q. enjoyed reading *The Stars and Stripes* so much, and had so many other things on its mind, that it forebore all unconsciously to annoy us.

Actually the gathering, writing and editing of copy for *The Stars and Stripes* was a rather less troublesome and recondite affair than is the assembling of an average issue of a morning or even an afternoon newspaper in any sizeable American community. As a weekly venture which went to press early Thursday morning and was distributed on Friday, *The Stars and Stripes* obviously could not hope to compete with the press of the world in the presentation of spot news. The dailies, whether in Europe or America, could hardly be expected to wait on us before divulging such essential historical data as the appointment of Ferdinand Foch as generalissimo of the Allied armies or the breakthrough on the Chemin des Dames, and so far as I know none of them actually did wait. But we could print a long account of Foch's career when no other newspaper in Paris at least, whether in French or in English, could devote space to such a comparative aside, and we could unearth and develop a quality of human interest in the war (once the A. E. F. was really in the war) that the dailies had to forego owing to the crush of the communiqués and the elaborate interpretations of them submitted by both sides. Thus

21

the time handicap, due to no special cleverness on our part, became an asset instead of a liability.

Visk went to Chaumont every weekend or so (he never took a day off throughout the war) and came back with interesting tips and a whole sheaf of general orders. A general order usually read as interestingly as the notice of a foreclosure sale in a town three counties away would read back home. But to turn a general order into a readable piece of news was a task that would not have caused grave concern to any rewrite man anywhere with three and a half minutes to make the edition. And every such story, obviously, was Grade A news to *The Stars and Stripes* audience, for G. H. Q. not alone exercised full suzerainty over our lives, our fortunes and our sacred honor but was likewise supreme arbiter of the length of our underdrawers.

The welfare organizations—the Y. M. C. A., the American Red Cross, the Salvation Army, the Knights of Columbus, the Jewish Welfare Board, and the American Library Association—were all news sources of the greatest importance. Covering their Paris headquarters was somewhat more routine than covering police in Fall River or Des Moines, though in those municipalities one would have missed the racy and not always evangelical asides of such Y publicity watchdogs as Maximilian Foster, J. C. Derieux, and Clarence Budington Kelland. We rarely had to worry about press handouts—all the welfare organizations were too busy supplying a real service (despite an occasional creak in the machinery), too busy making real news.

The city of Tours, headquarters for the Services of Supply and the most thoroughly Americanized community in France, was regularly visited by some member of the staff. Tours was easily the ranking A. E. F. news center. Here dwelt, among others, the supreme authorities in the Quartermaster Corps and the Medical Department, both springs of information which never ran dry. The Q. M. C. determined what we should eat and wherewithal we should be clothed; it more than determined these things—it provided them. We could go into the office of Brigadier General Harry M. Rogers, Quartermaster General of the A. E. F., shake the hand that fed us, and emerge with the exciting announcement of a new overseas cap, of a contemplated tobacco ration, or of a change in the construction of imported toilet paper from the cylindrical to the rectangular as an essential step in the conservation of tonnage.

But our main reliance everywhere was our possession of the Army's confidence. The higher an officer ranked the more freely would he talk. Some of this ready divulgence of what was going on doubtless sprang from the fact that the confider liked the paper and trusted it, for he knew that despite its informal presentation it was actually as official a document as the declaration of war itself. But more of this trust, I think, was owing to our uniforms—to the obviousness of our being part and parcel of the Army. I recall only a single instance in which an officer (he

"THE DAY BEFORE SKINNY RAFFLED OFF HIS KNITS," A VERY EARLY WALLGREN DEPICTING AN EXPERIENCE THAT BEFELL MANY OF THE VANGUARD OF THE A. E. F.

happened to be a lieutenant-colonel) drove a representative of *The Stars and Stripes* from his jurisdiction with instructions not to talk to the officers or men of his command under penalty of something or other and with strict injunctions to print nothing. Luckily the representative already had his story and was merely paying the colonel a sort of courtesy call. The story was duly printed and the heavens declined to fall.

The best test of the Army's confidence in its newspaper was the enormous bulk of contributions and correspondence that came in from the field. Appeals for information; suggestions for the conduct of the war; verse (which will receive the separate discussion it deserves); jokes, both brand new jokes and old jokes adapted to serve new ends; requests, indited more in anger than in sorrow, to know why we never mentioned the Engineers, or the Ammunition Trains, or the Umpth Bakery Company; enthusiastic endorsements or ironic disagreements—whatever the reader happened to have on his chest in addition to his issue undershirt and his two dog tags was removed therefrom and proffered to *The Stars and Stripes*. A soldier with the welfare of the nation deep imbedded in his heart submitted this pronouncement:

> To the Editor of *The Stars and Stripes:*
>
> Owing to the amount of tonnage the Government must dispatch every day, we lose the privilege of receiving packages from home.
>
> My solution to this perplexing problem is this: Let every man who receives the daily home town paper pledge himself to cancel the subscription.
>
> We all know that the papers are from a month to six weeks old, and when they do come, not only is the news stale, but they come in such bunches that it is hopeless ever to wade through them all.
>
> This morning two of our men received between them about 75 papers, needing a special bag for transportation from the postoffice. When you figure the weight of 75 papers, and see in your mind's eye thousands of our men going through the same performance, then you can see where our tonnage is being wasted.
>
> What do you think of the idea? If it is any good, *get behind it.*
>
> Arthur M. Vogel,
> Central Med. Dept. Lab.

As soon as the issue that made this suggestion public was out a dissenter took pen in hand:

> To the Editor of *The Stars and Stripes:*
>
> In your last issue I read a letter from a man in the Central Medical Laboratory suggesting that we cancel all subscriptions to home papers, since the news is old when received, and thus make way for packages. I want to protest against anything like this most vigorously.

The gentleman who wrote that letter is no doubt comfortably situated where he can obtain the current newspapers. He is probably in touch with the Y. M. C. A., or other places where reading matter can be had; hence he is, and should be, satisfied. With us here, however, it is different.

I am one of a detail of five radio men who have spent the larger part of the last three months on the front. We are generally out of touch with the Y. M. C. A., mails are infrequent, and reading matter at a premium. One man is on duty all the time, and during the long hours of the night, when little outside of test calls is to be heard, duty becomes tedious without something to help pass the time. Here is where the newspaper comes in, even the advertisements furnishing enjoyment.

There is another phase of the question, to me, at least. It seems as if the city in which I live is writing me a personal letter through the medium of the newspaper. What do we care for the war news? It is the little personal notes, bringing to mind people or places that one's parents or friends might not know of or mention. It helps to bring close the atmosphere of home and forms a bond with home nearly as strong as that formed by home letters.

So I am, I believe, voicing the sentiments of many men when I say, "Rather the papers than the packages." I know that at least 50 of my associates agree with me, for we discussed the question.

Pvt. Peter M. Walsh, F.A.

Enter now the spirit of conciliation:

To the Editor of *The Stars and Stripes:*

I see where one of your correspondents objects to the sending to France of home town newspapers because they waste valuable cargo space. Another wants them to keep coming, because they are like letters from home.

I think both of these men are right, and therefore I am in favor of doing the only thing possible to show them both that they are right—that is, to compromise.

How about passing up our daily subscriptions, and having one paper sent us a week?

Reader.

The universality of the cootie was repeatedly celebrated in song, story and cartoon. Back home a soldier whose soldiering days had ended half a century earlier offered practical advice from the depth of his own experience:

To the Editor of *The Stars and Stripes:*

In reading some experiences of the boys over there with cooties, I am very forcibly reminded of our experience during the War between the States, '61 to '65 and especially during the Siege of Petersburg, Va., where the pits and the whole earth seemed alive with what we called "graybacks." We were alive with them also, and the soldier that did not have the opportunity of ridding himself of these pests at least once in every 24 hours would find himself in very bad condition. Just at this time I made a discovery which proved to be of great benefit to thousands. I will relate it here as a suggestion for the boys in the Army and in the trenches.

As we were marching along I saw something bright sticking out of the dry sand in the road and picked it up. It was a piece of wire eight or ten inches long and about 3-16 of an inch in diameter, probably a piece of telegraph wire. It was bright and clean and I kept it, although at that time I had not thought of a use for it, but when the opportunity came for making war on this ever-increasing army, securely encamped under the seams of our pants and all other places of shelter, it struck me that to heat the end of this wire to a good white heat so as not to burn the cloth, and draw it slowly along under the turned-back seams, and all such places, would make it too hot to live for the old ones, and sure death for the nits which defy most everything, even hot water.

The result was so perfect and complete that I jumped up and down with joy and I had cleaned all my clothes (which of course would not require a trunk) in about three minutes. Then others saw it and it was loan, loan so often that I had a hard time finding it for my own use, but as fast as possible every soldier would get one of his own, until one would seldom see a soldier without one. I believe that I am within bounds when I say that hundreds of thousands of these simple little pieces of wire were in use at the close of the war.

If clothes are made about the same, and cooties and "graybacks" are the same, this is the quickest and most complete remedy ever found.

J. Sumner Welch,
Ex-Lieut. 10th and 6th N. Y. Artillery
Houston, Texas.

A correspondent who was enjoying his first war offered an alternative solution:

To the Editor of *The Stars and Stripes:*

It has come to the attention of the writer that considerable difficulty is being experienced not only in the delousing of the men's clothing, but also the men themselves.

The disinfectors now in operation should care for the clothing problem, but the men present a more difficult problem, and it is to this end the writer offers a suggestion herewith.

If the officer in charge of *The Stars and Stripes* has ever visited a zoo, he has doubtless witnessed the various antics of the monkeys there. The writer calls to mind one very pronounced habit or custom, that of the monkeys picking insects from one another. It is suggested that a carload of monkeys could be easily purchased at small cost in Algiers or Northern Africa, where they abound.

These monkeys could be apportioned, say three to a company of Infantry, where they would quickly become useful pets.

A SUFFERER.

The following question was put and answered at a time when the problem under discussion had, in the main, a purely hypothetical interest to the A. E. F.:

To the Editor of *The Stars and Stripes*:

Kindly advise the writer or state in your next edition whether or not a soldier who has been gassed in action is entitled to a wound stripe. Is gassing under the heading of slight wounds? I see names I know are those of men who have been gassed appearing under the wounded heading.

READER.

["Disablement by gas necessitating treatment by a medical officer shall be considered to be a wound." That is the wording of the regulation governing the wearing of the wound chevron.—EDITOR.]

In its issue of May 24th *The Stars and Stripes* published this editorial, headed "Hail, Canada!":

This is Dominion Day, Canada's own. Perhaps we never realized it before, unless we wondered why it was that Toronto and Montreal always played double headers on their home grounds every May 24th.

Canada is playing a daily triple header this year as a visiting team, like ourselves. Canada has been playing it since the season opened in 1914. Canada has played it at Ypres, at Lens, at almost any hot corner you care to name along the British front.

Canada has shown the Kaiser how the sons of the western world can fight.

Closest of our Allies in traditions, in manner of life, neighborhood and neighborliness, the Canadians merit alike our affection and our admiration.

They not only merit it—they have it.

In due season the Army Postal Service brought this answer:

To the Editor of *The Stars and Stripes:*

As an ex-Canadian I was delighted with your editorial regarding Dominion Day, but always thought that it came on July 1st until now. Speaking of natives here getting mixed on American history, what do you think of an editor who confuses Victoria Day, May 24th, with Dominion Day, July 1st?

CHARLES H. SHERATON,
1st Lieut., Q. M. C., N. A.

[You win, Lieutenant. The date in that editorial was hopelessly wrong, but that's the only thing in it we're going to take back.—EDITOR.]

Of humorous filler there was always an abundance, some of it staff produced, some of it sent in from the field in the form of letters to the editor or in any form at all:

To the Editor of *The Stars and Stripes:*

How does this strike you? Chaplain Patrick Dunigan of our regiment was recently attached to the Sanitary Detachment, thus confirming the old adage that "Cleanliness is next to godliness."

PVT. S. B. HUGHES.

To the Editor of *The Stars and Stripes:*

I want to write to a young lady friend in America. Is it better for a soldier to write military style, like this:

From: William Hunter, Private.
To: Miss Katie Cullin.
Subject: Regards.

1. Attention is called to the fact that since my arrival in France my feelings have underwent no change. I am still yours.

2. Answer, by indorsement, at once, if my photo is still on your bureau.

3. I hope George Goldfish is drafted.

William Hunter, Private.

A reply in your paper will help many of us.

WILLIAM HUNTER.

[If you really have serious intentions, don't. The military method of correspondence is fine form and all that, but our feeling is that they would not appreciate its merits. In all matters of the heart, the ancient free and easy—or natural—style still remains the best and most effective.—EDITOR.]

———

This Really Happened

End of letter: "Goodbye, my dear, for the present. Yours, Jack." Then—
"x—x—x—x—x—x—x—x. P. S. I hope the censor doesn't object to those crosses."

Added by Friend Censor: "Certainly not! x—x—x—x—x—x—x—x!"

"In our hut," writes Corporal No. 3, "we were agreed that these magazine writers were all wrong on their so-called horrors of war stuff, and we would like to submit the following as a few horrors that have been omitted:

"The guy who tells you what a soft job he used to have.

"The bunkie who wants you to read the letters from his girl back home.

"The amateur French conversationalist.

"The guy who used to take a bath every day.

"The private who sleeps in pajamas.

"Our captain at the Saturday inspection.

"The man with the trombone snore.

"Shave in a French barber shop.

"Reveille in the winter.

"Loss of pass privilege.

"Loss of hat cord.

"K.P. on pass day.

"Army stew.

"L'addition.

"Beans."

Mother Goose for Doughboys

Ride a big truck, through mud, rain and muck,
To see a fat major get quite out of luck;
Leaves on his shoulders, and spurs on his heels,
The language he uses shows just how he feels.

. . . .

Jim stuck his mug out, right by his dugout,
Eating his rice and beans;
A Boche sniper spied him and sent one beside him,
And grazed off the seat of his jeans.

. . . .

Little Jack Horner sat in a corner
Op'ning his Christmas box;
'Twas then about the end of March,
But he found lots of heavy-weight socks!

That Toul Weather

There are places in the world where the weather has been better the last few weeks than in the American sector northwest of Toul, but the prevailing dampness never even tarnished the American sense of humor.

The colonel of a regiment, making a night tour of the trenches, was challenged by a sentry who had been standing at his post for two hours in a driving rain.

"Who's there?" said the sentry.

"Friend," replied his colonel.

"Welcome to our mist," said the sentry. And the most serious thing the colonel did was to laugh.

Tears filled the soldier's eyes,
Though brave and true was he,
For he was peeling onions
By the hour on K.P.

Well, How Does It?

(A Play in One Act and Several Convulsions, produced for the first time in the *Théâtre de la Guerre*. All slights deserved—by the congregation.)

The time—A certain Sunday morning, not long ago.

The place—A certain underground improvised chapel, up front.

Enter the chaplain. After mounting his improvised pulpit, he looks his congregation squarely in the eye, and begins:

"You —— —— —— ——s!"

(Gasps, wheezes, short panting breaths from the congregation.)

"You —— £££ ***** —— ——!!"

(Groans, sounds of men collapsing, near pandemonium.)

"You —— &&&&&&&***** !!! —— () () () (——!"

By this time the audience is so weak and faint and all in from suppressed surprise, astonishment and general takenabackness that it is quiet, hushed, passed-out. The chaplain proceeds:

"That's what I hear every day, going around among you! Now, I ask you, how does it sound?"

(Quick curtain.)

Horrors of Peace

I miss my three-tint neckties,
  I miss my silken hose,
I've really got to miss a lot
  While I wear army clo'es.
But when I think of garments,
  A load slips off my mind—
I'm not bereft, for I have left
  The sport-shirt far behind.

Their Geography

Two Californians sat in a Y. hut waiting for the movies to start. Beside them sat a Rhode Islander.

"There ain't a pretty city in the East," said Californian No. 1.

The Rhode Islander pricked up his ears.

"Oh, I don't know," said Californian No. 2. "Detroit and Minneapolis aren't so bad."

The Rhode Islander sighed, and recalled the Far Western trip he had once made to Erie, Pa.

Lorraine Limericks

There was a young fellow from ———
Who put on what Tommy calls swank;
  His canteen on the hike
  He'd hit when he'd like,
And sweat blood for each drop that he drank.

There was a young fellow from ———
Who doted on corn-willy hash;*
    But he always objected
    Whenever elected
The spuds for that same hash to mash.

There was a young man from (deleted)
Who up in an airplane was seated;
    His bombs he threw down
    On a Hun fact'ry town,
And its output was sadly depleted.

———

* Yes, there once was a man who did.

It was some time in May, and he was inspecting the box that had been mailed him (according to his Christmas letter) some time in November.

"What are you waiting for?" said his hungry bunkie. "Open it up! What you rubbernecking all over the outside for?"

"Looking for the service stripe," said the box recipient.

It's Pronounced Foch

The French will think it is a joke
    When bungling Yanks pronounce it Foch,
Yet will we make a sadder botch
    If we attempt to call it Foch;
Nor can we fail to pain and shock
    Who boldly try to say it Foch.
In fact, we have to turn to Boche
    To find the word that rhymes with Foch.

We had our own personal and professional columnist, Captain Franklin P. Adams, late of the *New York Tribune*. He came to us from America via Chaumont (French for G. H. Q.), reporting for duty on that Sunday before Easter of 1918 when the Germans were shelling Paris at tolerably regular intervals (stopping soon after twelve o'clock for a three-hour lunch). La Grosse Berthe had begun to function the preceding day, but nobody had known who she was until evening. By

Sunday morning she was so sure of her range and capabilities that the capital's somewhat haphazard baptism of fire may reasonably be said to date from that day. F. P. A. called it Bomb Sunday.

We already knew (with reservations) all the news from the front; F. P. A. brought us news from the back. "How They're Getting On at Home, by a Recent Arrival," which appeared in the first issue following his enrolment on the staff, was his:

I know a woman in Terre Haute, who, when I left, had a little cold; and a man I rode next to on the Sixth Avenue Elevated in New York had dandruff; but generally speaking I can say that the folks at home are well. They had a tough winter; make no mistake about that. It was just as chilly for the rich as for the poor; I saw ever so many who lived in fine apartments on Riverside Drive and Park Avenue, New York, who shivered during the cold spell, and whose landlords couldn't get coal for them at any price. Some of them grinned and bore it, and some of them beefed and bore it; but they did bear it.

Take the theatrical managers. When the coalless Mondays went into effect, the theaters were closed for one day a week, but were permitted to give an extra matinée, so that the total number of weekly performances remained the same as before. Well, when the order was first published the managers objected. They saw, they said, the ruin of the American stage, not to say the permanent flop of the show business. But the show business failed to flop. Instead, the theaters did a bigger business than before. I can't prove this, but I saw the statements of two Broadway plays, and they bore out the truth of this. When the heatless days were abolished, some of the managers again objected.

Nor are the folks at home starving, any more than we are. Practically everybody—housekeepers and restaurants—has signed the Food Administration card, and, with the exception of a gluttonous slacker or two, adheres to it. And the folks like it. The corn flour muffins we were getting about the time I left were better than any white bread I ever dipped in my coffee.

Wages are unusually high and business, as a rule, is good. As Mawruss Perlmutter would say, I seen it better and I seen it worse. The clerks in the stores average older than they used to; most of the peppy boys are in the Army. Nowadays the musical shows print the chorus men's names on the programs and, if they are more than 31, their ages. And sometimes their serial draft numbers.

By and large, the folks are going about their business. The one thing they are interested in is what we are doing over here, and how we are doing it. Whom we are doing it to they know.

There come times over here when we miss them acutely—times even when we envy them what we are pleased to call their comfort. And there are times when they miss us, and how they do envy us! I heard hundreds of goodbyes said in the last three months, and those who are left behind deem us who are

"SIRE, AGAIN THE PEOPLE ASK FOR BREAD," REPORTS THE ORDERLY. TO WHOM THE KAISER: "WELL, WELL, KERL; ISSUE A THOUSAND MORE IRON CROSSES." FROM THE CARTOON BY BALDRIDGE

chosen to go the fortunate ones. Some even refer to us, as they grip us by the hand the day or the week or the month before we embark, as You Lucky Guy.

Which we are.

F. P. A.'s column, called "The Listening Post," ran for the ten weeks or so he remained with us before he was reassigned to Chaumont and subsequently transferred to counter-espionage work in the United States. That Brooklyn Bridge still stands and that the Statue of Liberty stands still is, for aught I know, his doing. The following selections from his column are chosen without (or possibly with) regard for a topicalness that age may have withered and uncustom staled. An exiguous French sun did, in a manner of speaking, shine occasionally; the original overseas cap, though definite matter for anguish in the spring of 1918, was soon but a pallid memory; one or two hamlets in the Marne and Meuse valleys were beauty spots even in the déshabille of war. But to affirm these truths in that far-off day would have been to deny three fundamentals of the A. E. F. credo. F. P. A. was not doing that. He probably held to these fundamentals himself—the rest of us did.

LINES ON TAKING A NEW JOB

When I was a civilian in the typing days of peace,
I spilled a column daily, *sans* vacation or surcease.
I whittled many a mournful wheeze and many a halting rhyme ,
To cop the fleeting jitney and to snare the elusive dime.
I jested by the carload and I frolicked by the bale,
When I used to write a column on the

> New
> > York
> > > Mail.

The years continued flitting, as the years are wont to do,
Until one New Year's Eve I went and shifted my H. Q.
I wrote a ton of trifles and a mass of metric junk
To give me daily ammunish for my Barrage of Bunk.
Oh, many a paragraph I pulled and many a sassy squib,
When I ran a daily column on the

> New
> > York
> > > Trib.

Goodbye, O dull serenity! Ye days of peace, farewell!
I went—oho!—to fight the foe and hear the shot and shell.
Yet once again I find that I must hurl the merry josh,

Though I now command a column set against the beastly Boche.
But the grandest, proudest job I've ever had among the types
Is this job to run this column in

THE

STARS

AND

STRIPES.

IF THE POETS HAD BEEN MEMBERS OF THE AMEXFORCES

The free, unbridled manner of most of the poets was well enough in its day, but, as Ruggles of Red Gap used to say, it would never do with us. The way the bards of an elder day used to hand out military information is almost unbelievable. Take, frinst, the author of "Bingen on the Rhine." If he— or maybe it was she (out here in East Somewhere Junction one has no reference books, and one's memory simply won't get warm this morning)—had been an Amexforcer, the chances are that the poem would have thundered down the ages thus:

A soldier of —— Infantry lay slightly wounded in a Mediterranean port;
There was lack of woman's nursing, there was dearth of woman's tears.
"Oh, tell my folks," he said, "that I am at Base Hosp. Number 9—
For I was born at A. P. O. 842, at A. P. O. 842 on a certain German river."

And Old Ma Goose might have written "Banbury Cross" this way:
Ride a cock-horse to a certain British suburb,
To see a fine lady ride on a fine horse!

While Tennyson, whether he liked it or not, would have had his stuff treated by the censor thus:
A certain distance,
A certain distance,
A certain distance onward!
Into the eastern sector
Rode a certain percentage of the —— Division.

The Elis would have to sing it like this:
Here's to a good old Connecticut university founded in 1701,
She's so hearty and so hale,
Drink her down, drink her down, drink her down!

And we should all be singing:
My bonnie lies somewhere in Europe,

In the dear S. O. S., L. of C.;
My bonnie lies somewhere in Europe—
  She's at A. P. O. 843.

  And:
'Way down upon a certain Florida tributary
  Far, far away—

As to a thing like "London Bridge Is Falling Down," that info would give the enemy so much comfort that any censor would be justified in not letting it pass.

THE STRANGE CASE OF EDGAR ALFRED ALLEN AND OSCAR A. McGINNIS

When Edgar Alfred Allen was a little boy with curls,
He used to cut out paper dolls and play around with girls;
He never did a naughty thing, he never was a knave;
And all the people on the block said: "My, he *does* behave!"

At school he always studied till he got the highest mark;
At college Edgar never went with boys upon a lark.
He never lost his temper, and no matter what occurred,
He never would articulate a naughty, naughty word.

Now, Oscar A. McGinnis was a different sort of lad;
He was the kind of whom the neighbors said: *"That* boy *is bad!"*
He pulled the hair of little girls and gave them all the creeps,
And people used to say he played at marbles—and for keeps!

When Oscar went to college he was captain of the team,
Although the old professors held him not in high esteem,
A virile, brave, intrepid, fearless man was Oscar A.,
And one who everybody said was sure to make his way.

Well, Oscar joined the Army, as the brave men always do,
And Edgar Alfred Allen? Why, he joined the Army, too.
And after several months in camp they both achieved the chance
To come and fight the glorious battle over there in France.

Edgar Allen, who in boyhood's days was never known to swear,
Displayed conspicuous valor, and he got the Croix de Guerre.
And Oscar A. McGinnis, who'd been fearless all his life,
Likewise achieved the Croix de Guerre for bravery in the strife.

MORAL

This is the little story of two soldiers overseas.
As to the moral of it, it is anything you please.

It takes all kinds of warriors to comprise a great army, including the dough-boy who asked for some blotters and a calendar when he took out his War Risk Insurance.

It occurs to us why baseball never has been the national pastime of France. The double-headers would pile up so that when a sunny afternoon came along there'd be about thirty-two games to play off.

The weather in the States used to be so changeable that it wasn't safe to write about it. By the time the paper was on the street, the comment would no longer be pertinent. But it is safe to take a chance here, even if you write your stuff a month or two ahead.

"Michigan," observes the *Chicago Tribune*, "won the most points and was declared the victor in the meet." Which proves that things have not changed much at home. The winners of the most points still are returned victors.

You may miss that noble institution, the American drug store, but you don't have to buy postage stamps, use the telephone or the directory, or ask where the Whoozis family lives. All you really miss is the soda fountain.

Things here have a way of reminding you of things at home. Our billet, for instance, these warm mornings isn't a bit chillier than the Yale Bowl or the Harvard Stadium in late November.

The difference between American and French automobile driving is this: In America when your tire blows up, you say, "Good Heavens! There goes our tire!" and in France you say, "Hooray! That was only the tire!"

Speaking of names, which is a habit hard to jettison, B. Worthy is a Y. M. secretary in New York, and will soon sail for this sunny, as they call it in the fairy tales, nation.

"Soldiers who are married and do not state the fact are subject to penalties," says an American dispatch to the *Daily Mail*. Especially, we surmise, if certain parties find it out.

Bill's fighting for his country,
  He rises to explain;
Lorraine is where he's fighting—
  With the accent on the rain.

Pay $1,500,000 Yearly for Gas They Don't Get.—New York *Evening World* headline.
Things sort of even up. Over here we get a lot of gas the Boche has to pay for.

A doughboy's notion of a Perfect Day: The war over, a box-seat at the Polo Grounds next October, and General Pershing throwing out the first ball.

If Charlie Chaplin joins the Army, as the cables say he is going to, the Q. M. will probably have to devise the issue custard pie.

All of us have had our shot at stating America's war aims, but our favorite is the Kansas man who says, "Yes, but what good is your wealth, or your honor, or your position going to do if you are forced to say 'Wie geht's?' every morning?"

There are duller things than war. Think, for instance, of being a traveling salesman in France and landing in one of these little burgs about three o'clock on a Sunday afternoon.

"I don't know what you could be a traveling salesman for," commented the soldier to whom the foregoing observation was made, "unless it was for pitch-forks."

Most of us never see the home papers any more, but the odds are 10 to 3 that these are some of the headlines we are missing about now:

War Forced on Germany, says Kaiser
Cobb's Homer Wins for Tigers
Peach Crop Ruined by Frost
McGraw Says Elis Have Great Team
Miss Bjurstedt Nabs Net Title
Not a Candidate, Says Hearst

THE INTREPID BARD

When shells are bursting around the front,
I hate the old typewriting stunt.

And when the bullets whizz, why, then
I find it hard to hold a pen.

I find it hard, in a shell-torn land,
To hold a pencil in my hand.

In fact—there is no need to stall—
I do not like to write at all.

Discovered, the Perfect Simile: As perfunctory as an officer's return salute to a Y. M. man.

The second lieutenant wheeze is getting as numerous as Ford stories used to be two or three years ago. To a comment to this effect a second lieutenant said,

"Well, all right. Maybe we're the Fords of the Army. We give the best service for the money, at that."

What will be in the peace compact it is hard, at this s. of the g., to forecast; but the guess is hazarded that this proviso will be in it: that if, after the war, anybody says "Potato" to a German hostilities will be considered on again.

The carrier pigeons are arousing the interest of the Yanks. A private suggests that the pigeons be crossed with parrots, in order that the birds may deliver their messages orally instead of by "flimsy."

One of the Washington State boys over here is so attracted by the French and their ways that when he gets back he is going to try to have the name of his home town changed to Voilà! Voilà!

After the Salvation Army had given a certain company some cocoa, the company advanced successfully against the enemy. After the war the S. A. will be justified in telling folks how many miles the boys got to the gallon.

Sign on the wall of a stevedore regiment's barracks: "You must not uese Bad Languis around Quartes. EF caught WILL deprive of a pass for 48 oures. mens going to YMCA, coats must be button up, and keep that way while there, Before going on Passes your shoes must be cleain, button on your clothes and cleained." The result, as to neatness of appearance of the regiment, is just as good as—probably a whole lot better than—if Henry James had written the notice.

FRANCE FLICKERINGS

**Ye scribe had a French hair cut last Saturday and is doing as well as could be expected.

**Several of the overseas caps are adorning the heads of our boys. Well, it is the war, as our Allies so well say.

**Pvt. —— —— of —— spent —— day in ——.

**When we get home again we are going to suggest to Ted Shonts that he put cards in the subway cars showing what the next station is, like they do in the Paris Metro. It is a lot easier to read them than to guess what a guard means when he hollers "Se'ndy Segon' the nex'."

**Ye scribe went to see a show last night, enjoying same, despite it being in a foreign tongue. Well, there was many an actress at home we couldn't understand, also.

**Straw hats are beginning to be seen on the boulevards of Paris, but most of our boys forbear to rush the season and stick to the more conservative tin derby.

**A warm spell of weather is expected next month.   tf

**Quite a little rain fell yesterday, and it was pretty cold.   tf

**Fred Ludendorff has had a very busy week of it, what with 1 thing & another.

**Some of the houses hereabouts would look better with a new coat of paint is the opinion of ye scribe.

**Ye scribe enjoyed his April bath yesterday afternoon.

**A certain party in a certain regiment got a letter from a certain party on a certain day last week. Have a care, Bert.

**Charley Hindenburg, the w.k. night editor of the Potsdam Offensive, has a little cold. Gossip has it that Charley is suffering from insomnia also.

**There is plenty of news this week, if we were allowed to print it and if we knew what it was.

———

The Stars and Stripes had its own American correspondent—J. W. Muller—who cabled weekly a long dispatch which, no fault of Mr. Muller's, it was agony to translate. It reached us pared to the bone, and in the stress of war it was occasionally garbled, but we inserted the obvious articles, prepositions and conjunctions, guessed what fgrph might mean, and slapped on a head. In the early numbers all of Mr. Muller's dispatches ran under a New York date line, but this was soon changed to the less provincial "America." Mr. Muller tried to send us (and succeeded, I think) a serial conspectus of the United States—a semi-news, semi-editorial survey of what our conglomerate old home towns looked like, how they were taking the war, how the war was taking them. In addition he cabled some hundreds of words of trivia that were far from trivia to news-hungry hundreds of thousands of Yanks. It is of little moment now, perhaps, that Prince Charles, a chimpanzee, was found "wandering about in male garb" in the old Hotel Knickerbocker in New York; that Nat

400 LIBERTY MOTORS TURNED OUT IN JULY

Orders for 50,000 Placed,

[By Cable to THE STARS AND STRIPES.]

AMERICA, Aug. 15.—The Dayton airplane. works has celebrated the completion of its thousandth battleplane.

John D. Ryan, Federal director of aircraft production, announces that orders have been placed for 50,000 Liberty motors.

He says that four hundred Liberty motors were turned out in July; he estimates that this month s production will be five hundred, and says that the peak of production will be reached in November or December.

Mr. Ryan further announces that the United States is now producing giant airplanes equipped with four Liberty type motors.

THE ONLY STORY IN THE STARS AND STRIPES TO WHICH THE CENSOR APPLIED THE CHISEL. TWO LINES OF THE SECOND DECK OF THE HEAD AND TWO LINES OF THE TEXT WERE EXPUNGED. HEAVEN ALONE KNOWS WHAT THEY SAID, BUT IT SEEMS REASONABLE TO ASSUME IT HAD SOMETHING TO DO WITH LIBERTY MOTORS

Goodwin, according to testimony divulged in a motion-picture suit, "takes baths in a mixture of bicarbonate of soda and vinegar to soothe his nerves"; that a painter in a Hudson River village caused at least one community temporarily to forget the war by taking a contract to refurbish a church and then painting the wrong church. Some of Mr. Muller's minor dispatches may serve as definite proof to the doubtful that the trail which leads back to 1918 is already a long one:

SCORE ONE FOR CHICAGO

NEW YORK CROWDS TO HEAR SINGER SHE PASSED ON TO RIVAL

[By Cable to *The Stars and Stripes.*]

NEW YORK, Feb. 14.—The great musical sensation of New York has been the appearance of the wonderful Italian soprano, Amelita Galli Curci, at the Lexington Avenue Opera House. There has been a tremendous spontaneous outburst of enthusiasm over her performances, which reminds old timers of the receptions accorded to Jenny Lind, Patti and other stars.

This gives Chicago a great laugh on New York. Galli Curci had been singing with the Chicago Opera Company for more than a year past. Chicago hailed her as a soprano conflagration, but New York disbelieved. New Yorkers now stand in line for several blocks to buy tickets.

Galli Curci is twenty-eight years old. She sang in Italy five years ago and then went to South America. She began singing in Chicago for $300 a night; she now gets $1,000. Her income this season will probably be $200,000, within $50,000 of Caruso's.

Women Preparing to Vote

NEW YORK CITY CONGRESSIONAL ELECTION GIVES FIRST CHANCE

[By Cable to *The Stars and Stripes.*]

NEW YORK, Feb. 21.—New York City women are greatly delighted over their first chance to vote in New York state on March 5. Four city congressional elections are to be held, and the women are preparing to make a big campaign.

In the meantime, the predicament of Miss Hay, head of the women's suffrage party in New York City, is being recounted. Miss Hay, one of the most active workers for suffrage, will not have an opportunity to vote with many of her co-workers. Owing to the fact that she does not reside in any of the congressional districts in which elections will be held she will not be able to cast a ballot. Six colored women employed in the kitchen at the city headquarters of the party will vote, however.

Carrot to Outshine Rose

[By Cable to *The Stars and Stripes.*]

NEW YORK, March 14.— Cabbage and carrot may be the queens at the flower show here next week. Fashionable exhibitors are to show war gardens.

A Fifth Avenue florist made a hit last week by displaying a big bouquet of beets, radishes, beans and carrots.

The smart milliners are now thinking of making edible hats for summer.

Injianny Goes Dry!

[By Cable to *The Stars and Stripes.*]

NEW YORK, April 11.—The Illinois township local option elections have resulted in gains for prohibition. Only three of the formerly dry townships voted to become wet, and 13 of the wet townships went dry.

Indiana has gone dry by State statute, the law taking effect on April 2. The wets have asked the State supreme court to declare the law unconstitutional, but in the meantime complete drouth will prevail.

The only Hoosier font now running full blast is the literary one, the spout of which is at Indianapolis, with Booth Tarkington, George Ade, and Meredith Nicholson as the main spouters in favor of the crystal pure *eau simple*.

Souse Bend no longer lives up to its name.

LOUNGE LIZARDS MUST GO

[By CABLE TO *The Stars and Stripes*.]

NEW YORK, April 18.—New York is preparing to enforce the anti-loafer bill compelling every able-bodied male between 18 and 50, rich or poor, to hold down a regular job.

The city police will look after the lounge lizards and similar ornaments in particular.

LIGHT ON MAIL DELAY

[By CABLE TO *The Stars and Stripes*.]

NEW YORK, May 2.—The first gun has been fired in Congress in the inquiry into the mail delays.

Every one in America has been loudly asking why it takes such an enragingly long time for letters to travel to and fro between the States and the A. E. F. Now Congress has taken the matter up and, to judge from the preliminary skirmishes, it looks very much as if the Post Office Department were about to pass the buck to some one in France.

LOSES CITIZEN'S PAPERS

[By CABLE TO *The Stars and Stripes*.]

NEW YORK, May 23.—A New Jersey court has revoked the naturalization papers of a German who has been an American citizen for 35 years for disloyal utterances. A bill has been introduced in Congress to make such revocations mandatory in similar cases.

Col. Roosevelt Signs Up

[By Cable to *The Stars and Stripes*.]

NEW YORK, June 6.—The Republican Club of New York has taken Colonel Roosevelt back into the fold, and he has accepted the invitation.

Beer May Hold Out

[By Cable to *The Stars and Stripes*.]

NEW YORK, June 13.—Food Administrator Hoover opposes the bill now in Congress which would prohibit the further manufacture of beer and light wines. This will probably kill the measure, leaving whisky, gin and similar redeye stuff as the sole outlaws.

There is lots of whisky in storage, however, and probably the whisky drinkers' only suffering will be the acute pain brought on by having to pay 25 to 40 cents per hoist.

We carried advertising, but not for revenue only. The revenue, in fact, was so much fungus. Every centime which *The Stars and Stripes* took in—and it took in fifty of them per copy, one dime American—vanished eventually into the unheeding maw of the United States Treasury. We carried advertising solely in order that *The Stars and Stripes* would look like what it was—a newspaper. This was a major premise in the original manifesto which Visk had drawn up. Another premise, equally important, was that *The Stars and Stripes* was not to be given away. Later a certain number of copies was reserved for distribution to men in hospital, but long before that the principle of paying for the paper—of paying for a paper that printed paid advertising—had been soundly established. *The Stars and Stripes* was not to carry the curse of the gift horse. It might, as a no-cost publication, have still been free of the slightest adulterant of propaganda and still been suspect. No one —at least no American—would or could feel anything except good will toward something that not only cost him money but was costing other people money and was making money on its own account.

Our original advertising manager was Lieutenant William K. Michael, already identified as one of the earliest tenants of the reconstructed chamber in the Hôtel Ste.-Anne. Michael had come over as an infantry officer to fight Germans and found himself fighting sales resistance. A. W. Erickson of New York City was our American representative, serving without commission and commissions as his bit toward the winning of the war, and the Dorland Agency of London sent in copy that added to the international flavor of the advertising columns.

As a result of all this activity we became one of the very few periodicals in history that frequently turned down advertising and didn't give a particular hurrah about such copy as we did use. Once, while making up page seven (a desirable position, since Private Wallgren adorned it regularly), I deliberately held out an inch ad and substituted a joke (probably something of Hawley's) just so that I could say I had once done it.

"ALL THE COMFORTS OF HOME," BY CAPTAIN WALLACE MORGAN

Our advertising, thus, fulfilled an editorial function. It was good for A. E. F. morale to know that Ivory Soap had not surrendered its floatability, that Mr. Walkover was still making one kind of shoe and Mr. Firestone another, that the Adams family was still engaged in the express business and in the manufacture of chewing gum, that the Wrigley flavor also was lasting right through the war, that sundry great American banks were not only doing business at the old stands but had established newer stands in France and England, that Fatimas and Bull Durham and Lucky Strikes (then little more than a year old) and Murads of a pre-nonchalant era enjoyed devoted followings in the midst of alarms. The doughboy doing bunk fatigue in the heart of a wood with only the wan French sky above could gain soul stimulus from the knowledge that somewhere heads continued to be sheltered by Barrett roofing.

Much of this familiar copy looks singularly commonplace and uninteresting after the lapse of years. It looks so by very reason of its familiarity. In France it wore all the glamorous trappings of high romance, for it stood for home. War and distance oddly transmuted the most ordinary facts of existence. That Bill Smith of the Eighteenth Infantry, for example, had won the D. S. C. for annihilating a machine-gun nest did not seem nearly so exciting as the fact that back home in Ottumwa Bill Smith used to drive a grocery wagon. So it was with advertisements extolling the virtues of Mennen's talc and Colgate's shaving cream, of Boston garters, of the *Outlook*, of Auto-Strop and Gillette razors.

Some of the smaller notices, however, have an individual flavor even at this late date. Two or three enterprising real-estate salesmen saw in the A. E. F. a potential market for French châteaux, with what results I know not. A London draper courageously advertised pyjamas, but even his optimism was exceeded by that of the Parisian shopkeeper who ran an inch notice about umbrellas. One could (and doubtless did) buy maps of the front, paper-bound Editions Nelson that had taken the place of unexportable Tauchnitzes, local chamber of commerce paper money, flashlights, camera film.

At the head of the editorial page in the first issue of *The Stars and Stripes* had appeared this notice:

> *The Stars and Stripes* is printed at the plant of the London *Daily Mail's* Continental edition in Paris. The paper stock is supplied by *La Société Anonyme des Papeteries Darblay*. Only the hearty co-operation of these two institutions, one British, one French, has made it possible for the A. E. F. to have a newspaper all its own. Unity of purpose among the representatives of three allied nations has succeeded in producing *The Stars and Stripes*, even as it will succeed in winning the war.

Of the good work of La Société Anonyme des Papeteries Darblay I am not technically qualified to speak. I know that in the beginning the paper supply was one of the biggest problems that confronted Visk. I know that our paper was clayey, tawdry, wretched, but que voulez vous?—there was, after all, a war. But I know that Visk got the paper, which was the main idea.

Mention of the Continental Edition of the *Daily Mail* arouses in this demobilized bosom a more responsive chord. All of our composition and most of our presswork (toward the end the plant of *Le Journal* was used as an auxiliary) was done at the *Daily Mail* plant. One of my functions was to assist in putting the paper to bed, and on most Wednesday nights I regularly toiled, in a manner of speaking, at the *Daily Mail* until three or four in the morning. We had a noble crew of our own in the composing room who labored in hearty good fellowship with their cross-Channel associates, earliest of whom were Sergeant Richard S. Claiborne (a veteran of '98 and of the Bureau of Printing and Engraving, and the Nestor of our whole outfit), and Privates Frank J. Hammer, Herman J. Miller, and Sigurd U. Bergh. Bergh read proof and saw to it that no non-American compositor tried to slip in civilise, honour, kerb or tyre. Later he joined the editorial staff and had a cushy assignment with the troops on the Rhine.

With the Anglo elements of this Anglo-American alliance those of us who had business with it built up as fine an entente cordiale as ever existed between Briton and American. It was the more real because there was not a trace of self-consciousness in it. It might have been otherwise if we had all been in London, but we happened to be in Paris—exiles all of us, strangers in a strange land.

The viceroy of this little cellar dominion in the Rue du Sentier, just off the Boulevard Poissonnière, was John H. Roscorla. If the name does not connote immediate Anglicity, let it be explained that Mr. Roscorla was a Cornishman. His next in command was James W. Faithfull, rechristened Jacob by Hawley. Mr. Faithfull, unless all auditory signs failed, came from London. Both Mr. Roscorla and Mr. Faithfull and all the rest of their staff spoke French like English printers marooned in Paris. It was mostly accent, but it was fluent and it was understood. Such rowdy scraps of true Parisian argot as I was able to acquire I had from the lips of Mr. Faithfull.

There were other practical advantages in knowing the *Daily Mail* outfit. A hundred feet away was the office of *Le Matin*, and across the Rue du Faubourg Poissonnière from *Le Matin* was a café which was permitted to open at three a.m. or thereabouts to accommodate the newspaper crowd—a benison known to almost no one in Paris outside the *Matin* and *Daily Mail* crews. It was pleasant to finish work just before dawn and drop in for a thick pâté sandwich and a glass of coffee or a menthe blanche.

Lord Northcliffe, as was his right, was an occasional visitor at the *Daily Mail* plant, and, whether he visited it or not, seemed to read every issue of the paper. His dictated comments on what he liked and what he did not would be put in type and proofs sent to his staffs. Apparently there were no secrets around a Northcliffe plant. "Have sent this wire," he would write, "to our correspondent with the ——s: '—— man [the representative of a rival Paris daily in English] beat you badly yesterday. Please explain.'"

Northcliffe was in Paris just after the Armistice and gave a tea at the Ritz for the

ENFANTS DE LA PATRIE (ANY ONE OF WHOM WAS WILLING TO SMOKE AMERICAN TOBACCO)

American correspondents who came over with President Wilson. Woollcott suggested that it would be interesting to meet him, and so four of us blandly requested invitations from the always accommodating Peter Goudie, editor of the *Daily Mail*. We went—three American privates and an American sergeant—and met our first lord. Mounting a chair, he talked quietly, intimately, earnestly to the group gathered about him. "We look upon President Wilson," he said, "as the man who has come over to stop the things that have been going on here for four years." Tea, chocolate and champagne were served. Our quartet had chocolate. We could have champagne any time we cared to pay for it.

Our engravings were made at an establishment far over on the left bank of the Seine—I have forgotten its name; some société anonyme, presumably. We are all wont to regard French as a far more compact language than English. Yet we are content with "inc" and an Englishman with "ltd" where a Frenchman has to take time out to unburden himself of "société anonyme". The word cliché itself, transplanted bodily into English, is familiar and comprehensible to anyone whose French extends far enough to cover chic, tour de force and naïveté, but it will never mean to such an one what it means to me. For to me a cliché will forever be nothing more nor less than a photo-engraving.

It is always open season on engravers in any country and in any language. When an engraver, be it in Odessa or Omaha, picks up a telephone he does not really listen to the first half-minute's conversation because he knows it consists simply of cusswords. The rule admitted of no exceptions in France. Nor was it necessary to know French in order to maintain the fine old traditions of the craft. One simply unleashed a few well-chosen Americanisms and roared "Cliché!" at the end.

I do not know that this particular société did particularly bad by us, all things (a war among them) considered. It did prove gloriously undependable in one crisis. For the July 12th number, in which we planned to celebrate the first Bastille Day on

AS DEPICTED BY BALDRIDGE FOR THE FRANCE NUMBER OF THE STARS AND STRIPES

which the A. E. F. had had a newspaper, Visk contrived to get statements from Marshal Joffre and President Poincaré. The Joffre statement, in French, was translated and spread across seven columns at the top of page one. The Poincaré letter was written in his own hand in English. From an authoritative source it was made known to Visk that it was the presidential wish that the statement be displayed in facsimile. It was intimated, moreover, that page one would be a desirable location and that there would be virtually no ill feelings if the Poincaré statement had obvious precedence over that of Marshal Joffre.

Not ours to attempt to ungnarl the tangled skeins of French politics. We knew little of what it was all about, but it was patent to the least internationally-minded among us that the spirit of jealousy was abroad in the land—a war within a war that might explode an unpleasant little skirmish right on our own doorstep.

The Poincaré letter was sent to the engraver with orders for a facsimile. Visk, I believe, had not actually made up his mind where to place it at the time. I do not think it would have made page one even if the whole French cabinet had appeared to plead the presidential cause in person.

It was late afternoon—Wednesday afternoon, closing day for the issue. The cliché had been due hours before. A group of us were sitting in Visk's office.

"I hope that damn cut gets busted," he said.

The telephone rang. Someone with an ear attuned to the nuances of engraver's French answered it. A thousand regrets, monsieur. The cliché had become broken. Would he make another? It would take some time. Ah, it was too late to attempt it? What damage! Another thousand regrets, monsieur. The broken cliché should be sent over? But yes, instantly. A third thousand regrets. To the next, monsieur.

The wrecked cliché duly came to hand, to be preserved against any possible governmental crisis. None developed. The war performed an about-face a week later and M. Poincaré had delights to compensate for the publication of his statement, five columns wide, in type on page two.

CHAPTER FOUR

CAME THE WAR

DURING the early weeks of 1918 the Western Front, particularly so little of it as appertained to the A. E. F., was laudably quiet. Credit for this exemplary condition was in no wise due to the A. E. F. itself. The American conception of war-waging was to fire off a gun. This not wholly original idea was frowned on by the tutelary French, and the frowning produced frequent outbursts of blasphemous and ironic protest. The French were right. Fire a gun by all means, was their view, but fire it only when and where it would mean something, not as a mere gesture of impetuous youthful exuberance. The French were old soldiers— they had been fighting for three and a half years, and a year on the Western Front was not altogether like a year on the calendar.

As the winter of 1918 swung toward spring it did not seem probable that *The Stars and Stripes* would require extensive representation at the front. A single envoy was, however, dispatched. He was Lieutenant Charles Phelps Cushing, and he went virtually AWOL to get there. Cushing had come to France with the Sixth Marines. As soon as he joined *The Stars and Stripes* staff (and he joined before there was a *Stars and Stripes*) he inaugurated an insidious campaign of Marine propaganda. In the first issue, which he made up and much of which he wrote (as much as Private Hawley left room for), he inserted at least one Marine story on each of the eight pages.

One of Cushing's earliest contributions was a moving little picture of the French family with whom he had been billeted before the fortunes of war made him an editor:

It wasn't my fault—I had nothing to do with the billeting arrangements— but every living creature in the old house, and everything inanimate, seemed to cry out that first day against my intrusion. The rusty hinges of the gate protested shrilly before I could set foot in the yard. The billeting sign, done in stencil on a piece of new packing board, seemed to be a desecration of the charm of the grey stone wall. Madame B—— met me at the door and failed to accept my proffered handshake. (How could I know, then, the reason for her seeming coldness?) Grey-headed Monsieur, bent over his cane and shuffling along in wooden shoes, wearily led the way upstairs.

Once in my room, the little knicknacks on the mantelpiece, the prayer chair and the rosary beside the bed and the shelf full of well-worn books smote my conscience again. Those books, in particular. I took one down—Montaigne! The man who had lived in this room and whose personality had colored it, the man who had gone out from here to die, perhaps, for la Patrie, had loved Montaigne! I am not ashamed to say it; as I closed that book and stealthily replaced it on the shelf the tears stood in my eyes.

How was I to know, then, that the Man of That Room was still alive and gallantly fighting for his country? How was I to know, then, that Madame B—— did not take my hand because, through illness, her sight was nearly gone?

Next morning Madame and Monsieur invited me to their little cellar-like living room downstairs. It had a tiny stove, two chairs, a table covered with oilcloth. An aged terrier, addressed as Moose, hopped up to the shelf on the front of the stove, hugging the fire. All seemed so old, so wintry, so pitiful!

Little by little, we grew better acquainted. I gave Monsieur a package of American pipe tobacco. That did much to break down barriers. I told him it came from Virginia and he looked up the State in a tiny school geography which treated of the whole of North America in a one-page colored map, with three-quarters of a page of text opposite.

Madame followed me to the door that morning and whispered: "He has not had tobacco to smoke these two months, Monsieur. Ah! He will now be *bien content*."

And, truly, he was. It warmed one's heart to see him sit by the fire and puff at his old black briar pipe.

Soon I learned about Madame's illness and had one of our Navy medicos pay her a professional visit. It was wonderful to see how she began at once to pluck up hope and spirits. The doctor's cheerful manners (bluff old mariner) did as much as his medicine to effect the transformation. Within a week she declared her sight was clearer. Doubtless it was, too, for her ailment was one which quickly affects the eyes.

My morning calls became an institution. I was shown through the other rooms of the house, closed since the war—the "company" kitchen, with copper pots and pans of every shape and size shining on the walls; the parlor, with a grand piano which had been mute since the first days of the war.

I learned, then, about the daughter in Paris—"you should hear her sing, Monsieur, and you would say, as all do, *ravissant*!" And, lastly, in a more hushed tone, Madame told me of the son away at the front; how hard he had worked, and how he had climbed, grade by grade, from the ranks to a lieutenant's commission.

Gradually, the place seemed to grow more friendly toward me. Aged Moose showed he could be taught new tricks; at least, he learned to bark a friendly greeting every morning when I came downstairs for a pitcher of hot water. The fragrance of Monsieur's pipe bade me daily welcome, too. Madame could smile, now—she could see so much more clearly, thanks to the good sea-doctor from America. One day she was even persuaded to put on her Sunday black silks and fare forth to hear our Marine band play in the village square.

"You must not think me over-critical," she reported later, "but your sea-soldiers should practice harder on the 'Marseillaise.' They already do really well with 'Madelon.' And they are really wonderful when they go at those happy American pieces."

We pledged the entente that evening in a bottle of twenty-year-old port from the cobwebby cellar, sipping slowly, and talking the while of the happy days to come, with peace in the world again and all the church bells clanging joyously.

When the hour arrived that I must shoulder my pack and bid good-bye to my billet, I took down Montaigne again. This time the good old book was like my good aged hosts and venerable Moose and the rare old wine. I chanced on a passage of philosophy about wars. . . . I closed the book reverently after a while and put it back, *bien content*.

Madame and Monsieur followed me to the gate, wrung my hand and wished me the best of luck. Moose barked excitedly.

"We shall not forget you, Monsieur Charles. We have learned to love you. Long live America!"

Neither shall I forget you, good old friends, nor be ashamed of the love I bear you—you and your friendly land that tries so bravely to be gay.

"Vive la France!"

I blurted it out, choking.

They understood and tried to smile.

The old gate creaked as it closed after me—this time not so shrilly.

It was Cush's old buddy Montaigne who said: "It happens as with cages: the birds without despair to get in, and those within despair of getting out." Once in Paris, Cush too despaired of getting out, and despaired to such good purpose that before long he was virtually roving footloose among the troops. Having an agreeable way with him, a smattering of Kansas City French and limitless quantities of tobacco, he made friends with the natives wherever he went—and France, even in its most thoroughly Americanized districts, was well supplied with natives. On one occasion he completely won the devotion of a French lieutenant who insisted on bearing Cush off to his battery and introducing him to the whole personnel, especially the captain. Cordiality was the keynote; food and drink were provided, and the vicinity reëchoed with vive-las. As a crowning gesture of hospitality the lieutenant insisted that Cush fire a shell from a seventy-five. But the captain, reasonably unwilling to rouse a sleeping war, drew the line, and Cush had to forego the honor of being the only representative of *The Stars and Stripes* to discharge a firearm in the face of the enemy.

But one distinction he did achieve—he visited a front-line trench and wrote a story about it that carried a by-line. It was no fault of Cush's that the war, at the moment, was tolerably decorous and house-broken—later, when the rest of us began to fare frontwards, the actual front had become a rather more imaginary line than the equator, and colonels and even generals were often uncertain as to exactly where it might be situated at any given instant. Cush's point of approach was Seicheprey, in the famous training sector north of Toul, and his hosts were the members of the Twenty-sixth Division. His account of the visit duly appeared in print as our first staff story from the seat of hostilities:

> Thanks to motor transportation, a correspondent for *The Stars and Stripes* had the chance to attend two Washington's Birthday parties the same evening. One, in the brightly lighted dining room of a little French hotel back of the front. Another, under murky skies, in the American first line trenches.
>
> The party in the hotel was conventional, but none the less picturesque. Half a dozen American officers, three young fellows in uniforms of horizon blue, two Italians and a stocky, good-natured Briton got to their feet and clinked glasses to the toast:
>
> "Washington, Father of His Country!"
>
> The toast had to be translated to the Italians via one of the French, and the Italians drank it first before they knew what it was all about; then again—and heartier—after they understood. This, of course, added to the merriment. The Briton then rose to confess that this was the first time he had ever toasted George Washington. And that, naturally, called for another round.
>
> There was only one woman in the room, an elderly French madame sitting at a little table alone and knitting. She looked up and smiled; then back to her stitches.

Outside it was chilly and raining. A single ray of yellow light filtered on to the wet pavement through the hotel shutters.

The press automobile, with dimmed lights, crept through the crooked streets to the outskirts of town and brought up beside a sentry box. There instructions were given that no lights should be shown and no motor horns sounded.

Along a long lonesome road lined with a double row of tall silhouetted trees, we set off for the front.

For an hour we had the road all to ourselves. The hum of the engine and the spatter of rain drops on the wind shield made the only sound.

Presently, a camion loomed up in the road and chugged past; then a rumbling train of ammunition wagons.

"*Our* boys," commented the driver. "Can tell 'em by the helmets."

All of a sudden, out of the murk, something rushed by on our right, and something else, bound the same direction, on our left. Zs-ss-t! Zs-ss-t! and both were gone.

"Our boys again," the driver chuckled. "Couple of machine guns on motors. Just racing, I guess."

By this time we had reached a crest from which we could see a long distance beyond. Dead ahead, some tiny lights, like fireflies, were flashing.

"Those are the big guns," the driver explained. He paused; then whistled. "Lots of 'em tonight. Something on, I guess. Like as not they're celebrating the holiday."

Not until we pulled up at brigade headquarters could we hear the reverberations. In the closed car, with the motor churning, the front had seemed noiseless. But the moment the engine stopped and the door of the car was flung open, the air suddenly became aroar. You have heard the same sort of sound when a telephone line goes aground.

We broke out our gas masks, donned our helmets and reported at headquarters. Two minutes later we were humming along on the road again.

We brought up at the end of the ride in the center of what once had been a village square. What used to be a town was now a few jagged walls and some heaps of debris. Four men came out of the blackness of a ruined house to meet us. Two were Army officers; two, newspaper correspondents.

"Hurry!" cautioned the conductor of the party. "This square is likely any time to be shelled again. Things have been rather lively around here this evening."

Along a muddy road, pocked with shell fire and occasionally as light as day from German star shells, we tramped in extended order until we came to another clump of ruins.

What seemed to be one of the most badly wrecked places of all—roofless and apparently about to crumble into a heap—sheltered our reception hall. In a little low-ceilinged place hidden in a corner of the ruin, we met the commander of the part of the line which we were about to visit. Less than an hour before our arrival a Boche shell had knocked a ton or more of debris down upon the bridge timbers of the ceiling and had dug up a big hole close by in the back yard.

Except for the fact that the concussion had put the office door out of commission and had jarred most of the furnishings down on to the deck, nothing had been affected. And, quite literally, nobody was losing any sleep over it. The runner who was to announce our "tourists" was fast asleep in his bunk in an adjoining room and had to make his evening dressing arrangements before he was presentable for company.

Meanwhile, the officers of the unit told us how pleased they were with the morale of their men. After the hard work of preparation back of the lines—so arduous that some of the boys had almost gone stale from overtraining—the trenches had "bucked everyone up" again.

"The hours are long here," the commander explained, smiling, "but this is a job to our liking."

The runner reported for duty and we set out in the night again down the main street. A ruined village has a certain beauty on a night like this—the beauty of seeming antiquity. Shell fire makes a Pompeii of it. None of us were surprised to see in the debris beside the road just such an ancient stone bath tub as the antique from Rome which the tourist finds in Paris in the Louvre. It couldn't have been a modern porcelain affair—not here in Pompeii!

The star shells heightened the illusion that this was, after all, a sort of Pain's fireworks exhibition, such as we used to see in boyhood days.

We came out into the open just as a star shell brightened the fields beyond and showed us the head of the communicating boyau leading to the trenches. The American artillery was blazing away in a sort of Fourth of July celebration, with an occasional sulky reply from the Hun, who didn't appear to have much heart for the proceedings.

The boyau deepened and we felt our way along the duck boards in single file. Yes, it was muddy. No one was sorry he had put on rubber hip boots. A slip off of the boards on a wet night such as this may drop you in water up to the knees.

Here and there we stopped—to pass the countersign with a guard, to watch a sniper at work, to allow two soldiers with a marmite of hot coffee suspended on a pole to pass by.

Whee-ee! Whee-ee! from overhead. Those were random shots. No one made any comment. The trenches became almost a maze as we got farther along. The visitors lost all sense of direction. Presently, the conducting officer halted us in a crossing, where there was room enough to crowd close around him, and made a brief comment on what was going on:

"Probably won't be much more doing tonight. You notice that the artillery seems to have decided to take things a bit easier. What you're seeing now is just a typical night in this sector. Typical weather, too."

We went on more slowly until we reached a point not more than 200 yards from the German trenches; there the orders were "no talking." A little farther on we took turns at having a glimpse of No Man's Land through a loop hole. The scenic features were simple, consisting chiefly of tangles of wire and a few flashes of gun fire from the dark background.

A stop in a platoon commander's dugout for hot coffee served in canteen cups varied the program of tramping through the maze of trenches.

As the artillery action kept dwindling, the trenches began to take on more the air of this-is-just-our-ordinary-job. Except for an occasional clip from a machine gun at objects of suspicion in No Man's Land, nothing further disturbed the night as we made our return journey to the communication boyau. The tools of the trade—rockets, *chevaux-de-frise,* hand grenades, automatic rifles—were ready for action, with silent doughboys standing beside them, but nothing happened.

We could have had a first class party in the trenches on Washington's Birthday, but the Hun didn't choose to celebrate. Maybe he thought the weather wasn't just right.

———————

The correspondent who made the visit to the trenches (described above) carried with him a bundle of copies of *The Stars and Stripes* which had just come off the presses. The papers were distributed the following morning to the men who had spent the night in the trenches.

Not long afterward Cush was transferred to the Signal Corps as photo news editor of the A. E. F., acquiring thereby a knowledge of the pictorial history of the war which still finds him a ranking expert in that field.

The long-anticipated "spring offensive" became a devastating actuality in the third week in March. It sent a million or two Parisians scurrying south and west and found *The Stars and Stripes* personnel pleasantly distressed over the possibility that the whole outfit might be obliged to retreat in good order to the neighborhood of Bordeaux. We devised pictures of the staff evacuating the capital in a motor truck, with Lieutenant Michael on the tailboard in charge of a machine-gun crew whose function would be to screen Private Hawley, who, stationed under the driver's seat, would pound out a running narrative of the withdrawal. In the emergency that the ammunition supply failed, Hawley's copy was to be periodically baled and tossed in the path of the onrushing enemy.

REFUGEES THRONGING THE GARE DE L'EST, PARIS, AFTER THE SUCCESSFUL GERMAN THRUST
FROM THE CHEMIN DES DAMES THAT BROUGHT CHÂTEAU-THIERRY INTO AMERICAN HISTORY.
FROM THE DRAWING BY BALDRIDGE

The war, it appeared, was not quite over. Two anxious months later it appeared even less over. On May 26th came the unpredicted lunge between Soissons and Reims along the Chemin des Dames, and within two days, for the first time since 1914, there reappeared in the communiqués the ominous name of the Marne.

But at the very moment when skies were darkest a heartening flash of sun appeared, by a meteorological freak, due north. The First Division, A. E. F., was rushed to the Montdidier front and on May 28th captured the village of Cantigny. The tactical value of this success was not of tremendous importance, but its sentimental value was overwhelming. American troops had already had several tastes of front-line service, but this was more than a taste—it was a real bite. For the first time in the war an American division had attacked in force and had won and held its objective. Americans could fight. No American had ever entertained the slightest doubts about this, but it was something, after all, to convince one's self. The French may have had no doubts about it either, but their assurance could well stand being doubly assured. Allied morale rose visibly and audibly at the neat little triumph.

With Cantigny won and held, American and French eyes could revert to the crisis along the Marne, where the hitherto insignificant town of Château-Thierry was winning tempestuous and eternal renown. Château-Thierry straddled the Marne much as Paris itself straddled the Seine, but Château-Thierry got along with fewer bridges. Through Château-Thierry ran the main highway from the heart of France to the Rhine—the Paris-Metz road. On May 31st elements of the Third American Division went into action here, and rifle and machine-gun blazed in the streets of the hapless city.

Geometrically, the result of the March and May battles was a quadrant extending roughly from due north to due east of Paris which brought the fighting line to within forty miles of the city walls—those useless, romantic, now no longer existing walls the moat surrounding which was farmed out to adjacent residents for gardens, so that wartime Paris was girdled about with a belt of vegetables.

It was all a great convenience to *The Stars and Stripes*. The staff could now close successive issues and spend its weekends at the war.

I have forgotten by what special Providence it fell out that Woollcott and I were the first to be bustled out of Paris with orders to see what all the shooting was for. Out of somewhere was evolved for the argosy an imposing gray National sedan. It was so immediately obvious that this elaborate conveyance would produce a running fire of salutes which neither Sergeant Woollcott nor Private Winterich would be entitled to return (and would not return) that Lieutenant Michael was temporarily released from his duties as advertising manager and ordered to live up to the car. The prestige of the expedition was still further enhanced by the presence of Correspondents Arthur Ruhl of *Collier's Weekly* and W. S. Ball of the *Providence Journal*. We followed the route now so familiar to any tourist who devotes a day of his Parisian allotment to the Château-Thierry bus trip—Meaux, La-Ferté-sous-Jouarre, Montreuil-aux-Lions, which latter hamlet was serving as Second Division headquarters, with the commanding general and his staff established in the maire and the mess sergeant of the headquarters troop comfortably billeted in the town hearse.

Beyond Montreuil the road stretched white and hot and dusty into nowhere—nowhere except the front. Animate life vanished—there may have been birds and butterflies, but there were certainly no cows or pigs or chickens—either the fleeing population had driven them to safety or else they had gone the way of all edible flesh with the help of God and a few Marines, not to mention Infantry, Artillery and Engineers. Meadow flowers (lord among them the effulgent poppy), grain, garden truck—these survived hardily. Even a thrifty French peasant, vanishing into the south to avoid the German steam-roller, could not carry a bed of young asparagus with him. Yankee cooks took up the good work, and many a shattered doughboy was brought back to a dressing station to be confronted by the miracle of petits pois only minutes out of the pod.

It was such a day as the French weather bureau should have commandeered and maintained in perpetuity as a goal for the rest of the calendar to aspire to— a day whose sunny placidity was a divine rebuke to man and the silly enterprise on which he was engaged up ahead.

Late that afternoon, after we had visited Twenty-third Infantry headquarters in the little cluster of farmsteads called Coupru, the National turned back toward Paris with Michael, Ruhl and Ball aboard. Sergeant Woollcott and Private Winterich were left alone with the war and the Second Division. We walked down a side road to a wood where a reserve battalion of the Twenty-third Infantry was taking its ease, presented ourselves to Captain Green of Company M, and let it be known that we had his colonel's permission to spend the night there. Captain Green was a shy, courteous West Pointer who had graduated smack into Armageddon. He would be happy to let us bed down in his woods. He turned us over to his company clerk, a temporarily retired Cleveland wall-paper salesman, and we were fed, watered and provided with blankets. Night fell—a balmy pre-summer night whose eerie stillness was intensified by the occasional boom of a gun. We sat and talked with a dozen members of Company M—talked until long after it was possible to see a face even as a pale smudge against the darkness. In the morning we breakfasted well (in war one breakfasts well if there is coffee and if it is hot), shook hands with our hosts, beginning with Captain Green, wished them godspeed, and set out afoot for division headquarters. A week later half of the little group with whom we had made friends the previous evening were dead.

The division P. C. at Montreuil-aux-Lions was three or four kilometres ahead, the railhead at La-Ferté-sous-Jouarre perhaps ten kilometres further. The ease with which the American soldier accommodated himself to the kilometre as the unit of road measure has always seemed to me a perfect expression of the adaptability of the American temperament. As soon as the transport docked one discarded the mile along with the dollar. This ready adoption of an alien system of computing distance may have been a deliberate piece of self-deceit—the long, long trail seemed so much

"SPIRAL PUTTEES," BY WALLGREN. DESPITE THE DISTRESSING INCIDENT HERE PICTURED, SPIRALS
WERE MUCH PREFERRED TO THE CANVAS GAITERS OF ROOKIE DAYS

shorter every time one consumed eight units which back home would have been
only five.

So in time we came to a field hospital. It sat on a hill overlooking La-Ferté-sous-
Jouarre—the modest country villa of some Parisian business man whose business, at

the moment, was fighting Germans. The villa was called, with peculiar fitness, the Château du Gardien Ange. The house itself, a cottage of seven or eight rooms, white stuccoed, with red tile roof, was given over to the needs of the medical staff —operating rooms, supply storage, kitchen, the regulation hospital paraphernalia. In the garden a large tent had been erected in which patients evacuated from the front awaited transport to the base. Beyond the tent was a sheltered arbor where the more ambitious of the injured could enjoy the shade and the spectacle of replacements marching grimly up to the line.

Two or three soldiers were lolling comfortably in the arbor—two or three patients and a setter dog and a couple of pups. The setter dog, presumably French, looked like any other setter. There is a peculiar imperviousness to nationality about animals.

The setter dog lay on a cot next to one occupied by a sitting Marine. (Of course it had to be a Marine.) I fell to talking with the Marine and asked him about the dog. It was his dog. Now an army is a communistic organization; property rights, beyond cigarettes and combs and toothbrushes and razors, are not generally recognized, particularly in active sectors. A soldier does not own his uniform any more than he owns his will. Aside from the exceptions noted plus a few keepsakes of small dimension, everything he wears and carries has been lent him by his government, and it is all expendable, including himself. The government does not issue dogs. Therefore it seemed highly irregular that this setter should be any one soldier's dog. I asked how this was. The Marine said that the dog's name was Belle and was beginning to tell me Belle's story when Woollcott, who had been foraging around for some extra lunch or telling the medical officers all about the New York doctors, strutted into the picture. Woollcott immediately went into ecstasies about the dog and spoiled the Marine's story; then he insisted that the Marine begin all over again, and as the Marine had nothing to do and Woollcott looked impressive, the Marine did.

An hour or two later a car picked us up and we headed toward Paris. On the way we set about dividing the work we were to do. Displaying the very nastiest aspects of his disposition, which was no mean feat of selection, Woollcott insisted on writing the story of Verdun Belle.

In the years that have intervened since the war I have many times determined to throw discretion to the dogs and put on paper a philippic which I had already decided to call "The Truth About Verdun Belle." That truth can be stated in few words: Ever since the late spring of 1918 Verdun Belle has been supporting Alexander Woollcott. Her story has become a byword and a barking; I have heard it in the watch-fires of a hundred circling camps; others have heard it around as many poker, bridge, cribbage and dinner tables; it has appeared in print (under various titles, but always over the signature of Alexander Woollcott) in virtually every American periodical except the *Wall Street Journal* and the *Harvard Alumni Monthly*. The original Belle (it was Woollcott who wished the Verdun on her) has long since been gathered to a canine Valhalla along with Beautiful Joe and Bob, son of Battle, but her soul goes marching on. Her erstwhile owner, more prosaically, is now selling real-estate or insurance in Los Angeles. Here is her basic story —the mythos whence sprang the whole Bellian cycle—as it appeared in *The Stars and Stripes* for June 14, 1918:

> This is the story of Verdun Belle, a trench dog who adopted a young leatherneck, of how she followed him to the edge of the battle around Château-Thierry and was waiting for him when they carried him out. It is a true story.
>
> Belle is a setter bitch, shabby white, with great splotches of chocolate brown in her coat. Her ears are brown and silken. Her ancestry is dubious. She is under size and would not stand a chance among the haughtier breeds they show in splendor at Madison Square Garden back home. But the Marines think there never was a dog like her since the world began.
>
> No one in the regiment knows whence she came, nor why, when she joined the outfit in a sector near Verdun, she singled out one of the privates as her very own and attached herself to him for the duration of the war. The young Marine would talk long and earnestly to her and every one swore that Belle could "compree" English.
>
> She used to curl up at his feet when he slept or follow silently to keep him company at the listening post. She would sit hopefully in front of him whenever he settled down with his laden mess-kit, which the cooks always heaped extra high in honor of Belle.
>
> Belle was as used to war as the most weather-beaten *poilu*. The tremble of the ground did not disturb her and the whining whirr of the shells overhead only made her twitch and wrinkle her nose in her sleep. She was trench broken. You could have put a plate of savory pork chops on the parapet and nothing would have induced her to go up after them.
>
> She weathered many a gas attack. Her master contrived a protection for her by cutting down and twisting a French gas mask. At first this sack over her nose irritated her tremendously, but once, when she was trying to claw it off with her forepaws, she got a whiff of the poisoned air. Then a great light dawned on Belle, and after that, at the first *alerte*, she would race for her mask.

You could not have taken it from her until her master's pat on her back told her everything was all right.

In the middle of May, Belle presented a proud but not particularly astonished regiment with nine confused and wriggling puppies, black and white or, like their mother, brown and white, and possessed of incredible appetites. Seven of these were alive and kicking when, not so very many days ago, the order came for the regiment to pull up stakes and speed across France to help stem the German tide north of the troubled Marne.

In the rush and hubbub of marching orders, Belle and her brood were forgotten by everyone but the young Marine. It never once entered his head to leave her or her pups behind. Somewhere he found a market basket and tumbled the litter into that. He could carry the pups, he explained, and the mother dog would trot at his heels.

Now the amount of hardware a Marine is expected to carry on the march is carefully calculated to the maximum strength of the average soldier, yet this leatherneck found extra muscle somewhere for his precious basket. If it came to the worst, he thought he could jettison his pack. It was not very clear in his mind what he would do with his charges during a battle, but he trusted to luck and Verdun Belle.

For 40 kilometres he carried his burden along the parched French highway. No one wanted to kid him out of it nor could have if they would. When there followed a long advance by camion, he yielded his place to the basket of wriggling pups while he himself hung on the tail-board.

But then there was more hiking and the basket proved too much. It seemed that the battle line was somewhere far off. Solemnly, the young Marine killed four of the puppies, discarded the basket and slipped the other three into his shirt.

Thus he trudged on his way, carrying those three, pouched in forest green, as a kangaroo carries its young, while the mother-dog trotted trustingly behind.

One night he found that one of the black and white pups was dead. The road, by this time, was black with hurrying troops, lumbering lorries jostling the line of advancing ambulances, dust-gray columns of soldiers moving on as far ahead and as far behind as the eye could see. Passing silently in the other direction was the desolate procession of refugees from the invaded countryside. Now and then a herd of cows or a little cluster of fugitives from some desolated village, trundling their most cherished possessions in wheelbarrows and baby-carts, would cause an eddy in the traffic.

Somewhere in this congestion and confusion Belle was lost. In the morning there was no sign of her, and the young Marine did not know what to do. He begged a cup of milk from an old Frenchwoman, and with the eye-dropper from his kit he tried to feed the two pups. It did not work very well. Faintly, the veering wind brought down the valley from far ahead the sound of the cannon. Soon he would be in the thick of it, and there was no Belle to care for the pups.

Two ambulances of a field hospital were passing in the unending caravan. A lieutenant who looked human was in the front seat of one of them, a sergeant beside him. The leatherneck ran up to them, blurted out his story, gazed at them imploringly and thrust the puppies into their hands.

"Take good care of them," he said. "I don't suppose I'll ever see them again."

And he was gone. A little later in the day, that field hospital was pitching its tents and setting up its kitchens and tables in a deserted farm. Amid all the hurry of preparation for the big job ahead, they found time to worry about those pups. The problem was food. Corned willy was tried and found wanting.

Finally, the first sergeant hunted up a farm-bred private and the two of them spent that evening chasing four nervous and distrustful cows around a pasture, trying vainly to capture enough milk to provide subsistence for the new additions to the personnel.

Next morning the problem was still unsolved. But it was solved that evening.

For that evening a fresh contingent of Marines trooped by the farm and in their wake—tired, anxious, but undiscouraged—was Verdun Belle. Ten kilometres back two days before, she had lost her master and, until she should find him again, she evidently had thought that any Marine was better than none.

The troops did not halt at the farm, but Belle did. At the gates she stopped dead in her tracks, drew in her lolling tongue, sniffed inquiringly the evening air and like a flash—a white streak along the drive—she raced to the distant tree where, on a pile of discarded dressings in the shade, the pups were sleeping.

All the corps men stopped work and stood around and marvelled. For the onlooker it was such a family reunion as warms the heart. For the worried mess sergeant it was a great relief. For the pups it was a mess call, clear and unmistakable.

So, with renewed faith in her heart and only one worry left in her mind, Verdun Belle and her puppies settled down on detached service with this field hospital. When, next day, the reach of the artillery made it advisable that it should move down the valley to the shelter of a fine hillside château, you may be sure that room was made in the first ambulance for the three casuals.

In a grove of trees beside the house, the tents of the personnel were pitched and the cots of the expected patients ranged side by side. The wounded came —came hour after hour in steady stream, and the boys of the hospital worked on them night and day. They could not possibly keep track of all the cases, but there was one who did. Always a mistress of the art of keeping out from under foot, very quietly Belle hung around and investigated each ambulance that turned in from the main road and backed up with its load of pain to the door of the receiving room.

Then one evening they lifted out a young Marine, listless in the half stupor of shell shock. To the busy workers he was just Case Number Such-and-Such, but there was no need to tell anyone who saw the wild jubilance of the dog that Belle had found her own again at last.

The first consciousness he had of his new surroundings was the feel of her rough pink tongue licking the dust from his face. And those who passed that way on Sunday last found two cots shoved together in the kindly shade of a spreading tree. On one the mother dog lay contented with her puppies. Fast asleep on the other, his arm thrown out so that one grimy hand could clutch one silken ear, lay the young Marine.

Before long they would have to ship him on to the evacuation hospital, on from there to the base hospital, on and on and on. It was not very clear to anyone how another separation could be prevented. It was a perplexing question, but they knew in their hearts they could safely leave the answer to some one else. They could leave it to Verdun Belle.

Visk was so delighted with the story of Verdun Belle that he dispatched Woollcott to the front again the following week with Private Ross as escort. It was probably only the restraining influence of Ross which prevented Woollcott from immediately appointing himself pound-keeper to the A. E. F. The following Saturday, by some unfortunate accident, I was the sole editorial representative in the zone of combat. I slept that night in the tent outside the Château du Gardien Ange, and I would have slept longer and sounder if solicitous Medical Corps men had not awakened me every fifteen minutes to inquire where I had been hit. It would have been embarrassing but for the fact that two cots away lay a soldier whose disability consisted of a sprained ankle suffered by walking into a shellhole in the dark.

By the time the great Allied counterstroke of July 18th turned the tide of battle we had become veterans in interpreting the war to the men who were fighting it and to the men who were supplying them with the means to fight. That we had hit upon the only possible way to do it was a fortunate and unavoidable accident. An oddly unorthodox democracy prevailed at the front—a democracy born of common perils and common inconveniences, and in war the inconveniences are harder to bear than the perils. Major X might have been a dashing figure on the Boulevards—undoubtedly would one day be a dashing figure there if shot and shell spared him. Major X, turned boulevardier, resplendent in whipcord trousers and polished boots, would exact the ultimate jot of respect due his ranks and dignities. But at the front Major X, clothed in issue O. D., with the oak-leaves on his shoulders smeared into meaningless knobs by mud or dust, was likely to bear a striking sartorial resemblance to Private Y. Both, moreover, felt a definite bond of kinship with Colonel (or perhaps Corporal) Z. The mutual dependence of the one on the other produced a spirit of practical camaraderie; it was the foulest of weather, but for all that it had brought good fellows together. The closer one approached the front, the more visibly did the army hierarchy broaden slowly down, if not from precedent to precedent, at any rate from major general to kitchen police.

They were all willing to talk—to tell us not what they had done, but what the next man had done. There was no vain excess of modesty in it. What had happened to them seemed, by quick acceptance of the condition of war, like a very ordinary thing, but this same war, they assumed, must still be a remarkable phenomenon to the other fellow. It became our privilege, therefore, to see the army as a group which at a touch resolved itself into its fascinating units, with every unit a good story. Happily it never occurred to any of us to look for types.

Our frontward jaunts produced an undiminishable stream of copy through all that vivid summer of battle. When the German advance touched the Marne at Château-Thierry units of the Third American Division had been flung into the fight, and two days later the Second Division was astride the Paris-Metz road west of the city. In the days that followed half a dozen tiny French hamlets leaped flaming into American history—Torcy, Lucy-le-Bocage, Bourèsches, Vaux, Givry, Belleau and its wood. By the time the last great German blow of the war fell—that *friedensturm* of July 15th that was the Prussian's last desperate bid for victory—America was ready to make her might felt. Three days later the initiative passed into the hands of Foch with the delivery of the thrust south of Soissons that spelled the beginning of the end of the Marne salient—and the beginning of the end of the war. The First and Second American Divisions, with the First Moroccan Division of the French Army, were the tip of the lance. Around the nose of the salient the Twenty-sixth and Twenty-eighth Divisions were ready to close in on both sides of Château-Thierry, which operation, for the two latter organizations, involved the passage of the Marne itself. By August 6th, nineteen days after the launching of the offensive, eight American divisions, a quarter of a million men, had borne the brunt of a cam-

"THE HAND OF MANKIND," FROM THE DRAWING BY BALDRIDGE. BY A HAPPY COINCIDENCE THAT NO ONE COULD FULLY APPRECIATE AT THE TIME, THE FOCH COUNTER-OFFENSIVE, WHICH WAS NOT TO END UNTIL THE ARMISTICE, BEGAN THE DAY BEFORE THIS CARTOON APPEARED

paign that had pushed the German armies back virtually to the point from which they had set out on May 26th. The Fourth, Twenty-sixth, Twenty-eighth, Thirty-second and Forty-second Divisions had played a valorous and essential part in regaining for France the pleasant, rolling country inside the salient over which the breathless German hosts had swept down to the Marne.

As the front receded further and further from Paris the business of covering it for *The Stars and Stripes* became less and less like spending a Sunday at grandma's. No longer was the battle line a mere hour and a half's ride from 1 Rue des Italiens; the way thither, also, lay across territory which had been battled over twice in as many months, and along roads where lines of supplies and replacements had the call over roving reporters. The necessity of providing Woollcott's text with a rational allotment of commas and of permitting him to use "bitter" and "tortured" only in alternate paragraphs kept me pretty well confined to Paris save for occasional excursions into the S. O. S., but this defection did not prevent us from being adequately represented between the Marne and the Aisne. Woollcott and Ross continued to urge on the conquering divisions and they were frequently abetted by Sergeant Seth T. Bailey, a fighting soldier whose "Henry's Pal to Henry" letters, sent in from the field, had earned him a place on the paper.

And so, week by week, we got to be a newspaper. Our function, it has been said, was to foster morale, and it became the easiest job in the world. It became so because the Army was fostering our morale. If we had been chronicling the deeds of a losing army, or even of an army that was standing still, we might none the less have come upon glowing little epics of courage that would have made good reading, but in that event we could hardly have imparted to their delineation that cocky élan which was reflected regularly and unconsciously in our pages. We simply rode with the tide.

The true spirit of the front, it has always seemed to me, shone bright not alone in the extended narratives we printed but also in the by-products that all of us turned out after our exercises in major composition were completed. These little oddments, ranging in length from fifty words to perhaps a fifth of a column, were regularly grouped under a general heading, sometimes to the extent of half a page. I think, all in all, that they made the best staff-produced reading we had.

All of them passed through my hands, yet only occasionally, by some tell-tale scrap of internal evidence, can I surmise now who may have written them. And this, I think, was the chief glory of *The Stars and Stripes*. The staff grew to be such a cohesive, single-purposed unit that there was evolved a composite style—a style to which we each contributed a filament or two, but of which the pattern wove itself. Ever since the paper started I had been sending home a copy of each issue, dutifully blue-pencilling my own contributions so that all else might be ignored by an admiring (I trusted) family. Glancing at such of these copies as have survived, I find it difficult at times to accept what should be unimpeachable evidence of author-ship. Of unpencilled material, I can only assume that, if a story occupies three col-umns, it was the work of Hawley, and that if four adjectives crowd one short line they were indubitably inserted by Woollcott.

Follows a selection of these very short short stories covering the battle period from the beginning of the defensive fighting along the Marne through the destruction of the Marne salient and the establishment of the line along the Vesle:

"Say," said an infantryman. "Do you want to hear about the worst piece of out-of-luck that ever happened in the A. E. F.? A pal of mine went into the fight with 2,000 francs in his pocket—you know.

"Now he's reported missing."

A batch of German prisoners was being marched along the road under convoy of a sergeant. They swung past a little audience of Yanks.

"Hello, boys!" called one gleeful captive in regular English. And pointing to the line he added just as gleefully: "It's hell up there!"

Following a night skirmish, a Yank appeared at a field dressing station.

"Got a bullet in the leg," he declared.

"Where?" asked the doctor.

"That's the funny thing about it," said the soldier. "I didn't feel it, and I can't find it, and I walked all the way here, but my leg is all blood from the hip down."

"Come into the light," commanded the doctor.

Investigation disclosed a punctured—and empty—canteen. The water had seeped down the soldier's breeches, and he had decided that it was blood.

When the civil population left Xville, it took along with it everything it could. But it could not take its potted geraniums. The potted geraniums, how-ever, still bloom in the red ardor of June. The Yanks see to that. Even dignified and not-to-be-trifled-with M. P.'s have been surreptitiously caught watering them.

The most valuable commodity at the front is matches. There comes a time when the last drop of gasolene or the last inch of tape is gone from the patent lighters, and the conservative fellows known to have matches can be counted on the fingers of one hand. These become the most popular men in the command.

There is a case on record of one regiment which went three weeks on 12 boxes of matches. When these were gone some bold soldier discovered a way of knocking the ball out of a cartridge, pouring out the powder and igniting it. This lasted until some of the officers began to wonder where their ammunition was going.

Then someone found that a tent rope, ignited at one end, would smoulder for hours. This worked until the supply sergeants found out about it.

Finally, a set of watches was arranged, and men were appointed whose duty it was to keep a light going for a certain number of hours. Everybody in the regiment is smoking without difficulty now, though there has been only that one carefully nourished light for a week.

They were loading up an ambulance for the long ride back from the field hospital. The patients were being classified into the customary groups of litter and sitting-down cases.

"How about you?" they asked a doughboy who had some shrapnel in his hip. "Can you walk?"

"Sure," he answered. "How far is it?"

"About 40 kilometers."

He scratched his head as though he hated to be shown up. So they explained that they expected him to walk only as far as the ambulance.

The Y. M. C. A. man in the field frequently is the banker for his unit. One was standing alone at the side of a road five or six kilometers behind the lines. All his pockets were obviously overtaxed, and his coat was bulging so that only the lowermost and topmost buttons could connect with their corresponding buttonholes.

"It's money," he explained. "Money and watches. I've got 17 watches and 90,000 francs. The boys got paid before they went in and most of them turned it over to me. I was going up with the battalion, but they asked me to stay behind and watch their valuables."

Y. M. men also keep an emergency fund for change. There is only one thing that a soldier needs change for 10 miles from the nearest store.

"Lemme have 20 francs in silver, please," requests one private.

"Can you give a 10 franc note for this chicken feed?" asks another.

"Sure," says the Y. M. man. "How's the luck running?"

A private of the buck species was watching a plane duel in the skies.

"Quite a sight," said a voice beside him, and his head nearly dropped off when he saw that it belonged to the general commanding the division.

There is a story in that same division, about the same general, which describes how he was seen one day recently walking along and chatting with a top sergeant. This shows that a use has at last been found for top sergeants.

That division did its share, and paid its price for the doing, when it helped to drive the Hun back across the Marne. That night someone softly opened the general's door, and then as softly closed it. And the word went around that he sat with his face buried in his hands, and his frame quivering with sobs.

The division commander in the above incident was Major-General Joseph T. Dickman, of the Third Division, later commander of the Third Army along the Rhine. He died in 1927.

Easy come, easy go.

One of the German regiments opposite the Americans, the members of which are, by this time, probably listed as "missing, believed prisoner," had just been paid when the curtain went down on their activity in *la guerre*.

Exactly 48 hours after the Germans marched before their paymaster and got their pay, they marched before an American officer, who relieved them of the modest collection of marks, pfennigs, and other things they had received.

American regulations for the handling of prisoners provide that all money shall be taken from them and placed in a fund which is devoted to the common needs of prisoners.

Rules specify that no P. G. shall be deprived of his personal effects—Iron Crosses and the like—but almost any captured German is willing to sacrifice anything he has for real tobacco.

When one Boche arrived before the examining officer and was told to empty his pockets, he laid out five partly filled sacks of American makin's, and not much else. For it he had traded off an Iron Cross, his helmet, a trench knife, and all the buttons he could spare.

A certain American private wasn't satisfied, however, with any modest vest pocket souvenirs of the battle. Nothing would do for him, he explained, but a German machine gun.

After his unit was relieved he went to a salvage pile, selected a weapon in good order, and carried it, in addition to his full pack and rifle, all the long, weary kilometers back to *repos*.

It was not until after he had arrived that he discovered it was a French and not a German gun he had seized. We won't repeat his remarks when he made the discovery.

———————

Be he a private or a general, "writing home" usually occupies the first leisure minutes of a soldier just out of action.

Parked near the headquarters of a unit back from the line was an impressive limousine, and in it sat a major general, pounding the keys of a small portable typewriter held on his lap. He had sought the privacy of his automobile to write home.

The embattled letter-writer was Major-General James G. Harbord, then commanding the Second Division.

———————

He was smiling, but pale, when they wheeled him in—a black haired youth of 20—and he was still smiling when they tenderly transferred him to a cot after the doctors had counted seven machine-gun bullet wounds, one in his ankle, three in his side and three in his chest. When a Y. M. C. A. man brought writing paper through the ward he took a piece and asked for a pencil. An attendant found him dead half an hour later with this beginning of a letter in his hand:

"Dear Mother:

"We made an attack on the Germans today and drove them five miles. I am in a hospital tonight. I was slightly wounded in the leg."

———————

Appareil in French can mean anything from an airplane to a moving-picture machine, but in our hospitals it means only the trellis-like arrangement over the cot of a patient whose arm or leg has to be held suspended.

A man lay with his left leg *en appareil* and his bare foot sticking up into space. A piece of shrapnel had pierced his leg.

He kept looking at that bare left foot lovingly. It was the first time he had seen it in 40 days.

———————

An American lying wounded in a wheat field was somewhat taken aback by the spectacle, in slow and stately approach, of a German officer. He was magnificent with medals and he wore a monocle.

Every once in a while his impressiveness was spoiled by a nervous turn of the head and the suspicion of a squirm—just as if someone were tickling his tail with a bayonet.

Someone was, for looking beyond, the wounded American saw a great, big, husky American negro prancing along, showing every tooth in his head.

"Hi-yi, boss," he called out jubilantly, "Ah don' know what Ah's got, but Ah's bringin' it along!"

———————

In the midst of the battle one young lieutenant, running into a pal of his, showed him under the flap of his pocket a little gold brooch.

"If anything should happen to me," he said, "try to get hold of this pin, will you, and when you get time ship it back home to my mother."

The other promised, and the lieutenant went his way. He had not gone 20 feet when he was struck by a shell and killed instantly. The pin is on its way to America.

———————

The captain looked suspiciously at his left trench-shoe.

"A machine-gun bullet went through the heel near the Marne," he said, "and yesterday another went straight across my foot between the sole and my stocking. It didn't do more than scorch me. But if they hit this darned shoe again, I'm going to get a new pair. They seem to think I'm Achilles."

———————

Listing prisoners is always interesting work.

Ernst Herman wore the insignia of an aspirant. In his pockets he had the epaulets of a second lieutenant. His period of probation over, he was to have become a lieutenant the next day. Had he been captured 12 hours later he would have been an officer and—he wouldn't have had to work all the time he remains in captivity.

"Kaiser," said the next prisoner when asked his name.

"Holy Smoke!" exclaimed the doughboy who brought him in. "I've captured the main show."

"Kaiser," repeated the prisoner. "Conrad Kaiser, and I'm 36 years old."

Up to the time that Germany's dwindling man-power caused the military finger to beckon him, Kaiser had been a college professor.

"Will they send us to America?" asked the next prisoner, an artillery captain. He was told that "they" wouldn't, and expressed regret.

"I had decided to go to America after the war anyhow," he explained. "There is nothing more for me in Germany. My father and mother were killed by an air bomb and my two brothers died in action. I'm the only one of the family left."

The generation of American mothers that have trained their boys to care for their teeth as the people of no other country do would glow with pride if they could trek up in the wake of our Army in action and see the whole rear area dotted at sunrise with Yankee soldiers, just out of battle, and every man brushing his teeth. Often most of his possessions have been jettisoned in the rush of the advance.

And now abideth these three, the rifle, the shovel, and the tooth-brush. And the greatest of these ——

An Artillery officer who had been a fairly well-known golfer and a keen enthusiast back home was looking out across a rolling plain that only recently had been heavily pounded by heavy shell fire.

"I've seen some well-trapped courses," he said, "but I must say this is the best bunker course I've ever run across. There's a pit every 20 feet. Par here must be about 200."

It would do Mr. Hoover's heart good if he could see—and probably he did—the harvest being brought in from the reconquered farms between the Marne and the Vesle. Marshal Foch's dashing counter offensive must be measured not only in territory regained, prisoners captured, guns netted, but in rich crops seized at the critical time.

The Germans, who are harder up for food than any other country, lost not only the harvest they held but the harvests they hoped to capture. Now, close behind the troops, the reapers and binders are at work.

The other day a battalion commander at the front, spotting a strange machine that looked like some fantastic tank wobbling along a crest across the valley, caught it in the focus of his field glasses and laughed outright. It was that eminently pacific engine, the land plow.

Here and there a threshing machine plays chorus to the song of the airplanes overhead. Old soldiers in faded blue, old women, buxom young wives, little children, all have been tugging away at the great stacks of wheat, and if you cross a newly harvested field at sunup, you are sure to see the women rolling out from under the hedges, shaking the dew from their hair, and going to work at the gleaning.

The Yanks in hospital, who got their wounds in the fields near Vaux and Bourèsches and Belleau Woods, will be glad to hear that from those fields a golden treasure has already been gathered, and the crickets in the stubble sing a song of peace.

Pvt. Herbert Ploughman, battalion runner in the thick of the fighting below the Vesle, carried his message forward to the platoon and dropped flat a few feet from the commanding lieutenant, who was helping bandage a wounded man's leg.

"What's the matter, are you wounded there?" the lieutenant asked. No, Ploughman was only playing safe. The message was important. Should he come out in the open and deliver it? The lieutenant nodded and Ploughman stepped to his side. He was just in the act of handing the message over when a shell crashed between them, tearing away the lieutenant's leg with a wound so grievous that he died before the day was spent. Somehow, Ploughman got back to his battalion commander.

"The message was delivered, sir," he said, and, from force of habit, saluted.

It was when the hand was thus raised that the major noticed two fingers had just been shot from it.

German officers and non-coms have frequently been detailed to line up prisoner detachments and, under the chaperonage of M. P.'s, march them to the rear. An incident which happened when one Boche non-com was instructed to form his company caused one sage American private to declare that a sergeant is a sergeant no matter what army he is in.

The German sergeant gave the command to fall in, and most of the prisoners obeyed with a clicking of heels that is the pride of the German army. One

Boche was late, however, and brought forth audible expression of the non-com's wrath which, when translated, means about this:

"What are you doing there, you boneheaded recruit? Come to attention! What are you trying to do, spoil our reputation before these Americans?"

A Prussian officer was being questioned at a regimental headquarters just back of Juvigny.

"Wouldn't your men rather surrender than undergo another barrage like the one we just put over?" the American officer asked.

"Never," was the answer. "My men will not surrender to the Americans." Just then five M. P.'s came in with nearly a hundred German prisoners. They were "my men."

At this late date some of the foregoing examples seem somehow to be characterized by a frisky effort at jazzing the war. There is that about them occasionally which seems to hint that *The Stars and Stripes* staff, at gushing editorial conferences, used to clap hands and shout: "Come, come! What shall we do today to help maintain the Spirit of the Troops?" But if there was any jazzing it was wholly unintentional. We simply wrote as we felt.

For we definitely admired this winning Army of which we were a part—admired it in all humility—and we felt a parallel distaste for the enemy. Inspecting ancient issues of *The Stars and Stripes*, I am appalled by our consistent addiction to the term Hun. I fear, and manfully admit, that I was largely responsible for this addiction, since I wrote probably ninety-five out of every hundred heads, and Hun was three letters better adapted to headline purposes than German, and two letters better adapted than Boche. Boche, of course, was much the better label. There was just the proper amount of absurdity about that ridiculous derivative of *l'argot des lou-cherbem*. Hun had a certain desperate impressiveness and dignity. A Hun was someone in a Prince Albert and a stove-pipe hat. A Boche was the same someone with his hat slightly dented.

We were certainly rough on the enemy at the beginning, and, by a perfectly comprehensible psychology, grew much less rough the harder we were fighting him. "Huns Starve and Ridicule U. S. Captives," "Hun's Brutal Policy Matter of Record," "Boiling Water One Instrument of Hun Torture"—these were among our early contributions to the reigning hysteria.

Copies of *The Stars and Stripes* got to Germany—got there, I suppose, through no more mysterious an agency than by mail through Holland or Switzerland. Sundry numbers thus came to the notice of *America in Europe*, a queer journalistic hybrid published at Frankfort-am-Main that was some *oberst commandant's* notion of a grand way to sap the morale of Yankee prisoners of war. The proprietors of *America*

THE ENEMY TAKES NOTE OF THE A. E. F.'S OFFICIAL NEWSPAPER—A CARTOON FROM AMERICA IN EUROPE, PUBLISHED IN GERMANY FOR DISTRIBUTION TO AMERICAN PRISONERS OF WAR. THE CARTOON WAS REPRINTED IN THE STARS AND STRIPES

in Europe seem to have watched and waited for an opening, and finally they found one in *The Stars and Stripes* for August 2nd. They then duly exposed us in an editorial which was set off with the cartoon reproduced herewith. The editorial, in *America in Europe's* own English, read:

> Under the illustrious title of *Stars and Stripes* there exists a publication characterizing itself as the official newspaper of the American Expeditionary Forces. A casual perusal of any of its numbers will convince the reader that the editors, in contradistinction to all gallant and chivalrous soldiers, have made it their general object to throw mud at their enemies in war. We absolutely refuse to believe that real American fighters are in any way responsible for the mad howl against the Huns set up in the columns of *Stars and Stripes* and for the sake of

America's good name we protest against this disgraceful employment of our beloved emblem.

But a simple protest won't do in the case of *Stars and Stripes* of August 2. In the six column of its front page, a bunch of lies is offered, so vile, so silly and —so stale that we must nail the name of the paper on our PILLORY FOR LIARS. It is up now to General Pershing, who despises vituperation of one's enemy, to stop the scandal and protect our *Stars and Stripes* against further disgrace.

This American newspaper wants to be up-to-date and yet indulges in warming up again that four-year-old English lie of German soldiers chained to their guns. Have these liars never bethought themselves of the gross nonsense to assume that cowardly soldiers do better, that is deadlier service against the enemy when they are chained to their guns? It takes all the impudence that only brazen ignorance and unlimited superficiality can provide to invent such lies. On account of its extreme absurdity this particular lie did not live long after its English birth.

To see its resurrection now in an American newspaper puts every good American to the blush. Of course the chained to their guns lie is entwined by smaller though not less violent lies. But no more of it; the liars have been caught and nailed.

I have forgotten (and neither tigers nor constitutional amendments would drag from me if I had not) who was guilty of the chained-to-the-guns charge. Certainly we should have known better. The heavy German machine gun was equipped with chains so that its crew could haul it from position to position with readiest convenience, and some adroit intelligence in the early days of the war, perhaps discovering a dead crew with the chains in their hands, had jumped to the chained-to-the-guns conclusion.

America in Europe did not make so much of this slip as it might have. Its irony labored and its cartoon looked then, as it looks still, too bizarre to be effective. The cartoonist's portrayal of our editor is an ideal rather than a literal likeness. It bears not the slightest resemblance to Visk even in his more critical moods.

The fact that a lusty proportion of the A. E. F. was now actively engaged in fighting the war by no means gave us leave to ignore that large fraction of it which fate or G. H. Q. had stationed south and east of Paris. For the harder the combat divisions fought, the harder the S. O. S. worked to keep up with them. At the head of the S. O. S. was a fighting general, J. G. Harbord, who had commanded the Marine Brigade at Château-Thierry and the Second Division at Soissons and who could have commanded an army had he not foresworn ambition when his friend and chief asked him to assume the arduous but unillumined task of heading the Services of Supply. As soon as General Harbord was appointed chief of the S. O. S. he made a tour of the whole vast area under his command, and Private Hawley was assigned a place on his special train. Thereafter, to our high envy, Private Hawley used frequently to get letters from General Harbord which opened not with the conventional military salutation of "From: To: Subject" but with "My dear Hawley."

Others of us, particularly Sergeant Philip Von Blon, who had joined the staff in July, made frequent journeys to Tours. Not Washington itself was a more thoroughly American city than General Harbord's own capital, and its supreme importance as an A. E. F. news center has already been noted. But apart from supplying news, the S. O. S. no less than the front offered a multitude of sidelights that presented in composite an accurate picture of a life which, no fault of those who lived it, had to be spent far behind the guns. Just as every flitting representative from the Marne salient brought back a sheaf of footnotes which may serve the ultimate war historian no less than the narratives on page one, so did the transient staff sojourner in the S. O. S. set down minor ana that were then and still are more graphic than impressive statistical summaries of troops and tonnage (which we couldn't print then anyway):

Colored troops from Louisiana have a linguistic advantage over other American soldiers. Many of them, through living in sections where French still is spoken, are more or less familiar with the language of this land when they get here. But they have their difficulties nevertheless.

"It's dis way," explained one. "Ah talk French puhfectly, but not de kind dey talk in dis country. You see, Ah learned French from mah fathah—de pure, classical, ole New Ohleans French—and dey don't speak dat kind ovah heah."

The French in the S. O. S. region have a delicious sense of linguistic values.

Witness this sign, in the window of a restaurant patronized by British and Yank toilers at two nearby depots:

"English spoken.

"American understood."

It is the duty of a certain Engineer sergeant to take half a hundred German prisoners out in the morning and see that, in the following eight hours, they do their bit toward winning the war—for the Allies.

For three days the sergeant had been troubled by the fact that the P. G.'s were not "hitting the ball". He had exhorted them and ordered them and they neither understood nor obeyed. Finally, he sent for an interpreter. The latter arrived when the sergeant was in a particularly angry mood.

"I want you to make these guys quit layin' down on the job," said the sergeant. "I want you to ask 'em how the hell they expect us to win this war by stalling around this way."

Second class mail is no more certain of arriving in the S. O. S. than it is anywhere else. So one man who likes, much as do the rest of us, to see his home town paper once in a while, has his wife cut out the news that will interest him and ship it along in a sealed envelope, postage paid. When he gets a letter from home his office looks like a clipping bureau. But he finds out what's going on.

Company censors in the S. O. S. haven't yet gotten entirely used to the rule permitting the mention of certain place names. More than one soldier's letter has started back over the ocean with the names carefully excised and then as carefully written in again over the gaping holes in the paper.

They were sitting around in the room wherein the company barber holds forth, in a camp not so very far removed from the seashore, where the old, coming out of hospitals, and the new, coming out of transports, frequently meet. After the immemorial custom of chaffing the man in the chair had been duly observed, the "nexts" started chaffing each other.

Over in a corner a shy young second lieutenant sat, not taking very much part in the chaffing. (Yes, reader, there is a new issue of shy young second lieutenants; have you got yours yet?) The old-timers, pausing in their fun, sought to include him in the conversation.

"You've just come over, haven't you?" ventured one of the two-stripers, with kindly inflection.

"Oh, no, sir!" protested the S. Y. S. L., bristling in an instant. "I've been over here two weeks!"

Of all scientific and mechanical products which make war possible, none is more important than tin. You might conceive of a big scale war without gas or airplanes, or a lot of other things, but you couldn't conceive of one without tin. A big fraction of the vast supply of food and medical supplies for the A. E. F. come in tin cans, and it would be impracticable if not impossible to handle most of it in any other kind of a container. On the docks at the base ports and in storage warehouses are stored literally millions of cans containing myriad articles.

Some day some one ought to write a poetic tribute to the old tin can—it has got it coming.

———

A prince of Prussia—genuineness guaranteed—who had rapiered his way through Munich or Heidelberg, bullied poor old cobblers and kept up generally the standing of his house, found himself ruffled, but intact, in a prison camp for German officers, somewhere in the S. O. S. zone.

An American captain, an engineering designer, who had been born in Switzerland and spoke German perfectly, was trying to extract military information from the line of prisoners when at last they brought in the royal lieutenant.

"Guten morgen, leutnant," observed the American officer pleasantly.

The Prussian made a noise deep down in his throat, and his lips shook with a rolling, gutteral exclamation of disgust.

"Address me as 'Your Royal Highness'!" he demanded, drawing himself up in his chair.

"Stand up!" roared the captain. "How dare you address a superior officer in that manner? Remember you are only a lieutenant."

The interview proceeded satisfactorily.

———

The Q. M. C. is shaking hands with itself again on this cargo-saving stunt. They're leaving the soup bones behind in the United States now, and refrigerator vessels are bringing tons of boneless beef to France. The experiment has worked very well, although dubious cooks think the next plan may be to send all fresh ground Hamburger steak.

———

The American soldier at leisure has proved himself about as much of a success as the American soldier at the front.

Since the first American leave center was established and opened at Aix-les-Bains, on the edge of the French Alps, along last February, just one man of the thousands who have come, had their stay, and gone, has committed a breech of deportment regulations serious enough to warrant his being returned to his company.

AMERICAN SOLDIER ON LEAVE AT AIX-LES-BAINS, AS SEEN BY PRIVATE WALLGREN, WHO WAS NEVER THERE

And this man (an ambulance driver) after returning, abandoned his ambulance in No Man's Land, walked back to headquarters and announced that he was a fish, and is now under observation that his mental condition may be determined. So he, probably, shouldn't be counted.

———

Ordinarily a soldier doesn't appear at the leave center with any more baggage than the law allows. One man arrived with a pair of extra socks and a rifle. Why the rifle? This was his explanation:

"It's a souvenir. Oh, it still shoots all right, and I'm going to use it for the rest of the war, and after that—well, this is one rifle no supply sergeant is ever going to get a hold of."

He exhibited the stock. There was a nick an inch deep at the top.

"Machine gun near Soissons. Shows how near a bullet can come without getting you."

———

Private Simp was in the train, starting back to his unit. The train was running beside the River Rhône, broad, placid and beautiful.

"I know how to end this war quick," he said to his buddy. "Change the o in Rhône to an i, and get out and capture it."

"Oh, piffle!" said Buddy. "I've got a better idea than that. Go back to the States, capture Berlin, Conn., hang the stationmaster, and call the war off."

———

There is a colored labor outfit in the S. O. S. engaged in quarry work near a base port. A few weeks ago, in the course of opening up some new ground, they discovered an old Roman burying ground with many skeletons, coins and relics. The find made quite an impression on the minds of the finders, and there were many speculations as to whether the shades of the departed legionaries still hover around in the vicinity of their last resting place. The general opinion was that a man ought to be on his guard when out late at night.

About that time the sum of 60 francs disappeared from the counter of a nearby Y. M. C. A. hut. The captain of this outfit doesn't know a great deal about classroom psychology, but he has learned a lot about it in the field. He called his outfit together one night in the Y hut and told them of the disappearance of the money. Then he outlined the history and characteristics of the old Romans.

"Boys," he said, "there was one thing a Roman hated worse than anything else, and that was a thief. If the ghosts of those old fellows who were buried up there on the hill should learn that somebody in this outfit had 60 stolen francs in his pocket, I don't know just what would happen. I'm going to put my hat here on the table and turn out the lights. The guilty man will know what to do."

There was quite a shuffling of feet and milling around in the hut, and then all was quiet. When the captain turned on the lights again and looked in the hat he found not only the 60 francs, but 300 more, and a few odd centimes for good measure.

———————

American Express officials in one branch in France say the enlisted men are banking more money per man than the officers. Well, well!

CHAPTER FIVE

MY COUNTRY, 'TIS OF THEE

A T THE beginning of its career *The Stars and Stripes* had sounded a clarion call for contributions. This was the only clarion used in the A. E. F., all other organizations holding fast to the conventional bugle. There was even an element of desperation in the appeal, which is hard to understand, since we were safe as long as Private Hawley did not lose the use of his fingers. The lengths to which this desperation could go may be measured from the fact that we specifically asked, among other desiderata, for verse.

As a result we got verse in an abundance that no periodical had ever got verse before. There was, I think, at least one other reason for this abundance besides our asking for it. Poetry is compounded in an emotional crucible, and so many of us contrive to edge through life without ever laying hands on an emotional crucible. The war placed this essential receptacle in nearly five million pairs of American hands. Many of the recipients gaily tossed theirs away in favor of the less sentimental messkit, which was reasonable enough. If every American soldier and sailor had written or tried to write poetry they would have had little time for fighting, and our boys and girls today might be calling a spade a schaufel.

There were a dozen poems in the first number of *The Stars and Stripes*, most of which will one day appear in the definitive edition of the works of Hudson Hawley. Hawley welcomed competition, however, as the true artist should, for in the second number appeared the following editorial (to ascribe which to Hawley may be an injustice to Cushing) under the title, no less, of "The Urge to Poesy":

Not so very long ago an American poet who really ought to be better known (his name is Richard Hovey and he died in 1900) summed it up this way:

"Three secrets that never were said:
　The stir of the moth in the spring,
　The desire of a man for a maid,
　The urge of the poet to sing."

With the first two we are not particularly concerned. The spring isn't here yet, for one thing, and the authorities differ as to when it will be. The second needs no explanation. The third—ah, that's the one that puzzles us! Why is it that a man who was a paying teller or a housepainter or a dog-catcher in civilian life becomes, the minute he dons khaki, a fervent would-be poet possessed of a highly irrepressible urge?

To be sure, an American soldier, if inclined to take serious thought, has about the most wonderful theme in the world to adorn with real poetic treatment—a nation, seeking no material advantage for itself, going to war that the world may be forever rid of tyranny and the consequent menace of future wars. But it's seldom he tackles so lofty a theme. Usually he contents himself with putting into verse the new and interesting thoughts that come to him from his contact with a country and a civilization which have hitherto been a closed book to him; in jotting down rhymes about his bunkmates, his officers, his chow, his drill,—in short, all about this great life of soldiering. Usually, be it said, he does a pretty good job of it, for the poetry that gets close to the every-day realities of existence is far more apt to live and thrive than is the poetry which deals with abstract virtues and principles.

For our own part, we hope the American soldier will not hold in his poetic urge as closely as he holds in his chin at " 'Ten-Shun!" It's nothing to be ashamed of, that desire to "bust into song"; everybody's felt it at some time or another, and has felt better for giving in to it. And, the chances are, if a man feels strongly about what he writes he will also want to have other people feel strongly, too; so he seeks to have his work printed.

Send 'em along then, you Amex versifiers! *The Stars and Stripes* wants to see your warbles.

The immediate results of this appeal were not impressive. Hawley and a pair of scissors continued for the next few numbers to be our chief lyricists. But as the weeks ran on there developed a gradual infiltration of response, and the quantity soon grew to such an extent that late in April, Visk, who I don't suppose ever built a lofty rhyme in his life, decided to devote a column in each issue to this overflow of sentiment.

One day he summoned Woollcott and me into the presence and asked us to help him select the copy for this first appearance of the column that was thereupon christened, and remained to the end, "The Army's Poets". Visk picked up the first chance scrap of paper and read it aloud:

I will be the gladdest thing under the sun;
I will touch a hundred flowers, and not pick one.
I will look at cliffs and clouds with quiet eyes;
Watch the wind bow down the grass,
And the grass rise.
And when lights begin to show up from the town,
I will mark which must be mine,
And then start down.

Spring had come to France—spring comes to France a few weeks earlier than it does to Connecticut or Iowa. Here, then, plainly, was a soldier who had gone out on a slope of the Vosges or in the valley of the Loire—ducked a detail, perhaps, to do it—and seen spring come, had drunk the beauty of an April day, had thought him of a hillside in Vermont or Pennsylvania or Wisconsin and set down the lyric essence of his home-longing in words that, so far as Woollcott and I were concerned, were going to be deathless.

"That's no good," said Visk, possibly to test our critical acumen, and forthwith he tore the manuscript in two and tossed it in the wastebasket. More lissom than Woollcott, I gained the wastebasket first. Together we smoothed out the crinkled folds, matched the torn edges together, and proclaimed that no captain in the A. E. F. (Visk had been promoted two grades a few weeks earlier), nay, no General Staff, could prevent that golden fragment from appearing in *The Stars and Stripes*.

Visk yielded in the face of this rhapsodic approval, and the scorned composition duly appeared as the first entry in the first column devoted to "The Army's Poets". It was credited to a private in the Quartermaster Corps.

Two weeks later an illusion faced the firing squad. From the field came a communication that moved Woollcott, in his most indignant manner, to compose the following open declaration that all the lowlifes who were devoting their time to the war were not in the German, Austrian, Turkish and Bulgarian armies. The name of the offender is charitably concealed—it was duly emblazoned in the original editorial and even in the heading: "Private —— to the Bar":

> We are in receipt of the following letter from Ord. Sgt. Launa W. Holland, A. P. O. 717:
>
> "In the May 3rd issue of *The Stars and Stripes* in column 1 on page 5, under the caption 'The Army's Poets,' there appears a poem, 'The Hill Back Home,' credited to Pvt. ——, Q. M. C.
>
> "I do not want to rob any one of due credit, but the verse referred to was written and published in the States early last summer by a woman, though I do

not recall the name, and entitled 'An Afternoon on a Hill.' The only difference is the word 'quiet' in the third line, which was originally 'kind.' The poem was reviewed in a July or August issue of *The Literary Digest* as an example of a poem written at that time and not inspired by the war and this was where I saw

"FROM: TO: SUBJECT", ANOTHER AUTOBIOGRAPHICAL INTERPRETATION BY WALLGREN

it. And in writing a friend back in the States I quoted it in a letter during the latter part of September."

It should be added, by way of further evidence in the case of the A. E. F. *vs.* Pvt. ——, defendant, that when he sent in this singularly beautiful poem (not

only signed with his own name, but with the explicit statement that he had "composed" it), it bore the title "One Afternoon on the Hill." That title was changed in this office in the belief that "The Hill Back Home" lent to the exquisite imagery of the poem some color of the war.

It would seem from this *prima facie* evidence, Pvt. ——, that, unlike your accuser, you are not one of those who "do not want to rob any one of due credit." What have you to say to the charge that you are a thief?

So far as I recall, Private —— had nothing to say. But it is interesting to note, for the benefit of those who may still regard the A. E. F. as a ragamuffin horde which sprang to arms in an ecstatic rush in order to avoid going to a school for defective children, that it included among its enlisted personnel at least four early admirers of the work of Edna St. Vincent Millay.

The Q. M. C. private was not the only uniformed offender against literary ethics— he can claim for himself only the distinction of having been the first in the history of *The Stars and Stripes*. A few weeks later appeared an editorial called "Just Thinking". This had been the title of a poem which had been published on page one of the second number under the unequivocal by-line of Hudson Hawley. Somebody paid Hawley the tribute of plagiarism, and the riposte of *The Stars and Stripes* (unquestionably, from internal evidence, the work of Hawley himself) exhibits a pardonable annoyance resulting not so much from the simple fact of the theft as from the garbling of the loot. Here again blanks may charitably be used where name and address were given in full in the original:

We are in receipt of a copy of a poem, sent us by Pvt. Melvin Ryder, which, according to him, purports to have been "passed on from soldier to soldier, and edited somewhat," and to have been written by [name and home address], whose A. E. F. address is unknown.

The poem in question is, with the exception of a paltry few words and punctuation changes (one of which destroys the rhyme which the original had), a direct duplicate of "Just Thinking," written by a member of the editorial staff of *The Stars and Stripes*, on the afternoon of either February 4 or 5, in the office of the Chief of the Press Division, I. S., G. S., at ——, France, and printed on the first page, top of second column from the left, of the second issue of *The Stars and Stripes*, on February 15, 1918.

From the nature of the copy—even the same title, "Just Thinking," is used— the "poem" purporting to have been written by —— is manifestly a taking down of the original; probably, from the nature of the changes, an attempt to reconstruct it from memory, or, more uncharitably, an attempt to cover up the adoption of it as his own by a slight switching of the phraseology.

The Stars and Stripes isn't calling ———— to account—yet. It is "just thinking."

Just what penalty *The Stars and Stripes* purposed to exact in addition to this exposure of the culprit was not subsequently disclosed. Private Ryder, later Sergeant Major Ryder, himself afterward became a member of *The Stars and Stripes* staff and a prop of the circulation department.

Not quite a year later, with the war well over and a good share of the A. E. F. already restored to the homeland, it became necessary to return to the attack. Once more the name of the alleged offender is ruthlessly suppressed—the editorial excoriating him, appearing in the issue for April 4, 1919, was headed "Petty Larcency":

A bit of fooling having been submitted to this newspaper as the work of ————, Company —, — Machine Gun Battalion, was printed on this page three weeks ago under the heading "M. D. R." Immediately there poured in information to the effect that it was originally printed in "Life" and written by Neal O'Hara, a Boston newspaper man now in the Navy.

The theft of which said ———— thus stands accused is a form of weak-mindedness, rather than criminality—a curious form from which many members of the A. E. F. seem to be suffering during these trying days. For instance, *The Stars and Stripes* has, within the last month, received, one at a time, between 50 and 60 copies of a poem beginning

Silver threads among the black—
Darling, I am coming back.
Now that Europe's peace appears
I'll be home in seven years.

The copies never vary except in one striking particular—that of the signature. Each time it comes in, it appears to be the work of a different man.

It should be obvious by now that we of the staff held plagiarism to be a somewhat less mitigable offense than treason. It should be obvious, as well, that we attached far more importance to the business than it merited. Plagiarism is a highly technical and professional offense. It becomes grand larceny only when committed by someone who should know better, and the number of men and women who do not know any better is amazing. The average non-professional sees something in print (almost invariably a poem) that he likes tremendously; he cuts it out and puts it in his pocket, or laboriously copies it with a stubby pencil and puts it in the same pocket, or sends it home, or shows it to his buddies, or transmits it to his favorite newspaper not as a production of the creative instinct but as something he has admired and wants to share with his fellows. Thus, substituting word of mouth for pencil and paper, was English balladry perpetuated; thus was the *Iliad* composed. True, there are exceptions like the Q. M. private who specifically asserted the composition of Miss Millay's verses, but certainly the offense of the fifty men who submitted transcripts of "Silver threads among the black" is hardly comparable to his.

Lumping them all together, the felons and the more or less innocent bystanders, they constituted a tiny fragment of the vocal impulse of the A. E. F. This fragment aside, we were ready and eager to indorse the great bulk of our lyrical contributors, and did so handsomely not long after the end of hostilities:

Although we speak without the confirmatory authority of Smith's Classical Dictionary, which is not to hand (you can't have all the comforts of home even during an armistice), we believe, none the less, that we are spelling the name correctly when we say that it was Tyrtaeus who, ousted from Athens because he was a poet and therefore presumably poor soldier stuff, forthwith journeyed to Sparta, composed a new set of battle anthems for the war-loving folk who adopted him, and sent them singing into victory against the people who had exiled him.

The Tyrtaeuses of our day are legion. But their influence—witness Rupert Brooke, Francis Ledwidge, Alan Seeger—is as potent, as direct, as definite as was that of their forerunner. And we of America, though this is not the place to discuss whether or not America has produced a warrior poet in her own armies, like to think that the inspiration of song, our own song, has had its share in our share of the victory.

All of which is only a modest way of calling attention to the Army's Poets, who conduct their column forum this week, as usual, in the same place and at the same length. They need no apologists. We of the paper know only this: that no part of the paper is read more religiously, studied more sedulously, clipped more consistently.

It has surprised us. We did not expect that O. D. poems would come in at the rate of 70 a day, with no further hope of reward for the writers than the appearance of their brain-children in print. We did not guess that that part of the Army which does not write poetry (we are convinced that it is a minority) reads it to a man.

All of which goes to show that when you go to war you learn about a lot of things besides fighting.

There were those among us who thought at the time that "Tribute," by Second Lieutenant F. M. H. Dazey, was the finest piece of verse *The Stars and Stripes* ever printed. Perhaps it was. I would not damn it with faint praise, for I once thought so myself and may yet. But I prefer to wait ten more years before coming to an unalterable decision. Here is "Tribute" to speak for itself:

There's tumultuous confusion a-comin' down the road,
    An' the camouflage don't nearways hide the dust,
An' it ain't no flock of camions, though some's carryin' a load
    (I guess the provos winked—or got it fust).
But now it's comin' closer, you can tell 'em by the roar—
It's the Umpty Second Infantry, a-goin' in once more.

        Oh, they've met the Hun at the length of a gun,
        And they know what he is and they mind what he's done,
        So that's why they sing as they slog to more fun!
        You doughboys, you slowboys,
        Here's luck, an' let her go, boys—
        We like you, Infantry.

Now us in the Artillery don't live no life of ease,
    Nor yet particular security,
For the present that Fritz sends us one can't dodge behind the trees,
    Unless trees was much thicker than they be.
But we know our lot is doughnuts, Orders Home and Gay Paree
To what you march to singing, Umpty Second Infantry.

        Oh, there's numerous blanks in your company ranks,
        But there's two in the Boches' for one in the Yanks',
        An' all that he guv, you returned him with thanks,
        You doughboys, you slowboys,
        Here's luck, and let her go, boys—
        We like you, Infantry.

Lieutenant Dazey did not write "Umpty Second"—he wrote "Hundred Second", but to have said so in *The Stars and Stripes* would have been to disclose to the enemy the fact that New England was loyal to the United States and was represented in the A. E. F. by a division all her own.

I don't know who wrote "Camouflage". It appeared in print signed simply M. G., which might have meant Machine Gunner or might have been the author's initials.

Whoever wrote it, "Camouflage" will always rank with me among the first dozen
poems of the war:

> They tell us tales of camouflage,
> The art of hiding things;
> Of painted forts and bowered guns
> Invisible to wings.
>> Well, it's nothing new to us,
>> To us, the rank and file;
>> We understand this camouflage
>> —We left home with a smile.

> We saw the painted battleships
> And earthen-colored trains,
> And planes the hue of leaden skies
> And canvas-hidden lanes.
>> Well, we used the magic art
>> That day of anxious fears;
>> We understand this camouflage
>> —We laughed away your tears.

> They say that scientific men
> And artists of renown
> Debated long on camouflage
> Before they got it down.
>> Well, it came right off to us,
>> We didn't have to learn;
>> We understood this camouflage
>> —We said we'd soon return.

> We understand this camouflage,
> This art of hiding things;
> It's what's behind a soldier's jokes
> And all the songs he sings.
>> Yes, it's nothing new to us,
>> To us, the rank and file;
>> We understand this camouflage
>> —We left home with a smile.

Lieutenant Dazey was not the only non-Infantry officer who had a good word for infantry. Lieutenant L. W. Suckert of the Air Service contributed "As the Trucks Go Rollin' By":

There's a rumble an' a jumble an' a bumpin' an' a thud,
As I wakens from my restless sleep here in my bed o' mud,
'N' I pull my blankets tighter underneath my shelter fly,
An' I listen to the thunder o' the trucks a-rollin' by.

They're jumpin' an' they're humpin' through the inky gloom o' night,
'N' I wonder how them drivers see without a glim o' light;
I c'n hear the clutches roarin' as they throw the gears in high,
An' the radiators boilin' as the trucks go rollin' by.

There's some a-draggin' cannons, you c'n spot the sound all right—
The rumblin' ones is heavies, an' the rattly ones is light;
The clinkin' shells is pointin' up their noses at the sky—
Oh, you c'n tell what's passin' as the trucks go rollin' by.

But most of 'em is packin' loads o' human Yankee freight
That'll slam the ole soft pedal ontuh Heinie's Hymn of Hate;
You c'n hear 'em singin' "Dixie," and the "Sweet Bye 'N' Bye,"
'N' "Where Do We Go From Here, Boys?" as the trucks go rollin' by.

Some's singin' songs as, when I left, they wasn't even ripe
(A-showin' 'at they're rookies wot ain't got a service stripe),
But jus' the same they're good ole Yanks, and that's the reason why
I likes the jazz 'n' barber shop o' the trucks a-rollin' by.

Jus' God and Gen'rul Pershing knows where these here birds'll light,
Where them bumpin' trucks is bound for under camouflage o' night,
When they can't take aero pitchers with their Fokkers in the sky
Of our changes o' location by the trucks a-rollin' by.

So, altho' my bed is puddles, an' I'm soaked through to the hide,
My heart's out with them doughboys on their bouncin', singin' ride
They're bound for paths o' glory, or, p'raps, to fight 'n' die—
God bless that Yankee cargo in the trucks a-rollin' by.

All ranks from private to major were represented among "The Army's Poets". Colonels and generals may have been present behind the screen of anonymity. At least, if they did not sing of themselves, other ranks could sing about them. H. F., himself probably not a colonel, sent in "Somewhere in France":

> Why is it that from yonder tower
>   The Colonel's lamp is beaming still,
> Though it is past the midnight hour
>   And all's serene o'er vale and hill?
> 'Tis not the wisdom of the sages,
>   Nor army lore his mind enchants;
> An earthlier task his time engages;
>   He's sewing buttons on his pants.

Much of the verse that came in was light to the point of frothiness, but the froth was often atop bitter beer. Still a soldier could handle a serious theme tenderly without prating about death or devising elaborate abstractions concerned with patriotism, witness "Lines on Leaving a Little Town Where We Rested", by Corporal Russell Lord:

> We with the war ahead,
>   You who have held the line,
> Laughing, have broken bread
>   And taken wine.
>
> We cannot speak your tongue,
>   We cannot fully know
> Things hid beneath your smile
>   Four years ago.
>
> Things which have given us,
>   Grimly, a common debt,
> Now that we take the field
>   We won't forget!

A similar sentiment could agitate the nickel-plated heartstrings of the Military Police, as was proved by Private Steuart M. Emery in "The Lost Towns":

> Beneath the new moon sleeping
>   The little lost towns lie;
> Their streets are very white and hushed,
>   Their black spires tilt the sky.

Across the darkened meadows
  A plaintive night bird calls;
The sea of fog that clouds the fields
  Rolls softly to their walls.

Within their shuttered houses
  No midnight candles glance;
Their womenfolk are all abed,
  Their menfolk fight for France.

They dream, the little lost towns
  Of Alsace and Lorraine,
The vision of the patient years,
  The old frontier again.

Sleep on, nor cease your dreaming,
  Who pitted men and crowns,
We'll bring you back, we'll bring you back,
  Oh, little long lost towns.

Alsace and Lorraine were all very well in their way, of course, but the A. E. F. was fighting to regain not so much Metz and Strasbourg as Nashville and Minneapolis. Home-longing was a dangerous subject—one at which more than one militarized Pegasus shied or over which he stumbled into a bog of mawkishness. Captain Joseph Mills Hanson (of whom there will be more to say) managed the business with masculine delicacy in "The Little Dreams":

Now, France is a pleasant land to know
If you're back in a billet town,
And a hell of a hole for the human mole
Where the trenches burrow down;
But where doughboys be in their worn O. D.,
Whatever their daily grinds,
There's a little dream on this sort of theme
In the background of their minds:

"Oh, gee whiz, I'd give my mess kit
And the barrel off my gat
Just to take a stroll up Main Street

In a new Fedora hat;
Just to hit the Rexall Drug Store
For an ice-cream soda stew,
And not a doggoned officer
To tell me what to do."

Here's a youngster sprawled in an old shell hole
With a Chauchat at his eye;
There's some wide H. E. on the next O. P.
And a Fokker in the sky.
It's a hundred yards to his jump-off trench
And ten to the German wire,
But what does he hear, more loud and clear
Than the crack of harassing fire?

Echoed footsteps on the marble;
Throbs of a revolving door,
And the starter's ticking signal—
"Up! Express here—fourteenth floor!"
Click of coins on the cigar stand;
Two stout parties passing by—
"I sold short and took no chances;
Lackawanna's too damned high."

Here's a C. O. down in his dugout deep
Who once was a poor N. G.
The field-phone rings and someone sings,
"Red Gulch, sir. 12—9—3
Is spilling lach on Mary Black;
Have Jane retaliate."
Two minutes more and he hears Jane roar,
While he thinks this hymn of hate:

"That north forty must look pretty,
Head-high, now, and ears all set;
And the haystacks in the meadow—
Wonder if they've mowed it yet?
Crickets clicking in the stubble;

Apples reddening on the trees—
Oh, good Lord, I'm seeing double;
That's not gas that made me sneeze!"

Here's a Q. M. warehouse, locked and still,
At the end of a village street;
The sunset red on the woods ahead
And a sentry on his beat.
The hour chimes from the ancient spire,
A child laughs out below,
And the sentry's eyes, on the western skies,
Behold, in the afterglow,

Row on row of smoking chimneys,
Long steel roofs and swinging cranes,
Maze of tracks and puffing engines,
Creeping strings of shunted trains,
Asphalt streets and stuccoed houses,
Lots, with brick and lath piled high;
Whips of shade trees by the curbings,
Yellow trolleys clanging by.

These are tawdry thoughts in an epic time
For martial souls to own?
They are thoughts, my friend, that we would not mend,
That are bred of our blood and bone.
A mustard shell, it is very well,
And an egg grenade's O.K.,
But we get our steam from our little dream
Of the good old U. S. A.

Cotton fields along the river,
Night lights streaming from a mill;
Corn, with curling leaves a-quiver,
Dump-cars lining out a fill;
Presses roaring in a basement,
Woods, with waters gleaming through—
Kaiser Bill, we'll up and go there
When we've rid the world of you!

What, one wonders, ever became of the writer of this piece of propaganda—for its title, "For Back-Home Legislators," boldly stamped it such? Its author planned to wait only "a dozen years"—thirteen have passed—does he now tenant the "vine-yard-covered acres" of his heart's desire?

If the States go prohibition ere the year that we go home,
    And from Oakland to Hoboken are bone dry,
I will bide my time till muster out; then once again I'll roam
    And across the blooming ocean I will hie.
But I won't have any reveille aboard the blooming ship,
    Nor a life boat drill whenever there's a squall,
For by that time all the submarines will sure have got the pip,
    And I won't mind being seasick—not at all!

There's a farm not far from Somewhere, where we used to serve our time,
    And I know that I can buy it for a song;
There are pigs and geese aplenty, and the village church's chime
    Rings the hours and the quarters all day long.
But my hanker for the simple life is not because of these,
    But because of thirst—the means which thirst to quell
I shall find upon my petite ferme as easy as you please,
    And you bet that I won't find it in the well!

For the farm has vine-clad hillsides, and its luscious fruit I'll tend
    Till the time is ripe for pressing into vin,
And if I can be patient for a dozen years, at end
    I shall pull off quite some party there—oh, man!
Let the others marry Daisy, and the rest sing "Home, Sweet Home,"
    An outcast "bach" I'll happily remain
If the States go dry and dreary—and be quite prepared to show 'm
    My vineyard-covered acres in Lorraine!

Private Charles Divine could wax lightly romantic in the midst of alarms and offered "When Private Mugrums Parlay Voos":

                I can count my francs and santeems—
                    If I've got a basket near—
                An' I speak a wicked "bon jour,"
                    But the verbs are awful queer,
                An' I lose a lot o' pronouns
                    When I try to talk to you,

For your eyes are so bewitchin'
  I forget to parlay voo.

In your pretty little garden,
  With the bench beside the wall,
An' the sunshine on the asters,
  An' the purple phlox so tall,
I should like to whisper secrets
  But my language goes askew—
With the second person plural
  For the more familiar "too."

In your pretty little garden
  I could always say "juh tame,"
But it ain't so very subtle,
  An' it ain't not quite the same
As "You've got some dandy earrings,"
  Or "Your eyes are nice and brown"—
But my adjectives get manly
  Right before a lady noun.

Those infinitives perplex me;
  I can say you're "tray jolee,"
But beyond that simple statement
  All my tenses don't agree.
I can make the Boche "comprenney"
  When I meet 'em in a trench,
But the softer things escape me
  When I try to yap in French.

In your pretty little garden
  Darn the idioms that dance
On your tongue so sweet and rapid,
  Ah, they hold me in a trance!
Though I stutter an' I stammer,
  In your garden, on the bench,
Yet my heart is writin' poems
  When I talk to you in French.

Money is the sinews of war; without it even the humblest private is muscle-bound. Corporal (ultimately Sergeant) Tyler H. Bliss's "How It Works Out" is unquestionably an autobiographical fragment:

When Jonesy joined the Army he had all the dope down fine,
Said he, "I'd ought to land the cush, though serving in the line.
A private's pay is thirty, then by adding ten per cent—
  That's thirty-three,
  And now lessee,
  In this here now French currency—
  Five-sixty rate,
  Makes one-eight-eight—
  Or thereabouts, why hell! that's great!
  It's more'n enough
  To buy me stuff,
  And let me throw a swell front bluff.
  Because my chow
  Is paid for now,
  And I don't need but to allow
  A little kale
  For *vin* or ale,
  And maybe some day blow a frail
  To vo-de-vee
  In gay Paree
  Or some live joint like that city—
Why, I'll be flush—besides, Friend Gvt. is staking me the rent."

On pay day Jones was right on deck, an outstretched cap in view—
He thought by trusting to his hands some clackers might leak through.
He'd planned to split his wages among all the leading banks,
  But the Q. M.
  Just said, "Ahem!
  You'll find your dope sheet is a gem.
  Expenses come
  To quite a sum
  Though where the tin is coming from
  Is not my care
  But your affair.

We'll have to charge you for a pair
Of leggins lost,
Ten francs the cost;
On board the ship we note you tossed
A cigarette
Into the wet—
Subs might upon our trail have set.
That'll put you
Back ninety-two,
Insurance, bonds, allotments, too—
In short, you owe the Government just eighty-seven francs."

Food, too, was a perennial theme of the A. E. F. troubadour. Hawley, our ranking occasional poet, contrived a minor masterpiece to order, "Home Is Where the Pie Is," to accompany a Signal Corps photograph of a tin-helmeted Salvation Army girl making a pie:

"Home is where the heart is"—
    Thus the poet sang;
But "home is where the pie is"
    For the doughboy gang.
Crullers in the craters,
    Pastry in *abris*—
This Salvation Army lass
    Sure knows how to please!

Watch her roll the pie crust
    Mellower than gold;
Watch her place it neatly
    Within its ample mold;
Sniff the grand aroma
    While it slowly bakes—
Though the whine of "Minnie" shells
    Echoes far awakes.

Tin hat for a halo!
    Ah, she wears it well!
Making pies for homesick lads
    Sure is "beating hell";

In a region blasted
   By fire and flame and sword,
This Salvation Army lass
   Battles for the Lord!

Call me sacrilegious
   And irreverent, too;
Pies? They link us up with home
   As naught else can do!
"Home is where the heart is"—
   True, the poet sang;
But "home is where the pie is"
   To the Yankee gang!

Additional evidence that an army marches on its stomach was provided in "Hoggin' It", by Medical Mique:

Well, I've eaten food sublime, and I've eaten food that's rotten,
From Alaska's coldest corner to where the landscape's cotton;
At times there has been plenty, then there's times when there's been none,
And I've kept me upper stiffest, for complainin' I'm not one.
But it's now that I'm protestin'—oh, I've suffered silence long—
It's fancy food I'm cravin', for me system's goin' wrong.

   Oh, it's bacon, bacon, bacon,
     Till your belly's fairly achin'
For some biscuits or some hot cakes that in your mouth would melt;
   There's no German dog could dare me,
   No fear of death would scare me,
If I only had some chicken à la King beneath me belt.

Now I read where Mr. Hoover tells the folks to lay off hoggin',
We'll be needin' lots of grub to put the Fritz on the toboggan;
And the way that they've responded makes you feel so awful proud
That you'd like to meet old Bill to take his measure for a shroud.
Lord, it's plenty that we're gettin', but I'd be dancin' jigs
If they'd pass an order home to stop a-killin' off the pigs.

   For it's bacon, bacon, bacon,
     Till your very soul is shakin'—
If I could pick me eatin', it's a different song I'd sing;

I'd not miss a raidin' party,
For patrol I'd be quite hearty,
Oh, I'd swap me chance of Heaven for some chicken à la King.

Further testimony to the universality of bacon was supplied by Corporal Vance C. Criss in "Toujours le Même":

No matter how wise or how foolish
  The company's cook may be,
When down at the table we're seated,
  Two things we all plainly can see;
    When we look at the chow,
    There's the bosom of sow,
    And beans—beans—beans.

If quartered in city or country,
  The cook never misses his aim;
If messing in swamp or on mountain,
  Two things will remain quite the same;
    Though it may cause a row,
    We get bosom of sow,
    And beans—beans—beans.

When tasks for the day are all ended,
  And weary are body and brain,
Small matter it makes if we're eating
  Indoors, or outside in the rain,
    The cook makes his bow
    With bosom of sow,
    And beans—beans—beans.

Of all that I've learned in the Army,
  This fact I am sure I know well—
And others are certain to tell you—
  The soldier's worst picture of Hell
    Is thrice daily chow
    With the bosom of sow,
    And beans—beans—beans.

We printed no more effective panorama of the march into action than "Me,—An' War Goin' On," by Sergeant (later Second Lieutenant) John Palmer Cumming,

who saw the war out with the Seventy-seventh Division and later joined the staff of
The Stars and Stripes:

Me!—a-leadin' a column!
Me!—that women have loved!
Me, a-leadin' a column o' Yanks, an' tracin' Her name in the Stars!
Me, that ain't seen the purple hills before, all mixed in the skies
With the gray dawn meltin' to azure there;
Me that ain't a poet, growin' poetic;
An' the flash o' the guns on the skyline,
An' red wine—an' France!
An' me laughin'—and War!
An' Slim Jim singin' a song;
An' a lop-eared mule a-kickin' a limber
An' axles 'thout no grease hollerin' Maggie at me!
Me, that women have loved—
    An' War goin' on!

Mornin' comin',
An' me—a-leadin' a column
Along o' them from the College,
Along o' them from the Streets,
An' them as had mothers that spiled them, and them as hadn't,—
Lovin' names in the Stars—
An' Slim Jim singin' a song,
An' Folks to Home watchin' them, too,
An' Maggie that never had loved me, lovin' me now,
An' thinkin' an' cryin' for me!—
For me that loved Maggie that never loved me till now—

Mornin' comin',
An' me—a-leadin' a column,
An' a town in the valley,
Round the bend in the road,
An' Ginger strainin' his neck
An' thinkin' o' Picket Lines—
An' me an' the rest o' them, thinkin' o' home and eggs down there in the
        village—
An' Coney startin' to close at Home

An' Maggie mashed in the crowd—
An' me a-leadin' a column—
    An' War goin' on!

Me that hollered for water,
With a splinter o' hell in my side;
Me that have laid in the sun a-cursin' the beggars and stretchers
As looked like they'd never a-come;
Me that found God with the gas at my throat
An' raved like a madman for Maggie,
An' wanted a wooden cross over me!
Me—an' Slim Jim back o' me singin'
An' tracin' a name in the fade o' the Stars—

Me—knowin' that some'll be ridin' that's walkin' tonight—
Knowin' that some'll never see Broadway again—
An' red wine,
An' Little Italy,
An' Maggies like mine,—
Me!—a-murmurin' a prayer for Maggie
An' stoppin' to laugh at Slim,
An' shoutin' "To the right o' the road for the Swoi-zant-canze!"
Them babies that raise such Hell up the line, —
An' marchin',
An' marchin' by night,
An' sleepin' by day,
An' France,
An' Red Wine,
An' me thinkin' o' Home—
Me—a-leadin' a column,—
    An' War goin' on.

With the A. E. F. at last in the war up to its elbows, "the urge to poesy" became so compelling that every time we opened an envelope we expected a lyric to flutter out, which it usually did, except that sometimes there were two lyrics. The accumulation of verse eminently worth printing became so bulky that in the August 16th issue, in an effort to catch up with the output, we published, in addition to the usual column, a whole page of it.

Boxed in the center of it was one of the great requiems of the war—Joyce Kilmer's "The Woods Called Rouge-Bouquet". Woollcott, who knew Kilmer as a fellow-member of the staff of the *New York Times*, came back from the Ourcq fighting one day early in August with the news that Kilmer, an Intelligence sergeant with the 165th Infantry of the Forty-second Division, had been killed in action. Woollcott had with him a tattered manuscript copy, in pencil, of "Rouge-Bouquet". The verses, since become among the most familiar of the war, immortalized the death of nineteen members of Company E of the 165th who had been killed by a shell-burst in the Bois de Rouge-Bouquet, Forêt de Parroy, in the Lunéville sector, on March 7th, when the 165th was in its first tour of the front line. The poem had been read at a service in their memory by Chaplain Francis P. Duffy. The manuscript which Woollcott brought was one of several which had been made by the members of the regiment, and a few small errors had crept in in the transmission from one hand to another. All were trivial except one. One stanza, as published in Kilmer's collected poems, describes how, on the arrival of the nineteen souls on high,

> St. Michael's sword darts through the air
> And touches the aureole on his hair.

That is, St. Michael elevates his sword in a sweeping salute until it touches his own halo. In the transcript which Woollcott brought, which was used as copy by *The Stars and Stripes*, this couplet read:

> St. Michael's sword darts through the air
> And touches the arrival on his hair.

It was a natural error in copying—one of those confusing errors that still make sense. For by it St. Michael's sword touched not his own but the newcomer's head, as if with the benediction of heavenly knighthood.

"Rouge Bouquet," as it appears in the definitive edition of Kilmer's works published by Doubleday, Doran & Co., and as it was intended to appear in *The Stars and Stripes*, reads as follows:

> In a wood they call the Rouge Bouquet
>   There is a new-made grave to-day,
> Built by never a spade nor pick
> Yet covered with earth ten metres thick.
> There lie many fighting men,
>   Dead in their youthful prime,
> Never to laugh nor love again
>   Nor taste the Summertime.

For Death came flying through the air
And stopped his flight at the dugout stair,
Touched his prey and left them there,
   Clay to clay.
He hid their bodies stealthily
In the soil of the land they fought to free
   And fled away.
Now over the grave abrupt and clear
   Three volleys ring;
And perhaps their brave young spirits hear
   The bugle sing:
"Go to sleep!
Go to sleep!
Slumber well where the shell screamed and fell.
Let your rifles rest on the muddy floor,
You will not need them any more.
Danger's past;
Now at last,
Go to sleep!"

There is on earth no worthier grave
To hold the bodies of the brave
Than this place of pain and pride
Where they nobly fought and nobly died.
Never fear but in the skies
Saints and angels stand
Smiling with their holy eyes
   On this new-come band.
St. Michael's sword darts through the air
And touches the aureole on his hair
As he sees them stand saluting there,
   His stalwart sons;
And Patrick, Brigid, Columkill
Rejoice that in veins of warriors still
   The Gael's blood runs.
And up to Heaven's doorway floats,
   From the wood called Rouge Bouquet,
A delicate cloud of buglenotes

That softly say:
"Farewell!
Farewell!
Comrades true, born anew, peace to you!
Your souls shall be where the heroes are
And your memory shine like the morning-star.
Brave and dear,
Shield us here.
Farewell!"

On the same page with "The Woods Called Rouge-Bouquet" appeared "The Fields of the Marne":

The fields of the Marne are growing green,
The river murmurs on and on;
No more the hail of mitrailleuse,
The cannon from the hills are gone.

The herder leads the sheep afield,
Where grasses grow o'er broken blade;
And toil-worn women till the soil
O'er human mold, in sunny glade.

The splintered shell and bayonet
Are lost in crumbling village wall;
No sniper scans the rim of hills,
No sentry hears the night bird call.

From blood-wet soil and sunken trench,
The flowers bloom in summer light;
And farther down the vale beyond,
The peasant smiles are sad, yet bright.

The wounded Marne is growing green,
The gash of Hun no longer smarts;
Democracy is born again,
But what about the wounded hearts?

The verses were signed by Sergeant Frank Carbaugh, and below his name was this note: "Written while lying wounded in hospital; died August, 1918."

Our most famous contributor of verse (though he can hardly be credited with having been, in technical strictness, one of "The Army's Poets") was Rudyard Kipling. By special arrangement with Mr. Kipling and through the good offices of our London correspondent, George T. Bye, who did all the work except the composition of the poem, we were able to print "Justice" in the issue for November 1st. "Justice" was published in book form in the collection entitled "The Years Between" which appeared in 1919.

Now in the eyes of many of us the most envied member of *The Stars and Stripes* personnel was Corporal George P. Wrench, whose duty it was every Friday to chaperone several sackfuls of fresh papers from Paris to London, where he delivered them for distribution to our London circulation office. Traveling as a courier, Wrench enjoyed privileges which generals and colonels of any Allied army might and doubtless did sigh for in vain. After the Armistice I once accompanied him on the same exalted status, and we shared a luxurious stateroom on the Boulogne-Southampton packet while a British major slept on top of the saloon piano. I have always felt a little guilty about this because the British major had probably spent four years in the trenches. Well, by comparison a piano top was probably Heaven.

Visk commissioned Wrench to take over with him an extra bundle of *The Stars and Stripes* for November 1st for presentation to Mr. Kipling. Wrench, accompanied by a soldier stationed in the London office, went to the office of Mr. Kipling's publishers to deliver the papers.

"We'll be very glad to deliver them," said a courteous representative, "but wouldn't you like to present them to Mr. Kipling yourself?"

Corporal Wrench indeed would. So it was arranged that Corporal Wrench and his buddy would take tea with Mr. Kipling at Brown's Hotel that afternoon.

The two Americans went to Brown's and met an affable little man who asked them where they were from (it was Georgia and Texas, respectively) and who showed an amazing amount of knowledge of each State, to judge by the questions he put and which Wrench attempted to answer. For the Texan was dazzled into complete silence, and contributed no word to the conversation until the moment for departure arrived. Thereupon, shaking hands with his host, he delivered himself of this appreciative tribute:

"You know, Mr. Kipling, the book of yours I like best is 'The Rubáiyát of Omar Khayyám'."

Mr. Kipling handled this poser with due tact. He modestly disclaimed the authorship, thanked his visitors once more for their courtesy, and wished them well.

In the same issue to which Mr. Kipling contributed "Justice" *The Stars and Stripes* announced plans for the publication of "Yanks: A Book of A. E. F. Verse".

"Yanks" would consist of ninety-six pages of extracts from "The Army's Poets" column and would cost two francs fifty centimes a copy. The proceeds were to be devoted (and were devoted) to the purchase of delicacies for men in hospitals.

Visk had Hawley and me make the selections, and we had sufficient modesty not to exclude ourselves from the contents. Some contributors were represented more than once, and in these cases we used only initials for the second contribution, and, if there were a third, let it appear anonymously. Thus were we blandly enabled to conceal the fact that Captain Joseph Mills Hanson was the author of no fewer than six units in the anthology—a consummation not consciously aimed at, but one which speaks handsomely for our admiration of the Captain's particular muse.

"Yanks," despite what we considered the excellence of its contents, was an atrocious piece of printing, though hardly comparable in this respect to some of the outfit histories subsequently printed in Germany for units of the Army of Occupation, compounded of ersatz type and ersatz paper and set in English by German compositors to whom the copy was so much Ojibway. "Yanks" was set by an A. E. F. printer using a French-speaking linotype in the office of *Le Libre Parole*, and every time he came to the letter w he would have to confer with the foreman, requisition a letter, and jimmy it in by hand. The title-page was a triumph of typographical eccentricity; the presswork was uneven—some pages were almost white and in others half the letters were filled with ink. But everything was somehow readable, and the only error I can recall was that a left-handed accent got into the name Liège. But "Yanks" could look a hundred times worse than it does and it would still be my favorite volume of poetry.

The concluding poem in "Yanks"—"There's About Two Million Fellows", by Sergeant Albert J. Cook—was a whole history of the A. E. F. in epitome:

> There's about two million fellows from the North, South, East and West
> Who scurried up the gang plank of a ship;
> They have felt the guy ropes paying and the troopship gently swaying
> As it started on its journey from the country of the blest.
> They have washed in hard salt water, bucked the Army transport grub,
> Had a hitch of crow's nest duty on the way;
> Strained their eyes mistaking white caps for a humpback Prussian sub
> Just at twilight when "the danger's great, they say."
> When their ship had lost the convoy they were worried just a bit,
> And kinda thought the skipper should be canned;
> And the sigh of heartfelt feeling almost set the boat to reeling
> When each of those two million sighted land.

There's about two million fellows that have landed here in France—
They're scattered God and G. H. Q. knows where;
By the cranes where steamers anchor, schooner, tramp or greasy tanker,
There's an O. D. outfit waiting just to make the cargo dance.
They are chopping in the forest, double-timing on the roads,
Putting two-ways where a single went before;
In the cabs of sweating engines, pushing, pulling double loads
When the R. T. O.'s in frenzied tones implore.
For it's duty, solid duty with the hustling men behind,
From the P. of E.'s on up to No Man's Land;
And there's never chance of shirking when the boys up front are working—
Night and day must go the answer to the front line's stern demand.

There's about two million fellows and there's some of them who lie
Where eighty-eights and G. I.'s gently drop;
Where the trucks and trains are jamming and the colonel he is damning
Half the earth and in particular the Service of Supply.
They have had a stretch of trenches, beat the Prussian at his best,
Seen their buddies fall like heroes right beside;
But—there's nigh two million fellows from the country of the blest
Who know the cause for which their comrades died,
Who have crossed the sluggish shallows where their little life-streams ran
And broadened just a trifle, you will find;
And their vision's cleaner, clearer and they hold just that much dearer
The great and glorious land they left behind!

CHAPTER SIX

FIRST AID

MARCH 29, 1918, was the most miserable Good Friday the world has known in our time. The great German offensive in the north had won back in days, almost in hours, territory for which British and French had battled yard by yard for nearly two years. The gigantic Amiens salient bellied out over the Allied world like a portentous thundercloud about to rain down doom on civilization. Big Bertha had begun to shell Paris, and while the results were moderately ineffective except to whatever and whoever happened to be directly underneath, it was on that identical Good Friday that the Boche had the good or ill luck to land a fluke hit against a column in the Church of St. Gervais. The column collapsed, the roof fell in, and nearly one hundred members of the congregation were killed.

On that bad Good Friday *The Stars and Stripes* led the paper with a two-column head which urged units of the A. E. F. to "Take As Your Mascot a French War Orphan". The story occupied the entire sixth and seventh columns, and the nub of the business was summarized below it:

A company, detachment, or group of the A. E. F. agrees to adopt a child for a year, contributing 500 francs for its support.

The children will be either orphans, the children of French soldiers so seriously crippled that they cannot work, or homeless waifs from the invaded districts. The adopting unit may select its child from any of these classes and specify its age and sex.

The money will be sent to *The Stars and Stripes* to be turned over to a special committee of the American Red Cross for disbursement.

At least two hundred and fifty francs will be paid upon adoption and the remainder within four months thereafter.

All of the money contributed will go to the children. The expenses of administration will be borne by the Red Cross.

A photograph and a history of each child will be sent to its adopting unit, which will be advised of the child's whereabouts and hereafter notified monthly of its progress.

The Red Cross committee will determine the disposal of the child. It will either be sent to a practical agricultural or trade school or supported in a French family.

The Red Cross committee will regularly visit the schools and homes of the children and supervise the expenditures of the money upon them.

No restrictions are placed upon the methods by which the money may be raised. It may be gathered by an equal assessment upon the members of a unit, by passing the hat, by giving an entertainment—in any way the unit sees fit.

The funds may be handled through the C. O., the top sergeant's office, or by any one in a unit designated for the purpose.

Address all communications regarding these children to War Orphans' Department, *The Stars and Stripes*, G2, A. E. F., 1 Rue des Italiens, Paris, France.

It needs to be explained now, as it needed frequently at the time, that the word adoption was not to be taken literally. The explanation was the more necessary at the time because the A. E. F. was already preparing to take every portable object in Europe back to America as a memento of its experiences.

The idea of the campaign was Private Ross's; credit for its execution must be divided between the A. E. F., who supplied the funds, and Miss Marie Perrin of the American Red Cross, who headed the bureau which the Red Cross established to superintend the selection of the children and the distribution of the money.

Before the next issue of the paper went to press five adoptions had been recorded. *The Stars and Stripes* staff, holding example to be as good as precept, dived into its communal pockets and became sponsor for Marie Louise Patriarche, three years old, who lived (and lives today, a mademoiselle of sixteen) in a village near Dijon. Her father had fallen in battle in 1915. The captain of an Infantry company requested for his outfit "two children, a boy and a girl, preferably brother and sister." The unit was accommodated with André and Simone Lamulle, aged eleven and ten respectively, of Aubervilliers, on the edge of Paris. An Engineer company wired: "Reserve for adoption one boy, aged six, total orphan from occupied territory, northern France. Mailing check today." The staff of the Intelligence Section at G. H. Q. were less fussy. They merely asked for a boy, age and habitat not particularized.

But they might have particularized as minutely as they chose—the want could have been filled. It was possible to reach a hand down into that multitudinous flotsam and fetch up, in a few chance hauls, almost any tiny relic of life that the specifications required. A few weeks later Herbert H. Knox of New York City (civilian and at-home adoptions were welcomed) requested "a boy of about seven whose father has fallen in battle and whose name is Samuel, which is the name of my youngest son". A Samuel was supplied as per blueprint. The campaign did run into one serious ethnological snag. A request for a red-headed youngster with freckles had to go over for several weeks but was eventually attended to.

Fourteen days after the inauguration of the campaign *The Stars and Stripes* was able to announce the adoption of thirty-three children. A week later the total stood at fifty, a week later still at sixty-six, then at 104, 126, 149, 171, 193. Then a single

"ME AND MY PAL," BY BALDRIDGE

regiment—the 166th (Ohio) Infantry of the Rainbow Division—took fifty-four, making the week's figure sixty-eight and swelling the grand total to 261.

Adoptions were itemized each week, with the adopters identified so far as the censorship would permit. In the issue which announced the then record-breaking seven-day total of sixty-eight the list read as follows:

TAKEN THIS WEEK

Enlisted Personnel, Base Hosp. No. 5	2
Co. A, —— Engrs.	1
Major J. W. Stillwell	1

Captain G. B. D. 1
Co. A, —— Bn., Tank Corps. 1
An Ohio Regiment. 54
Co. F, —— Engrs. 1
"Southern Officer" 1
"F. H." 1
Y. M. C. A. Secretaries, Base Camp No. 1 2
General John J. Pershing. 2
—— Aero Const. Squadron 1
    Previously adopted 193

    Total 261

General Pershing's contribution was thus inconspicuously recorded at his own request—or I should say (since after all he was in a position to have what he wanted) at his specific order. His name was not mentioned in the head or in the news story—nowhere except in the itemized list. This was, to my knowledge, the only occasion on which the Commander-in-Chief of the American Expeditionary Forces gave definite or even indefinite instructions as to what *The Stars and Stripes* should or should not print and how it should or should not print it.

After this late spring spurt the campaign settled down to a summer average of eighteen a week. America was in the thick of things; the Marne salient was rapidly disappearing from the battle maps; there would be plenty of time to adopt orphans (and plenty of orphans left to adopt) when the tumult had temporarily subsided.

Girls were running away from boys. This statement is set down not as a great pre-Freudian psychological discovery but as a simple statistical truth. When adopting units presented no specifications the Red Cross was supplying a luckless male in an effort to redeem the balance.

Thanks to the close and detailed supervision exercised by Miss Perrin's bureau over her forlorn charges Private Ross could present frequent reports concerning their progress. He was early able to announce that every child of school age who had been assigned to an A. E. F. unit was attending school. He continued:

> The knowledge that they are the wards of *les Américains* has had a noticeably stimulating influence on their study.
> The boys are inclined, at first, to be a little bit dazzled by having a unit of American soldiers as a parrain. In their particular circle they are the aristocracy

of French boydom. They outshadow millionaires' sons and girls' favorites and, upon learning of their selection, behave, usually, as an American youth would act if he had just been presented with a four ring circus.

"YES, THIS REALLY HAPPENED," BY WALLGREN

One such youth received a present of 10 francs direct from his new godfathers. Did he buy a new pair of trousers with it, or lay it away toward a pair of much needed shoes? He did not.

He bought a toy cap pistol for six francs and four francs' worth of caps, painted his face like an Indian and, in imagination, killed every other youth in that part of the country. He was going to be a cowboy, he explained, and was getting ready for his career.

It wasn't until he received a letter from his parrain expressing the hope that "he was getting along well with his studies" that he quieted down. But when he got the tip that he was expected to make progress with his books, he declared that he would become the best student in the class—and he did.

For any unit of the A. E. F., from a company up, to raise five hundred francs for the adoption of a war waif was a ridiculously simple task. We were, be it remembered, among the salaried elect of an embattled world. Our dollar and ten cents a day pay for privates seemed a fantastic guerdon to the Frenchman, who generally forgot that we left most of it with his relations. The rules governing the orphan campaign, it will be recalled, adroitly announced that "no restrictions are placed upon the methods by which the money may be raised." What more equable method than to kitty out of crap, blackjack and poker pots?

Many adoptions, however, were not corporate but individual obligations. The instance of General John J. Pershing has been cited; at the other end of the military spectrum appears such a figure as that of Private Charles Shuman, who proffered five one-hundred franc notes with, I make no doubt, an elaborately casual air.

Even more impressive, perhaps, were the instances of those who, somehow unable to participate in group projects and still less able to assume whole orphans on their own accounts, nevertheless offered their fractional bits to help the good work along. "Aunt Belle" of New York, God bless her, sent fifty francs; William Kimbaugh (military status, if he had one, not declared) contributed twenty; a Quartermaster captain sent a hundred, a sergeant of Engineers fifty. Before the campaign was three months old enough miscellaneous mites had come in to provide for two multitudinously step-fathered children.

By the eve of the Battle of the Meuse-Argonne adoptions had reached 514. The campaign was a conspicuous success. But Private Ross, rapt in Californian contemplation of the stupendous, was far from content. In the issue of September 27th *The Stars and Stripes* presented on page one a five-column box headed: "Offered to the A. E. F.—500 Christmas Gift War Orphans."

Seven days later this appeal had hardly had time to make itself felt—"37 Christmas Orphans Taken; 42 a Week Needed for 500," a somewhat disconsolate heading announced. This was the last ever heard of that 42 average. Next week's issue recorded a gain of 88—"Best Week of Whole Campaign." Another week and this best was beaten with a figure of 109, and another week brought another best with

144. And in the issue of November 1st—the day on which American troops broke through the Kriemhilde Stellung and initiated the march that was to halt only with

"THE BEST CHRISTMAS BOX OF ALL," BY BALDRIDGE

the Armistice, the paper led with the announcement: "514 Christmas War Orphans Taken; Three Months' Goal in Five Weeks."

The lid was off. Adoptions would continue, although the gratifying total of 1028 children had already been reached. The following week there were an even hundred new adoptions, then 133, 115, 294. And on December 6th everything went by the board when the S. O. S., which had stealthily organized itself into a gigantic orphan-adopting association, gaily tossed in 418,000 francs for the adoption of 836 fatherless French boys and girls. Even Private Ross was surlily satisfied. Even in San Francisco they would have called it an earthquake and not a fire.

The war was over. The A. E. F. would soon, so to speak, go home. It was decided to terminate the campaign on December 16th. In the final rush 462 new adoptions were recorded for a grand total of 3444—not a bad oversubscription of the original quota of a thousand. And in the issue of December 20th the customary weekly orphan story opened with this citation:

> *The Stars and Stripes*, in the name of the war orphans of France, has awarded the Distinguished Service Cross of the Real Christmas Spirit, of the $33 a month (or any other) class, to the following organization for the act of extraordinary generosity described after its name:
>
> *The A. E. F.*, France.—For extraordinary generosity all over France between March 29, 1918, and December 16, 1918, while helping hold the German at bay in the first half of 1918, and in the latter part of July, and in August, September, October, and the first 11 days of November, assisting the Allied Armies of the free nations of the world in driving back and defeating the German army in the hardest day-by-day fighting the world has ever known, and ever since in staying faithfully on the job to see that it won't have to happen again. *The A. E. F.* found time and francs to adopt 3,444 French orphans of the war whose fathers had died fighting for the same cause for which its members proffered their lives. Throughout the entire war orphan campaign *The A. E. F.* showed the highest contempt for destitution and poverty which, in many instances, followed its generous giving, and the concomitant thirst, hunger and loss of physical enjoyment. At all times and under all circumstances it was cool and collected—but for the most part collected. Home address: U. S. A. —"and a little child shall lead them."

When the adoption campaign was only a few weeks old *The Stars and Stripes* printed half a page of unsolicited testimonials from the adoptees or their mothers of which these are examples:

To Co. B.,—Supply Trains:

I must at first say that Henriette will be but five in July next and that, as regards writing, she only knows how to make marks; but she wants me to tell you that she can sing "The Petticoat's Dance." For one year at least it is her mother who will send you news and who will make you acquainted with Henriette's dispositions, qualities and defects.

I must say how glad I was to hear that a company of American soldiers was adopting my daughter. As those soldiers have come to avenge her father, I feel that they will bring good luck to her.

My mother was an American lady, and I think the little one has something of her blood in her veins. I shall send you soon a photograph, but, meanwhile, I shall just describe her:

Henriette is a blonde, she has very cunning blue eyes, a fat little turned-up nose, a mouth like a cherry, and a pink and white skin. Like all mothers, I think my daughter is pretty. She is a high-spirited girl, and laughs and cries with all her heart. Although very young, she is already a little woman as regards finery; she likes ribbons, laces and silks; she is curious and a little chatterbox; but, if she has the defects of her sex, she has also the qualities going with it.

She has a little brother, one year younger, who also has the defects of his sex; he is despotic and selfish. Well, Henriette yields to him in order not to make him cry; in a word, she is quite devoted to this little brother of four years. She likes sewing, and is always trying to do what she sees me doing; she will be clever.

Her little heart is not very large; she loves her mother, her father, who is in heaven; her brother, and little Jesus.

What she likes best are the little animals. Some time ago she wanted me to buy her a little fox to play with, and she keeps thinking about it still. When she goes to her grandmother's in the country her great pleasure consists in kissing the chickens and ducks.

I have told her that a company of American soldiers was adopting her; I am not sure that she understood, but she says she would like to see them to fondle them.

Let me thank you again for the kind interest you are taking in my little daughter's welfare, and believe me,

Yours gratefully,
V. THOMAS.

To Lieutenant Howard Conklin:

My little Marie-Thérèse being too small to write herself, being only 14 months old, I take her place to let you know that she is a cunning baby, never keeping still, very intelligent for her years, always sweet-tempered, and scarcely ever crying. Pride apart, I may say that she is admired by everybody who sees her. You will have seen from her photo that she is very healthy. She has fine features, thick, fair hair, and large blue eyes. If you could see her, I am sure that she would win your heart.

Now that I have told you how my daughter is looking, I must thank you for adopting her; I shall send you news concerning her and, later on, it will be herself who will thank you for your kindness to her.

You perhaps know that we come from an invaded country; we have left at Sedan all our possessions; we lived there very comfortably, my father having a trade in the town. What shall we find when we go there again! However, material losses were nothing, but I had the grief to learn that my husband had been killed in April, 1917; my little girl was just two months at that time, and

A LETTER OF THANKS FROM MARIE-LOUISE PATRIARCHE, THE STARS AND STRIPES' STAFF'S OWN ORPHAN, AND THE FIRST OF THE 3,444. MARIE-LOUISE'S MOTHER GUIDED HER HAND, FOR MARIE-LOUISE WAS ONLY THREE AND A HALF YEARS OLD AT THE TIME

her brother, Jacques, 28 months old. That boy wants to be a soldier like his father!

I took refuge in Charmes with my sister; we live there very sparingly while waiting for our country's deliverance. Owing to your help and that of your gallant soldiers, perhaps that deliverance will come sooner than is anticipated.

Warmly thanking you again, and with the children's best love.—I am yours sincerely,

VVE. A. AZEGLIO.

To the 2nd Brigade, M. G. Bn.,—Division:

I am a little girl who knows how to read, but cannot yet write well. I shall try and learn quickly in order to have the pleasure of writing to you and, when I am grown, I shall study so I can send you long letters in your own pretty language.

In the meantime, I beg Mother to tell you that you are very good to protect me and that I love you for it. There are many American soldiers at —— and, when I see them, I want to go and kiss them because they are your brothers, same as I have two little brothers Dédé and Jeannot.

We shall be very good. Every night we pray to God to make you victorious of those bad Huns who deprived us of our dear Father, and may God protect you all.

My dear and great friends, if you will allow me, I shall write to you often and you will be very kind if you will answer me.

I send you the sweetest kiss from your little   GERMAINE DUTHU.

With a pretty flower for you.

———

To Lieutenant E. L. Wheless:

I hear to-day that I have American friends! How glad I am! Although I do not know you, I should like to know at once what are your names and where you are. I wonder you selected me because the photo sent you was very bad and I look stupid on it.

I am ten years old and am born in Dakar (Sénégal). I go to school at Janson de Sailly and am in Class 6-A. I am a good pupil and am beginning to learn Latin. I learn English also and won a good place at composition, but I wish I knew it quite well in order to be able to speak.

I am pretty good at drawing and am always making sketches during my spare time. During the Pentecost holidays I intend making sketches for you, as I shall have time to do it then.

I shall make my first Communion on May 16 at Janson de Sailly. We shall be alone on that day, as all my family Trousselle has just left Noyon and has been evacuated in different parts of France. We shall sing hymns on my first Communion day; I am proud of it and like very much singing with my school-fellows.

I have a brother called Pierre. He is 12 years old and very good at gymnastics; he stands up for me when a bigger boy wants to strike me. I cannot live without him and am very unhappy when he is away. I have also a sister who is 15 years old and is called Renée.

On Thursdays we go to the Bois de Boulogne, where we all play together. Since Mother has died, we live with Grandmother and Auntie, who stays with us because Uncle is at the front. I don't know what I shall do when I am grown, but I want to be like my darling Father. We are not afraid of the Gothas or guns.

I shall try to send you a better photo of myself and send you all a big kiss. I am so glad to have friends like you!

Your Little Robert Trousselle.

The orphan adoption campaign was over, but the francs kept pouring in. The sequel belongs with the story of the post-Armistice career of *The Stars and Stripes*. A little child continued to lead them.

"A POILU DIED FOR HIM," BY BALDRIDGE

CHAPTER SEVEN

ARTS AND CRAFTS

THE more zealous student of this collection of notes will perhaps recall a passing allusion to Private Abian A. Wallgren. Private Wallgren, it was disclosed, reported for duty with *The Stars and Stripes* and then vanished into whatever time of day it happened to be. Three days later he was restored to us, apparently of his own volition (Wallgren was never the man to appropriate another's volition), and resigned himself to becoming the ranking comic artist of the A. E. F.

Wallgren had come to France with the Marine Brigade of the Second Division and had proceeded with that subsequently not unknown organization to a point which was close enough to the front to indicate that theirs was not to be purely an onlooker's part in the ensuing excitement. Wallgren's prowess with pen, pencil and brush was early recognized, and he was forthwith made company sign-painter. His superiors' belief in signs thereupon became itself hardly credible. Everything and everybody in the organization was labelled. So far so good, but Private Wallgren's frequent infractions of one or another Article of War soon had him in such consistent hot water that the war became for him a kind of perpetual Turkish bath. Confinement did not annoy him, because his unit was in a corner of France that offered little in the way of diversion even for the unconfined. Deprivation of pay would have been a more sensible hardship had it not been for the fact that, confronted by so dire an emergency, Private Wallgren would speed up production and turn out such an abundance of portraits at so much per head (an officer's head cost more than an enlisted man's) that he would often become, for several consecutive seconds, the richest man in the outfit.

The selection of Private Wallgren as cartoonist for *The Stars and Stripes* doubtless caused sighs of relief (assuming a Marine ever sighs) among his betters and unquestionably released whole platoons of officers from juridical duties for active service in the field. Endowed with such worldly goods as Marine supply sergeants customarily issue to their clientele, including a rifle, Private Wallgren entrained for

Paris. Invariably of sanguine temperament, he soon determined that the necessity for all this armament in a civilized community like Paris was virtually negligible, and accordingly abandoned it bit by bit all the way into the capital, disembarking with the clothes he had on and the heartfelt gratitude of the Chemin de Fer de l'Est. How, a stranger in a strange land, he made his way to *The Stars and Stripes* office has never been disclosed, but it was, perhaps, a fortunate coincidence that the office of *The Stars and Stripes* and the local military hoosegow were under the same roof. To transfer a cartoonist from the other to the one would have been, and perhaps was, the work of a moment.

The extraction of a weekly cartoon from Private Wallgren thereupon became one of the more monumental tasks of the war. Somehow it was accomplished, and

AN ALMOST UNKNOWN WALLGREN, SIGNED "A. A. ANDERSON" IN AN ATTEMPT TO MAKE THE
GERMANS THINK THE STARS AND STRIPES HAD A WHOLE PLATOON OF CARTOONISTS

it proved in the end, no less than in the beginning, to be worth all the pains it cost. Thanks to his deft and sympathetic handiwork the A. E. F. could spare itself the pangs of self-pity and laugh at the accumulated miseries that beset the path of him who goes forth to war.

No small share of the success of Wallgren's weekly strips was due to the involuntary and not over-hearty co-operation of other members of the staff. Since he was drawing soldiers for soldiers, and since the staff itself was all soldiers, why go elsewhere for models? Private Hawley was immediately elevated to a pedestal from which he was not to descend until the final issue of *The Stars and Stripes* was printed. Hawley, in his frequent peregrinations into the A. E. F., would visit a strange outfit to be greeted with the puzzled query: "Now where have I seen you before?" A look, a stare, a dawning conviction—"Why, you're the guy that's always in *The Stars and Stripes* cartoons!" Sergeant Woollcott and, less consistently, Private Ross, Sergeant Bliss and Field Clerk Britt were also brought forth wriggling from Wally's ink bottle to further an army's delight.

One Sunday soon after the removal of *The Stars and Stripes* office from the baleful precincts of the Ste.-Anne to the Rue des Italiens a tall man in a novel type of uniform walked in and spoke English. I reciprocated and the visitor, who said his name was Baldridge, exhibited some drawings. I said they were very nice but what in blazes kind of a rig did he think he was wearing. He explained that he was attired as a member of the Mallet Reserve, a sort of corps d'élite of truck drivers in the French Army who could wear practically anything they pleased provided they delivered so much net tonnage of ammunition at the front.

THE FIRST WALLY STRIP FOR THE STARS AND STRIPES. THERE WAS ONE IN EVERY ISSUE. ITS OMISSION WOULD HAVE JOLTED A. E. F. MORALE AS SEVERELY AS A LOST BATTLE

It developed (though not at this interview) that Reservist Baldridge had been a commercial artist in Chicago when the war broke out in 1914. He at once wrote to a transatlantic steamship company asking them to hold open a berth as steward or anything else and a day or two later presented himself at their New York offices prepared to sail. They were courteous but firm—they could not engage him as a steward for the reason that no passengers had signed up for the ship on which he had reserved employment. Undismayed, Baldridge drew on the savings of a lifetime and paid his way to the war as a first-class passenger.

He had acted with such promptness that he was in Belgium before the opposing armies had settled down into the deadly stalemate of trench warfare. Salvaging a bicycle whose disappearance was doubtless subsequently laid at the door of some unoffending hostile, he had a fine old time pedaling back and forth between the armies until the Germans, who had probably been thinking about it for several weeks, decided to arrest him. He managed to talk himself out of being shot and withdraw in good order to London, bought a package of Benson and Hedges ciga-

"WHAT WE'RE FIGHTING FOR"—PRIVATE BALDRIDGE'S FIRST APPEARANCE IN THE STARS AND STRIPES (MARCH 15, 1918). LIKE EVERYTHING ELSE THAT WAS NOT NAILED DOWN, THIS DRAWING WAS ACCOMPANIED BY VERSES FROM THE PEN OF PRIVATE HAWLEY

rettes with his last shilling, and cabled home collect for more money. Courage like this would brook no deterrent. Assuming, properly, that he was now persona non grata with the Germans, Baldridge crossed to France and cast his lot with the

Mallet Reserve. He drew and wrote and sent the product to *Leslie's Weekly* of sacred memory.

I told Baldridge his drawings were very nice but that he might be Rembrandt or Titian and it would be all the same unless Visk liked them. When Visk saw them he did like them and said he would be glad to have Baldridge join the staff if he would come into our army. Baldridge said that was fair enough and was forthwith transferred to the A. E. F. as a private of infantry unattached. He was, and remained to the end, a man without an outfit—the only soldier in the A. E. F. who enjoyed that status with the possible exception of Pershing, who really was a member of every outfit.

Wallgren greeted Baldridge with the cordiality typical of him who sees his weekly labors reduced by half with no corresponding decrease in salary. Up to this time Wallgren had been killing two birds with one stone, and the quarry had grown wary. He had been not alone our comic stripper but also our serious cartoonist. His comic strips were the stuff of history, but he will, I trust, forgive me if I say that some of his serious cartoons were simply terrible. Baldridge took over this sector and developed a technique of argument in crayon that echoed the effective idealism of embattled America. There would come occasions when a Baldridge cartoon would go forth with all the compelling clarity of a bugle call—and produce as speedy a result.

It was not, however, essential that an artist be a private in order to be represented in *The Stars and Stripes*. We had an occasional striking pen-and-ink drawing from Captain Wallace Morgan or a scrap of humor from Lieutenant Percy L. Crosby, whose rookie from the Thirteenth Squad in the home papers had sent many a doughboy chuckling aboard the transport, and we had one welcome cartoon donation from Captain Bruce Bairnsfather of the B. E. F. In later days Sergeant Hal Burrows joined the art department, and Captain Herbert Morton Stoops sent some last-minute cartoons from the distant Rhineside pastures of the Sixth Field Artillery.

Baldridge enjoyed one noteworthy advantage over the rest of us. With the exception of Field Clerk Barney Miller (no one could remember him as William T.), who, for reasons that have never been disclosed, brought a civilian suit to France, no one of us, before Baldridge joined the staff, possessed any other clothes than those which Uncle Sam had allocated to us. Baldridge brought with him the sombre and decorous investiture of the Mallet Reserve, arrayed in which he could (or at least did) occasionally emerge into the highways of Paris as effectively disguised as if he were an elderly frock-coated native behind a Niagara of whiskers. Astute M. P.'s would study his blond locks and blue eyes speculatively but impotently; the apparel did not proclaim the man, but not theirs to penetrate beyond the apparel.

As a military unit, *The Stars and Stripes* was definitely in and of the capital. The city and so much of its environment as was in any degree Americanized con-

A WALLGREN CARTOON THAT IMMORTALIZES THREE OF HIS FAVORITE MODELS: PRIVATE HAWLEY, SERGEANT WOOLLCOTT, AND (ACT 7 ONLY) PRIVATE ROSS

stituted in military geography the District of Paris, and the commander of the District of Paris was Brigadier General W. W. Harts. District headquarters had once been located in the Hôtel Ste.-Anne but eventually was transferred to an elegant mansion close to the Étoile. Lieutenant Adolph S. Ochs II, our painstaking and kindly treasurer, in whose bosom the seed of the martinet never took root, once had an errand at district headquarters and received there his chief and perhaps only fright of the war. As soon as he entered the door a corporal of the guard roared "Attention!" and a resounding clank which Ochs took for the dissolution of the universe reverberated through the corridors. It was only a multitude of sentries— one, apparently, before every doorway and on every stair-landing—coming to Present Arms because an officer had stepped in, which probably happened on an average of once every eight seconds. "If a mere shavetail can rouse all this hubbub," mused Ochs, "what happens when Pershing comes visiting?"

CAPTAIN WALLACE MORGAN HAS A LITTLE FUN AT THE EXPENSE OF THE "REGULATION" OVER-
SEAS CAP. IN THE SAME ISSUE IN WHICH THIS DRAWING APPEARED THE STARS AND STRIPES
ANNOUNCED THE ADOPTION OF A NEW MODEL

General Harts was more than Commanding General of the District of Paris. He was also chairman of a special committee which was charged with submitting definite suggestions for a new type of uniform. Anything that touched dress was news. A story on the gold service chevron led the paper and was worth it. "Insignia of Rank on Overseas Cap," "New Cap Ready for Whole A. E. F.," "Long Trousers Latest Decree of Army Tailor," "Non-Coms' Chevrons on Right Arm Only"—all these likewise, and many more like them, were front-page stuff. The original overseas cap had been an atrocity—if *The Stars and Stripes* had anything to do with laughing it out of existence its career was not in vain. Most officers had done what they pleased about it, contenting themselves with a not-too-approximate likeness— a tendency which Wallace Morgan gently satirized in the drawing here reproduced. But the enlisted man could not afford to take advantage of this latitude or did not want to run the risk, and so resigned himself to the crowning infamy.

The deservedly detested overseas cap produced an interesting collaboration from the field—the only one of its kind, I believe, that *The Stars and Stripes* printed. The verses were by Lieutenant Fairfax Downey and the drawing by Lieutenant James C. Lysle, Artillerymen both. The Downey-Lysle opus was called "By Way of Farewell":

> The war of the Trojans and all the Greek crew
> Was fought for the sake of a fair lady who
> Went absent without leave, for weal or for woe,
> And took her *permission* to Paris to go.

> All Greeks grasped steel helmets and trench knives and tanks
> And wheel teams and chariots and fell into ranks.
> Shipping boards gave no trouble with quarrels or slips:
> The beauty of Helen had launched all the ships.

ANOTHER BLAST AT THE OVERSEAS CAP, DRAWN BY LIEUTENANT JAMES C. LYSLE TO ACCOMPANY
VERSES BY LIEUTENANT FAIRFAX DOWNEY

> All cautioned their sweethearts that since they must go,
> To keep home hearths heated, on flirting go slow;
> For each warrior was off to the battle and strife
> To make the world safe for a good-looking wife.

> But they'd never have fought if they'd read Helen's note,
> Which just before leaving she hastily wrote:
> "Menelaus just entered our once happy home
> With an *overseas cap* on the top of his dome!"

The best thing that could be said for the issue uniform was that it was not so bad as the overseas cap, and a report that alterations were being projected filled the staff with dire forebodings. A change might be for the better but the chances were equally good (better, some of us thought) that it might be for the worse. The thing was eminently worth looking into.

The first intimation that a new uniform was being discussed was brought to the office by Sergeant Philip Von Blon, who had picked up the tip at Tours. Von Blon had left the staff of the *Cleveland Plain Dealer* to enlist in the Lakeside Medical Unit (Base Hospital 4), which became the very vanguard of the A. E. F.— its members set foot on French soil on May 25, 1917, exactly forty-nine days after America had entered the war, and were old soldiers before Pershing landed.

Von Blon had joined *The Stars and Stripes* staff at the end of July and had been assigned to the circulation department. The sterling service rendered by the circulation department has been blithely passed over so far in this chronicle, but will receive its due meed in season. By this time virtually every newcomer was being assigned to circulation. There was, for instance, Private John Black, late of the *Brooklyn Daily Eagle*, who had come to France with the Medical Department and whose newspaper connection had drawn him to us.

"What did you do on the *Eagle*?" Visk asked him.

"Usually, sir," said John, "I wrote dramatic and musical criticism."

"You're going to wrap papers here," said Visk, and John wrapped papers for the back-home subscription list until his talents brought him into the editorial department to aid in the busy after-Armistice task of covering the S. O. S.

Von Blon joined the editorial staff in ample time to be represented at the front and in the S. O. S. His outfit had been the first to reach not alone France but, before that, the first to reach England. From both England and France Von managed to send back to the *Plain Dealer* some forty stories of the experiences of this pioneer unit, to the great discomfiture of a rival newspaper which happened to be represented in the same outfit. The competing soldier-newspaperman employed all the artifices he could devise for getting his copy back to Cleveland ahead of Von, but Von continued to scoop him consistently. Von's program, it later developed, was simply to write his copy, affix a British or French postage stamp, and drop the envelope in the nearest postbox.

Among the multitude of Paris edifices turned over to the A. E. F. was the Élysée Palace Hotel on the Avenue des Champs Élysée—one of the largest hostelries in all Europe. It housed, among thousands of others, a personage of no less importance than Colonel Charles E. Stanton, Chief Paymaster of the A. E. F., who gave us every month a story that was read by everybody in the Army—the rate of exchange at which the current payroll would be made up. Colonel Stanton was a fine old soldier and a man of moment apart from his status of paymaster. For it had been Colonel Stanton who, standing at a grave in Picpus Cemetery on July 4, 1917, had placed a wreath on it and said, "Lafayette, we are here."

Von Blon entered the Élysée Palace and was soon an inconspicuous unit lost in the vastness of its uniformed personnel. By making discreet inquiries he reached at last the comparative seclusion of one of the upper floors, where apparently endless rows of corridors stretched out in every direction, flanked by cubicles each of which sheltered some abstruse activity aimed at winning the war.

Von found the room he sought. Luckily it happened to contain at the moment only a single American soldier and an assortment of tailors' dummies.

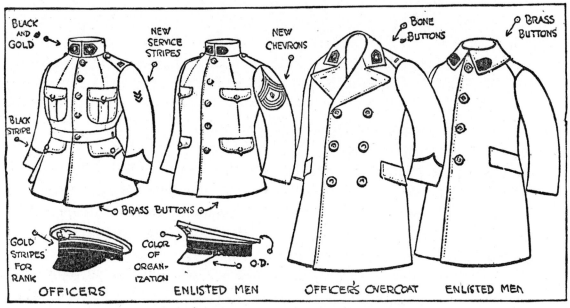

WALLGREN'S STILL-LIFE OF THE UNIFORM THAT NEVER WAS

The rumor, it was at once apparent, was only too true. For the principal tailor's dummy, standing at a more impressive attention than even Private Hawley, in his most punctilious moments, had ever been able to achieve, was habited in the new uniform. The hideous details will be presented in a moment in Von's own words.

The soldier was making a few adjustments on the new uniform and was slightly disturbed to find a stranger in the room, but as the stranger was wearing the familiar old uniform the man at the dummy was soon at ease again. He proved to be an Italian tailor who had got in the Army only to find that he was to a be a tailor still. His not to reason why when a sergeant came in to pass the time of day.

Von Blon saw all that it was necessary to see at the moment, hurried to a telephone, and suggested the immediate presence of Private Wallgren. By the time Wallgren walked into the room the little tailor was fully reconciled to the presence of visitors. Von Blon casually noted down the details of the new uniform and Wallgren as casually sketched the only fashion plate which was ever to appear in *The Stars and Stripes*.

The story led the paper in the next issue. It merits reprinting, together with Wally's sketch, as an example of one projected horror of war that never came to fruition:

Brass buttons, bright hued patches on collars of blouses and overcoats, caps with black visors and colored stripes denoting branch of service and rank, and colored piping, denoting branch of service, sewn in the seams of the breeches —all these are features of proposed uniform changes for the A. E. F. now up for approval by those who have the deciding voice in such matters.

The same plans include a change in the lines of the uniforms for officers and enlisted men. They call for an officer's blouse to be long and flaring at the bottom, with a deep vent in the back, and cut in and seamed at the waist-line. They provide a double-breasted officer's greatcoat, and a single-breasted overcoat for enlisted men to be cut on new lines, with a simple turn-over collar. They also call for an enlisted man's blouse simpler than the present one.

These changes have been under consideration by an Army board which has spent weeks in deliberation with tailoring experts. In its work the board had many sample uniforms tailored, and many proposals were debated, among them the adoption of the roll collar. It is thought probable, however, that the present collar will be retained.

If proposals under consideration are adopted, the uniform will show these changes:

Brass buttons wherever bronze ones are used at present. This change is considered necessary because of the growing difficulty in obtaining bronze in the quantity needed for the Army.

Patches of colored cloth sewn on the collars of all blouses and overcoats to show branch of service. Embroidered regimental numerals placed on the patches of color.

Black visored caps for officers and enlisted men. The officer's cap will be similar in lines to the present one, but the crown will be higher at the front and lower at the back. A broad colored stripe will show branch of service.

Gold stripes paralleling the service stripe will show rank—a single stripe for a second lieutenant, two stripes for a first lieutenant, three stripes for a captain, four stripes for a major, four gold stripes with a silver stripe in the center for a lieutenant colonel, and five gold stripes for a colonel. Higher ranks will have other distinctive markings. A gold eagle will be mounted over the visor on all officers' caps much in the position of the ornament on the present cap.

The enlisted man's cap will have a black visor and black band, with a single stripe of color at the top of band to show branch of service. It also will have an ornament in position corresponding to the one on an officer's cap.

The officer's blouse, to be worn with Sam Browne belt, will be longer than at present and very roomy below the waist, which will be form fitting with an in-seamed belt. The coat skirt will have a long vent at the rear, and the flaring effect will be pronounced all around. The breast pockets will have pleats. The lower pockets will be cut-in, only the flap marking where the pocket is, and they will have an inside-bellows effect, giving great carrying room but preserving an unruffled coat front. The present sleeve braid will become a sort of cuff, having an angle with piping in color of branch of service.

The greatcoat for officers will have a convertible collar, to be worn either roll down or buttoned up under the chin, with the new color patches on each side. It will be double-breasted and have two rows of large, composition buttons.

The blouse for enlisted men will be longer than at present, and cut so that there will be no gap at the bottom when it is buttoned. It also will have color patches. Pocket seams will not show on the outside, only the flaps marking the position of the pockets. The lower pockets will be bellowed inside, the same as in the officer's blouse, to give a maximum carrying capacity without bulging the coat front.

The enlisted man's overcoat will be single-breasted, with one row of brass buttons, with the pockets at the sides running at an angle. The collar will be similar to the collar of an ordinary raincoat, and fit closely at the neck. It also will bear the color patches.

In addition to the question of general uniform changes, the board may recommend changes in officers' insignia, chevrons for non-commissioned officers and service chevrons.

Samples of the new non-commissioned officers' chevrons are radically different from the present ones. They are much larger and wider and curved to a point. On the coat sleeve they look like the markings of a coast-line on a map, the edges of each stripe being black.

It is also proposed that service chevrons be much smaller and of dark or olive gray cord-like material, and that they be on the upper instead of the lower half of the left sleeve.

"THE STATUE—AND THE BUST," FROM THE DRAWING MADE FOR THE STARS AND STRIPES BY CAPTAIN BRUCE BAIRNSFATHER, B. E. F.

The news was a sensation. But it was a much greater sensation to General Harts than to anyone else.

That morning Visk, who was a stickler for punctuality and practised what he preached, did not reach the office until half past ten or so. He strode up to my desk breathless with anger, and there was that in his manner which told me that I was not the cause of it.

"Winterich," he said, "come into my office."

I followed him in and shut the door.

"I'm under arrest," he said, clipping his syllables in half in the stress of his emotion. "Harts called me. Furious about uniform story. 'Who wrote it?' said. 'I did!' said. 'Who drew pictures?' said. 'I did!' said. 'You're under arrest!' said. 'Go quarters!' Didn't go quarters. Came here."

The telephone rang. "Harts's aide," said Visk. "Wants to know if I'm here. Tell him hotel."

An officer under arrest (except, I suppose, for murder or arson) is supposed to proceed to his quarters and to remain there, performing no military duties, until he is hailed before a court martial or until his case is otherwise disposed of. General Harts, impressed by the Tartar he had caught, evidently had his suspicions.

I answered the telephone. It was General Harts's aide.

"Is Captain Viskniskki there?"

"No, sir. He's at his hotel—the St. James."

It was the only lie I was ever compelled to tell for my country.

Visk performed a few odd jobs around the office and then put himself under arrest. For the next few days the Hotel St. James must have been an interesting sector to those among its staff and guests who were not familiar with the ways of army newspapers. As page proofs became available at the *Daily Mail* I would take them to Visk's room for his inspection. Every footstep along the corridor set me quaking at the possibility of General Harts bursting in the door and ordering our instant execution.

Ultimately (and not very long thereafter) the affair was patched up. I believe G. H. Q. took a hand and let General Harts know that an affront to his dignity was not necessarily a high crime or even a misdemeanor. Visk was speedily unjailed, and the projected new uniform got no farther than Von's story and Wally's sketch and the tailor's dummy in the Élysée Palace. The war would one day be won, but not with brightly colored tabs on A. E. F. collars.

It was out of this incident, probably, that the rumor grew that Headquarters, District of Paris, had a special grudge against *The Stars and Stripes*. Or it may have been our own conceit. Or it may have been true. At any rate, we were not utterly friendless even in official Paris. One morning in October an alert major in the Provost Marshal's office who had a nose for news telephoned that he had in his charge an American soldier who had been a prisoner of war in Germany and who

"IT'S EASY IF YOU GET SORE," FROM THE DRAWING MADE FOR THE STARS AND STRIPES
BY LIEUTENANT PERCY L. CROSBY

had just escaped through Switzerland. If we cared to collect him we could have the story.

Now there had already been a few instances of Americans being temporarily held by the enemy in the scuffle of battle who had escaped back to our lines after a few hours or, in at least one case, a few days of detention. But not before had a member of the A. E. F. who had become a full-fledged prisoner of war, who had been conveyed to authentic Germany and held there, been able to win his way back to France according to all the best traditions of escaping prisoners.

Ross hurried down to the Provost Marshal's office and returned a few minutes later with a grinning little fellow in a private's uniform. He was Frank Savicki of the Thirtieth Infantry of the Third Division. Getting his story was a comparatively simple job despite Savicki's collapsible English. It was a good story. Exactly the things had happened to Savicki that should have happened to him. Ross let it ride.

But a serious problem remained. The English and American dailies in Paris were hardly our competitors, but it would nevertheless be pleasant to be able to keep the Savicki story in soak until we could print it. If we returned Savicki to the Provost Marshal's office there would almost certainly be a leak despite the alertness of the friendly major, for Savicki had committed no military offense and would not be detained—instead, a free agent, he would be returned to his outfit. The only thing to do was to keep hold of Savicki. Accordingly Ross and I assumed official charge of him, contracting to return him in good order to the A. P. M. as soon as the paper was out three days later.

Fortunately for his custodians, Savicki was the most amenable, tractable and good-natured creature it had been our lot to come upon in the Army. Everything we did pleased him; whatever we wanted to do he wanted to do. We got him a room in the Hôtel du Pavillon, conducted by the Y.M.C.A., tucked him in at night, yanked him out in the morning, gave him breakfast, and escorted him to the office. Luckily his recent experiences had provided him with such an abundance of excitement that he seemed to welcome the comparative calm of an army newspaper establishment. Neither did he have the slightest objection to three square meals a day.

The paper came out, the escaped prisoner story was a scoop, and Savicki was duly returned to the A. P. M. and through him to his outfit. The war was all but over —I hope Frank got back safely and is now a leading citizen of Shenandoah, Pennsylvania. Here is the record of his great war experience as Ross set it down:

> The first doughboy prisoner of war to escape from Germany after completing the cycle of experiences which befall American captives of the Boche is back in France. He spent two months and a half behind the German lines.
>
> He saw men robbed of their valuables and personal effects, even to their shoes. He went days without food or water. He was beaten several times by guards for trying to pick grass from the roadside to eat.
>
> He worked 14 and 15 hours a day for the Boche, first on military work,

later on a farm, when, for the most part, the daily diet consisted of two meals of a so-called soup made from grass and horse meat, a single piece of bread, and a substitute for coffee which hardly discolored the water in which it was made.

He went through the big internment camp at Rastatt, near the eastern Lorraine border, in which were quartered several hundred American prisoners. He saw it all, and more; he saw something of life as it is today in Germany, and escaped with his story.

This escaped prisoner of the Germans is a Russian Pole by birth, an American citizen by inclination, declaration and demonstration. His name is Frank Savicki. He is 24 years old, of less than average height, but sturdy and well built. He was born at Vilna, in Poland.

At 16, with a sister only a few years older, he sought a future in the United States. He arrived there, an immigrant, and joined his uncle at Shenandoah, Pa., where he got a job in a coal mine. He was a mule skinner, underground, and afterward a timberman.

He learned his English—still far from perfect—from the men about him, but before he had progressed far enough to learn the meaning of the word "bohunk," applied to many of his fellow-workers, he removed the danger of its application to him. He took the first step to become a citizen of the United States, and, afterward, when he had completed his necessary term of residence he raised his right hand and swore allegiance to the country he had adopted.

It was only a few months later that he got an opportunity to prove that allegiance. America declared war on Germany. A few weeks later, in April, 1917, he raised his right hand again and swore to defend the flag of the United States unto death.

It is a far cry from Shenandoah, Pa., to a shell hole north of Château-Thierry, France, but given a year and three months and a sacred cause to defend, fate worked it out with the same weird incongruity with which she has, in the last year, shaped so many American destinies.

In that year and three months she led Savicki through the recruit camp, through the intricacies of squads right and squads left, across the ocean, through the final training area, into the first line trenches of a "quiet sector," and, finally, in that memorable week in July when the Germans were started homeward, into the inferno of the Château-Thierry battlefield.

Savicki had been the liaison man between Company B of the —— Infantry and C Company, his own unit. With the Marne and the town of Château-Thierry behind, B Company was going ahead to maintain contact with the

Boche and C Company was following. It was uncertain going through scattered underbrush.

Suddenly B Company found the Boche. There was the roar of a dozen machine guns opening from concealed positions, a few shouted commands, the explosion of a score or more hand grenades. Savicki passed the signal back to C Company, and dropped into the shelter of a shell hole. A few minutes later he was joined by a corporal and a private of B Company. That company had fallen back to C Company's line, they explained, and they had been cut off. So they had crawled into the hole in what had suddenly become No Man's Land to await an opportunity to join their comrades.

This was about 2 o'clock in the afternoon. At 3 o'clock the corporal, peeping over the edge of the shell hole in an effort to locate the American positions, received three bullets in the head. He died instantly.

For two hours Savicki and the other private sat in the hole. Then the second private said, "We might as well make a run for it; we'll be killed anyhow."

Savicki agreed. They started. The second private was killed by machine gun fire before he was fairly out of the hole. Savicki dropped back unharmed.

Savicki continued his wait alone. Once he put his helmet on his bayonet and held it above the edge of the hole, to draw it back a moment later with six bullet holes in it. That decided him that escape in daylight was impossible.

He waited until nightfall, but as he was about to chance a getaway in the darkness, seven Germans surrounded his hole with fixed bayonets and took him prisoner.

Savicki was taken a mile to the rear to the support trenches, which were filled with Germans. He was turned over to an officer who spoke English.

"How many Americans are in France?" asked the officer.

"Five million," replied Savicki.

"How many American soldiers are there in the United States?" queried the German.

"Ten million," said the Yank.

The captain was impressed by these round estimates. He was so impressed that he gave Savicki a shove which sent him to the ground.

"Raus!" exclaimed the officer.

Savicki was taken two miles further to the rear. He was locked in one room of a French farm house after the Germans had searched him and taken three francs in silver, his watch, a safety razor, and his spiral puttees. Savicki had had almost nothing to eat for two days prior to his capture. His water had given out several hours before he was taken. But his requests for food from his captors were disregarded.

They left him in the farm house for two days. There was no article of furniture in the room, the only window was boarded up.

On the morning of the third day came two Germans. They made signs that the captive was to accompany them. Then started a hike which lasted all that day and all the next night, and ended at daylight of the second day at Laon.

Four days Savicki had been without food, but when he asked one of his guards for a piece of bread the latter only waved his rifle threateningly at him. They did, however, allow him water before they started. All the way to Laon the two Germans accompanied their lone prisoner.

At Laon, weak from fatigue and hunger, Savicki was put in prison barracks in which were quartered several hundred other Americans, French, British and Italians. The barracks had been converted from some large public building and was surrounded by a barbed wire fence. On the morning of his arrival, three days and 16 hours after his capture, Savicki was given his first meal.

All the prisoners were lined up and every seventh man was handed a chunk of black, sour German war bread, weighing three pounds. This was the daily ration for seven men. The man to whom it was handed shared it equally with six comrades. To supplement this, half a can of liquid was given each man. Savicki thought it was hot water until it was explained that it was supposed to be coffee. Whatever ingredient it had been made of hadn't destroyed the transparency of the water.

For a month and a half Savicki was at Laon, and this is how he describes his stay there:

"There were several hundred prisoners, about 50 of whom were Americans. We worked every day from 7 o'clock in the morning until 8 or 9 o'clock at night. We were divided into small gangs of from six to 12 to work on the roads, on the railroads or unloading supplies. Always there were almost as many guards as prisoners. If they sent eight men out, they had five or six guards.

"We had to walk one, two or three miles to our job, and usually we worked hard. Sometimes we would get a good bunch of sentries who would let us rest occasionally, but mostly we were made to work hard all the time. Those who did not work were beaten by the sentries with their rifle butts.

"Every morning we were given our bread ration—three pounds for seven men. At morning and at night we were given a can of the so-called coffee. At noon we were given soup made of some kind of grass and horse meat. There never was much meat in it, though. This noonday issue was the only pretense of a meal of the whole day. I lived on it for a month and a half, but I don't know how I did it.

"In the mornings and at night, marching to and from work, we used to try to gather grass along the roadside. We would take this back to camp with us and make soup of it. The Frenchmen cooked it in the prison yard, flavoring it liberally with salt. Salt is the only thing in Germany, so far as I know, of which they have plenty.

"But only infrequently would the guards let us gather grass. Usually, if we tried it, they would attack us with their rifle butts. Twice I was struck across the back for this offense.

"Living conditions were terrible. There were no beds in the barracks and none of us had blankets. We slept on the barn floor. There was cold water in the yard, but no means for taking a bath. No one had a change of clothes and there was no means of washing those we had. In all the month and a half I was at Laon I did not have my clothes off. Everybody was covered with lice.

"The Germans issued us nothing, not even a mess tin. We ate out of old cans, and if we happened to get a piece of meat in the soup too big to drink, we had to eat it with our fingers."

From Laon, Savicki was sent to the prison camp at Rastatt to which, early in the war, many French civilians were deported. He made the trip in a box car with 40-odd other Americans. They were three days and two nights en route, during which they subsisted on one piece of bread each and two drinks of water.

At Rastatt conditions were better. It had felt the effects of the work that the American Red Cross is doing for American prisoners in Germany. A shower bath had been shipped from Switzerland and it had been installed. Savicki got a bath and a change of underwear. Many of the Americans in the camp were non-coms. Non-coms, Savicki was told, are not required to labor. The American remained 15 days in this camp and received two boxes from the Red Cross, containing each 10 pounds of canned meat, beans, tobacco and hardtack. The Red Cross forwards one of these boxes each week to every American prisoner in Germany.

From Rastatt, Savicki was sent to work on a farm. The farm was near a little town of 50 houses. It was presided over by an aged German and his wife. Their son, 30 years old, was at the front. The old farmer put his charge to digging potatoes with a fork. Savicki worked from daylight until dark, about 14 hours.

After dark he had a late supper at the same table as the German couple. Sometimes the Germans had eggs and occasionally a little milk—never any meat—but usually their sole article of diet was potatoes, and potatoes was all they ever gave Savicki.

After supper a German soldier came for the prisoner and marched him to a sort of guard house in which were quartered a group of Russian prisoners who worked on other farms. These Russians, although peace between Russia and Germany had long since been signed, were still held in captivity despite their protests. They were treated the same as the lone American except that, whereas the latter was locked in his prison all day on Sundays, they were allowed the freedom of the farm.

Speaking their language, Savicki soon gained the confidence of the Russians. Some of them had been captives for nearly four years. All of them were restrained from efforts to escape by the rigorous punishment inflicted upon fugitives when caught. This punishment consisted of 20 days' solitary confinement in a bare room on a diet of bread and water—bread one day and water the next, alternating through the 20. You got this punishment if you were not shot, but, they explained, escaping prisoners usually were shot.

Despite this prospect Savicki decided to chance it. He learned from the Russians that a snow-capped mountain, visible in the distance, was in Switzerland; it would serve to guide him. On the fifteenth day of his stay on the farm came his weekly box of provisions from the Red Cross. He and the Russians ate it between them, all except two cans of corned beef and two packages of hardtack. This the American reserved for his flight.

That night, as usual, the guard came to the farm house for his charge. As usual, the Yank started to the guard house. As usual, the sentry followed about 20 feet behind, in fact, the only unusual thing that happened this evening was that Savicki stepped aside at the door of his jail, and when the guard entered, as was his habit, he shut the door and locked it. Then he quietly made off.

He cut straight across country avoiding all highways. His path lay over the tops of several hills, through knots of woods and stretches of ground heavy with underbrush, across several small cultivated valleys. He traveled all night, guided by the knob of the mountain. He paused when he saw before him, glistening in the moonlight, a little river which he knew separated Germany from Switzerland.

Dawn found him in a clump of shrubbery on a hillside, less than 300 yards from the nearest of the little vine-covered German sentry boxes spaced scarcely more than 100 feet apart along the international boundary. He breakfasted on corned beef, hardtack and water.

In the cover of the bushes he remained all day. Across the valley he could see the peasants tilling the soil. They, he knew, were in Switzerland. Before him, in the foreground, too, he could see the river and the difficulties before him in crossing it. Paralleling the river was a railroad, the string of sentry boxes and a wide belt of barbed wire, obviously put there to prevent the escape of such as he. At noon he saw the sentries changed, and again in the evening.

The sentries, he discovered, did not walk post, merely maintaining a watch from their boxes. The wire, he decided, he could get through. The river, he calculated, was too broad to jump—but it could be vaulted. He stirred during the afternoon just enough to get a sturdy stick and trim it for a vaulting pole.

"HOT STUFF—COMIN' THROUGH!" FROM THE DRAWING BY CAPTAIN WALLACE MORGAN

After dark he started. He crawled. So slowly and cautiously did he go that the trip to the edge of the barbed wire took five or six hours. There he rose and threaded his way through the strands, pausing after each step to unfasten the barbs which clung to his clothing.

He came to the railroad track and crawled over that. He could dimly discern the sentry boxes. He heard a guard cough in one of them. He crawled on, laying a course midway between two of them.

He gained the edge of the river. He stood on the bank. The other bank, ten feet away, was Switzerland and safety. He poised his vaulting pole and sprang for the further side. The pole sank four feet into the mud of the river bottom. Private Frank Savicki landed, belly deep, in the water with something of a splash.

There was a tense minute. Clinging to a clump of grass on the Swiss bank, Savicki waited for the bullets he was certain were coming. But none came. Evidently the Boche had not heard him. Finally, he pulled himself on to the land. He was a prisoner no more.

By daylight he made a little Swiss village in which he met an old man who dried his clothes before a fireplace and gave him breakfast. The town received him graciously and bought him a ticket to Berne. At Berne the Red Cross fitted him out in a new uniform, and the American colony outdid itself in affording entertainment worthy of an American ex-prisoner from Germany.

His trip through the prison camps, and especially his 15 days on the farm, gave Savicki a store of information on how the Germans themselves are faring. Soldiers and civilians alike are stolid, unsmiling and miserable. They have very little to eat and they seem to have little interest in who wins the war so long as it is soon ended.

"German soldiers actually on the line eat fairly well," said Savicki. "They all have bread, meat once a day, marmalade, coffee substitute and tobacco made of leaves. They do not have all they want, but they have enough to keep them in good health.

"The soldiers at the depots, 20 or 30 miles behind the line, however, do not get the same ration. They have meat only two or three times a week, and they subsist mostly on war bread and vegetables grown by themselves, French civilians forced to work in their gardens, and prisoners.

"In Germany itself there is little food of any kind. During the 15 days I worked on the farm I ate at the same table with the old farmer and his wife. They had chickens and cows, but only rarely did they have milk or eggs themselves, and never did they give me more than a boiled potato in hot water. With my box from the Red Cross I had a far better meal than they.

"Every week German soldiers came to the farm with a wagon and took off the week's accumulation of eggs and the weekly harvest of potatoes. Once they took, over the farmer's protests, two live chickens. They had a book with them which apparently contained an inventory of what he had on the farm.

"Once they were not satisfied with what he gave them and they searched the premises. For what they took they gave him a receipt, and I think the farmer exchanged this receipt for German paper money, which will be redeemable after the war in silver. There is no metal money in Germany now.

"After I had been on the farm a week the farmer's son arrived from the front for a furlough. As soon as he arrived he took off his uniform and all his equipment and sent it back to the front. This included his shoes. There is a shortage of all sorts of clothing and equipment at the front, he told me, and permissionnaires have to turn back all their government issue upon starting their leave.

"Of all the persons I met in Germany, the son was the only one who had a kind word for me. He gave me apples occasionally and told his father not to be too hard on me.

"America, the son told me, had turned the scales of the war, and Germany had no hope. He complained of shortages of everything at the front. He believed, however, that the United States was fighting for the money she would make out of it and he believed that the American soldiers were fighting because they were so highly paid.

"I heard many Germans condemning Hindenburg. Some of them said that if he were dead the war would be over and everything would be all right.

"I saw only two automobiles all the time I was in Germany. They were ammunition trucks at the front. Nearly all of the Boche transport is by horse-drawn vehicles. There are large numbers of horses behind the front. They are in fair condition. After I got away from the front I did not even see many horses. On the farms oxen and milch cows are used for hauling."

CHAPTER EIGHT

GAME CALLED

IN THE beginning there was a sports page. At the end there was a sports page. In the middle there was none.

The very first sports page was a distressful affair and admitted as much over the initials of its editor, C. P. C., which could stand for none other than Charles Phelps Cushing. Cush's defense, constructed in the manner of Kenneth C. Beaton (it was a day in which everybody was imitating K. C. B.), read:

THIS IS a poor apology for

· · ·

A LIVE SPORT page but it

· · ·

MAKES A beginning and

· · ·

SOMEBODY had to do it

· · ·

AND I was the goat but

· · ·

WITH YOUR help we'll

· · ·

DO BETTER next time if you

· · ·

WRITE US some notes from

· · ·

YOUR CAMP and send us

· · ·

SOME VERSES for

· · ·

ONE GUY can't handle this

ALL himself and

. . .

ANYBODY could do the job

. . .

BETTER than I can you know

. . .

WE WANT to find a

. . .

REAL SPORTING editor somewhere

. . .

AND WISH this job

. . .

OFF ON him and then

. . .

WE'LL buy a cable from

. . .

BACK home and tell him

. . .

TO HOP to it.

Our own George W. B. Britt wrote for this first sports page a story about a boxing bout up Neufchâteau way in which Judson C. Pewther, Q. M. C., had defeated one Kid Johnson of the Infantry. It was Cush's ill luck that this, the only available piece of honest sporting news in the A. E. F., concerned a fracas that had ended in a knockout inside two minutes, so that the most adroit master of words could hardly have spun it out to impressive dimensions. Britt managed to stretch the incident to five-eighths of a column, which was four-eighths too much. From somewhere was evolved nearly half a column more of miscellaneous sports dope. There was a full column about the Red Cross canteen service and another about the life of the Army postal clerk, and there were two fat advertisements. One of the advertisements said: "For the Most Cable and Mail News from the United States Read the American Daily Mail." The other advertisement conceded the virtues of "The Chicago Tribune: Get the News from Home in a Newspaper That Is American in Origin—American in Spirit." It looked as if the *Daily Mail* and the *Chicago Tribune* might be able to stage a more exciting party than Kid Johnson and Judson C. Pewther.

By the second number *The Stars and Stripes* was able to do somewhat better by its customers. Apart from advertisements announcing that Waterman's Ideal Fountain Pen could be had of all stationers in France and that the Guaranty Trust Company of New York had a capital and surplus of $50,000,000 and resources of more than $600,000,000 (plus a house filler to the effect that "the censor says you can mail *The Stars and Stripes* home after you have finished reading it"), the page was nearly all sports. Stuart M. Carroll initiated a column called "Star Shells" which repeated Cush's appeal of the preceding week:

> A homely versifier, I,
> An honest journalistic guy,
>   And born in old Mizzou;
> I'd like to dip my pen and write
> From milky morn till naughty night
>   Such stuff as this for you.
>
> But when ye autocratic ed
> With accent military, said:
>   "I need some sporting chat,"
> What could I do except salute,
> For I'm a buck and he's a lieut.—
>   A deuxième lieut. at that.
>
> So here we go, and you who read
> May see that we don't go to seed
>   By making it your biz
> To send us all the sport you know—
> Then watch the wicked wrinkles go
>   Forever from my phiz!

Carroll's calling himself a buck was an overdraft of poetic license, for he was a sergeant in the Q. M. C. and was later elevated to Quartermaster sergeant, senior grade, a rank just below that of field marshal. Carroll also took over the construction of streamers at the top of the page and of two quatrains, one at each upper corner, which were always the last copy to be handed in with the exception of Wally's cartoon. Carroll's streamers, assembled in order, would today form an epigrammatic history of the war. Some of the early ones read:

RUSSIA BENCHED; NO MORE WEAK HITTERS
HOOVER WORKS SQUEEZE PLAY ON YANKS
HUNS HIT .OOO AGAINST LORRAINE HURLERS
SCHUTZENGRABENVERNICHTURGAUTOMOBIL

UNCLE SAM PINCH HITTING ON WESTERN FRONT
HUNS MAY REQUEST WAIVERS ON KAISER
ALLIES AHEAD IN BIG EXTRA INNING BATTLE
BRITISH SCORE TOUCHDOWN AT ZEEBRUGGE
WET GROUNDS DELAY PLAY IN PICARDY
AN AID TO KULTUR—TRIGGERNOMETRY
YANKS NIP HUN RALLY IN BELLEAU WOODS
AUSTRIA GROGGY AT END OF FOURTH

Number Four on the above list seems to require a word of explanation. The accompanying Carroll stanzas at the top of the page made everything clear:

> The word between the boxes here
>   Won't puzzle Fritz or Herman,
> For, crazy though it may appear,
>   The thing means "Tank" in German.

> So if you were a Q. M. clerk
>   In some high Hun commission,
> 'Twould take about thirteen days' work
>   For one Tank requisition.

Stuart Carroll has gone on since the war, and some of the world's store of joy and friendliness has gone with him.

Occasionally we got hold of what we thought was a big sports story and dutifully put it on page one. In the fifth number appeared the "First Full Account of Moran-Fulton Go." It came by special cable and we appear to have thought enough of it to preface it with this editorial note: "The following account of the Moran-Fulton fight at New Orleans is the first detailed story of the big boxing event of the winter in America to reach this side."

All save the hardiest adherents of fistiana will probably have to stop and think at least twice to recall who Messrs. Moran and Fulton were (or at least who Moran was) and what became of them. The event, however, was of importance in its day; our story said the crowd was "huge"—"the spectators numbered 8,000." Mr. Fulton, dight the Plasterer, won by a knockout. The concluding paragraph of the cabled account read:

> Fulton may be challenged by Demon Jack Dempsey, who knocked out Homer Smith in one round, Jim Flynn in one round, and fought great fights with Gunboat Smith and Carl Morris. Dempsey is only 22 years old. He is an

aggressive fighter for the body, which appears to be Fulton's weakest point. In Milwaukee, the day before the Moran-Fulton fight, Dempsey licked Bill Brennan in the sixth round of a scheduled ten round bout, the referee stopping the fight to save Brennan from a knockout.

Publication of the round-by-round story of the Moran-Fulton imbroglio seems to have set the staff's introspective machinery in motion. The following week we carried an editorial called "Heroes in Wartime". "To our notion," it said, "the proper belt for a fighting man to wear in war time is of regulation canvas web or fair leather —not of green silk. . . . It is no excuse for a fighting man to plead that service in the A. E. F. would separate him from his family and a fat income. Thousands of other Americans in France and in the training camps back home are making such sacrifices and making them cheerfully. A trained athlete, particularly one who has had the opportunity to lay away a tidy fortune at fighting, owes it to his country to do something in return."

This was the opening salvo from *The Stars and Stripes* in what proved to be a fight to a finish.

Professional sport was dying hard, mainly for the reason that the civilian was having a hard time getting used to the fact of war. England had had to learn the same lesson more than three years earlier. Dispatches from London in the late summer of 1914 had told how the shops were courageously displaying "Business As Usual" signs on the mistaken theory that they were thereby bolstering morale. It is difficult for an individual to accept an abnormality, a violent rupture of routine, an utter reversal of habit; it is even more difficult for a whole nation to accustom itself to the supreme abnormality of war. Every country involved had gone through the same experience. London's "Business As Usual" signs had soon come down—business was emphatically not as usual. America had to learn the lesson. It was comforting (or it seemed so) to know that Fulton was going to fight Willard—God, in that event, must still be in his Heaven. We could not lose the war as long as Christy Mathewson was pitching for the Giants. (Mathewson himself thought different—so did a host of other true sportsmen—and came in. An old friend of Visk's, he was later one of the most distinguished visitors at the office in the Rue des Italiens.)

The A. E. F., however, did not need to perform any such sand-diving. We *knew* the times were out of joint. Most of us could not see boxing and baseball as essential industries. We were, perhaps, human enough to resent the fact that the man at home could see a good ball game and we couldn't.

Meanwhile casual driblets of sport news—a result of Cush's and Carroll's appeals—were beginning to come in from the A. E. F. It was not always permissible to tell who played whom, which must have been small satisfaction to the winners and anodyne to the losers. George Bye sent in sports stories from London, among them the news that "the famous National Sporting Club has given over Wednesday nights to American boxing." Blood was thicker than water and "prizes of medals and $25, $10, $5, $3.75 and $1.85 have been posted." The rewards, particularly in the lower brackets, do not seem tempting, but a man who was willing to risk being blown to bits for $1.10 a day was probably willing to risk having his nose pulped for $1.85 a night.

Meanwhile America's "Business As Usual" signs (so far as they appertained to the business of sport) were beginning to come down. In the issue for July 12th— a hair-trigger moment, with the last German offensive three days off and the Foch counter-thrust three more—appeared a special cable from America which began:

> Baseball teeters anxiously on the ragged edge, the players, owners and fans wondering if the "work or fight" ruling means that baseball is not work, and that, therefore, the players must fight.
>
> Many of the teams are pretty ragged already owing to the draft, and also because of the high wages paid in the shipyards, which have lured many diamond heroes from the teams. Cynical persons suggest that the shipyards are being used by ingenious players for extracting bigger salaries out of the managers, who see their teams dissolve.

Some of the signs stayed up—the same cable brought this intelligence:

> Jack Dempsey added one more K. O. to his long list when he stopped Porky Flynn in the first round of a scheduled ten round bout at Atlanta.
>
> The round was barely half over when Dempsey shot a left hook to the stomach, and followed it with a right cross to the jaw which sent Porky to dreamland.
>
> This was Dempsey's second knockout in a week, he having stopped Bob Devere at Joplin, Mo., in the first round of a 12 round battle. A left hook, after about two minutes of fighting, did the trick against Devere.

A week later there was further interesting sports news: "Babe Ruth, Red Sox, Is Year's Sensation," said a heading. Half a column was devoted to chronicling Mr. Ruth's prowess; the entire half column need not be quoted:

> Babe Ruth of the Boston Red Sox continues to be a regular Dick Merriwell. His exploits are becoming the talk of baseball back home. Ruth pitches, plays first and also the outfield, and besides that is among the leaders in the American league in batting. His feat of four home runs in four consecutive days is

THE COMPLETE LETTER-WRITER—

alone enough to make him famous. Ruth had some trouble with the owners of the club last week. He quit in a huff, but the trouble was soon patched up, and he is back clouting the ball again. . . .

Babe is a tremendously powerful man, who handles a bat as though it weighed no more than a toothpick. He takes a full swing and hits the ball out in front of the plate, giving him tremendous drive. Home runs are his specialty, and in any park that has a short right field fence he usually makes two or three in a series.

He is credited with the longest hit ever made in the American league, driving one into the center field bleachers at Fenway Park, Boston, in a game against Detroit last year with Bill James pitching.

That same week Lieutenant Grantland Rice of the 115th Field Artillery joined the staff of *The Stars and Stripes*, and in the issue following his acquisition the paper printed this announcement, three columns wide, under the title "The Sporting Page Goes Out":

This is the last Sporting Page *The Stars and Stripes* will print until an Allied victory brings back peace.

The reasons for the decision to discontinue an ancient institution are almost as numerically great as Allied shells crashing into German lines.

They are at least sufficiently thick to pulverize or blot out any objections that might be offered by those who have yet failed to see the light.

—AS SEEN BY PRIVATE WALLGREN

This paper realizes the great aid sport has given in the past in developing physical stamina and enduring morale among thousands of those now making up the nation's Army.

It recognizes the value of such training for the future. It was sport that first taught our men to play the game, to play it out, to play it hard. It was sport that brought out the value of team play, of long, hard training and the knack of thinking quickly at a vital point of the contest.

But sport as a spectacle, sport as an entertainment for the sideliners, has passed on and out. Its glamor in a competitive way has faded. Its leading stars are either in the iron harness of war—or forgotten—until Germany is beaten.

The Stars and Stripes appreciates in full sport's abiding value and the countless thousands of well-trained men it has sent into the line. But these men have given up the glory of the sporting page boost and the old action snapshot. They are not mentioned today because their job has taken on another hue.

There are tennis and golf champions, football players galore, track stars without number, boxers and ball players who have traded the easy glory they knew at home for the hard, unglorified grind of the S. O. S. or the bloody heritage of the western front. And their fame here belongs with the mass, not with individual mention.

Neither is there space, entertainment or policy in attempting to handle the scores of hundreds of ball games played all over France. A 40-page paper would not make a beginning. And those left out would remember the offense longer than those included would remember the space allotted them. . . .

The Stars and Stripes is printed for the A. E. F., not to help perpetuate the renown of able-bodied stars, who, with unusual qualifications for war or useful work, elected to hear only the "Business as Usual" slogan above their country's call for help in the greatest war she has ever known.

There is but one Big League today for this paper to cover—and that league winds its way among the S. O. S. stations scattered throughout France and ends at the western front. Any work that is part of the Big Job, either in the lines or back of it, from Château-Thierry to San Francisco, is of utmost value. But "entertaining the people back home" isn't part of the Big Job, nor do we believe the bulk of them want to be entertained in any such way.

When it finally came to a point where any number of able-bodied men were rushing into various occupations at the point of the boot, when the Secretary of War was forced to produce a ruling that would make hundreds of these men "work or fight" as the squabble and scurry grew day after day, this paper felt that it no longer had space left for such activities—not with so many events of far greater interest taking place within sight and hearing of its working staff. . . .

Back home the sight of a high fly drifting into the late sun may still have its thrill for a few. But over here the all absorbing factors are shrapnel, high explosives, machine gun bullets, trench digging, stable cleaning, nursing, training back of the lines and other endless details throughout France from the base ports to beyond the Marne.

Sport among the troops must go on—for that is part of the job. Sport among the youngsters back home must go on—for that, too, is part of the training job.

But the glorified, the commercialized, the spectatorial sport of the past has been burnt out by gun fire. The sole slogan left is "Beat Germany." Anything that pertains to that slogan counts. The rest doesn't. And that is why this is the last sporting page *The Stars and Stripes* will print until an Allied victory brings back peace.

And that was that.

To engage a Grantland Rice for a newspaper and then abolish the sports page may sound like carrying coals to Newcastle and then installing an oil-burner. Lieutenant Rice found plenty to do. He accompanied the staff delegations to the front and lent them a prestige of rank that had been lacking since those early days in which Lieutenant Cushing had visited a front-line trench. Meanwhile he conducted for a few weeks a column called "Chow" which printed, among other things, one of the most familiar ballads of the war—"Through the Wheat: The Sergeant's Story":

"There's a job out there before us,"
    Said the Captain, kinder solemn;
"There's a crop out there to gather
    Through the wheat fields just ahead."
Through the wheat of Château-Thierry
    That was soon to hold our column,
"There's a crop out there to gather,"
    That was all the Captain said.
(Oh, at dawn, the wheat was yellow,
    But at night the wheat was red.)

"There's a crop out there to gather"—
    And we felt contentment stealin'
Like a ghost from out the shadows
    Of a lost, old-fashioned street;
For the crop out there before us
    Brought a kinder home-like feelin',
Though the zippin' German bullets
    Started hissin' through the wheat.
But it didn't seem to bother
    As we slogged along the beat.

"There's snakes here," whooped a private
    As the bullets started hissin';
And we saw that Hun machine guns
    In the thicket formed our crop;
So we started for the harvest
    Where a bunch of them was missin',
But a bunch of them was hittin'
    Where we hadn't time to stop.
But we damned 'em to a finish
    As we saw a bunkie drop.

So we gathered in the harvest,
    And we didn't leave one missin';
(We had gathered crops before this
    With as tough a job ahead.)
Through the wheat of Château-Thierry,
    With the German bullets hissin',
"There's a crop out there to gather,"
    That was all the Captain said.
(Oh, at dawn the wheat was yellow,
    But at night the wheat was red.)

And an army could roar a heartfelt "Amen!" to these "Reveries of a Cannoneer"
—also from "Chow":

Could it ever have been, I wonder,
    That the barking guns were still?
That no one could hear their thunder
    Rolling from plain to hill?
That a man might sleep in the morning,
    Sleep with his dreams set free
From the endless flash where the H. E.'s crash
    With never a reveille?

Was there ever a life behind us,
    A life that we knew before?
With never a shell to find us,
    Crouching in mud and gore?
With never a pal to bury
    As part of the bitter test?
With never the cry of a last goodbye
    From a mate who is starting west?

Well, there's a dream behind us,
    And a life that is out ahead,
With never a shell to blind us,
    Far from the sleeping dead;
Yes, there's a happy morning
    Over the waiting foam,

When the game is won and we've licked the Hun,
And the good ship points back home.

Not until the final issue of 1918—December 27th—did the sporting page regain its place in the sun. The story of its resurrection belongs elsewhere in these notes, but it is not out of order to reprint here the editorial that heralded its return:

After being absent with leave for 21 issues, the Sporting Page comes back this week. It will have to make a modest rebeginning, like a man from replacement, and its destiny depends largely upon the co-operation it receives.

There was considerable comment when *The Stars and Stripes* expelled the Sporting Page last July. There was more in the States (possibly because there was more time for it there) than there was here. The comment in the A. E. F. was divided, but divided unevenly. Indorsements of the decision were far more numerous than complaints. Along in August, when the A. E. F. got up to its ears in the engrossing game of war, there was nothing apropos of sports but silence, deep and profound, which confirmed the justice of the decision.

This paper's opinion of sports is the same as ever. Proper recreation, exercise and amusement are prime necessities. The fighting over, sports in the A. E. F. are of high importance.

There is just one thing more. This paper's opinion of the leading figures of the world of sports is unchanged. On July 26 it was stated of sports:

"Its leading stars are either in the iron harness of war—or forgotten."

Some of the professionals—most of them—have been in the iron harness. Of them we can say nothing, except that they are of us and that we are for them.

Of the others it can be said that, so far as this paper is concerned, they will continue to be forgotten—and unnamed.

CHAPTER NINE

ST. MIHIEL

AT THE first breath-taking eruption of hostilities in the summer of 1914 the non-European world had suddenly been confronted with a confusing mass. of brand-new geography. Overnight there was catapulted into fame a cluster of trivial rivers which, unfortunately for millions of freshly recruited amateur strategists, did not show on most of the available maps. Chief among them were the Marne, the Ourcq, the Aisne and the Meuse, which last did not help matters by crossing over into Holland and getting itself called the Maas.

The Meuse had a clear priority to immortality. On its banks stood the "impregnable" forts of Liège and Namur, past which the German tide swept to the highwater mark of the Marne. The issue at the Marne decided, the Meuse came back into the news again. Late in September the Germans crossed the plain of the Woevre to establish a bridgehead on the Meuse opposite the town of St. Mihiel. The thrust was pivoted on the hills roundabout Verdun; the result of the attack was an ungainly protuberance some fifteen miles long on its western face and twenty-five on its southern. The amateur strategists may have wondered what the Meuse was doing so far away from Liège and Namur, but their attention was soon absorbed by the desperate race for the Channel ports and the inauguration of trench warfare in the north.

The St. Mihiel salient was thus established as a permanent institution, so far as one may measure permanency in a war. Not until a year and a half later, when the hosts of the German Crown Prince beat at the gates of Verdun, did the awkward significance of the salient make itself apparent to the lay observer. The salient itself, since 1915, had been an area of comparative tranquillity, and early in 1918 its sunny side (so to speak) was turned into a training school for battle for the earliest A. E. F. divisions.

The southern face of the salient thus became speedily famous throughout America as the sector north of Toul. Now, in September of 1918, the region was about to become more thoroughly Americanized than ever before. There were several good reasons why the salient should be reduced. Its presence was a continual threat to the sensitive area about Verdun. It covered the Briey iron basin and the bulwark of Metz, and no grand-scale offensive toward the east or the northeast could be initiated while the salient continued to exist. In their four-year tenancy of the salient the Germans had established themselves with typical thoroughness; a sudden application of the pincers would be likely, if successful, to pay rich dividends in prisoners and booty, and would restore to France hundreds of square kilometres and thousands of imprisoned civilians. Moreover the very presence of the salient was something of an affront to the prowess of Allied arms. A man from Mars, being shown the battle-line for the first time, would have been likely to point to St. Mihiel and say, "And what is *that* ugly looking thing?" Not inaccurately had the French long since christened the unlovely bulge "the hernia of St. Mihiel".

Along its western face the salient was bastioned by the heights of the Meuse—a chain of hills somewhat reminiscent of the lower Connecticut Valley. On the southern face the topography was far less impressive. Here the land was flat or gently rolling, though in general somewhat more broken than the chalky plains of Champagne further east. The only striking feature of the landscape was the towering knob of Montsec—Dry Hill, so called, perhaps, because no sooner did the rain fall on it than it ran off to increase the always superabundant quantity of French mud. But deep within the salient the contours were altered at some points with startling abruptness. A long escarpment was flung out from the heights of the Meuse into the Woevre, and on its eastern extremity the village of Hattonchatel stood like a lighthouse on a promontory flung out into the sea of the surrounding plain. From here, on a moderately clear day, were visible the roofs and cathedral tower of Metz.

Early on the morning of September 12th the freshly organized First American Army, with the news of its coming heralded in the most extensive use of artillery in American history, climbed out of the trenches on both sides of the salient prepared to remove it forever from the battle map. On the western face of the salient, close to where the line swung out across the heights that protected Verdun, were our Fourth and Twenty-sixth Divisions. To their right, around the nose of the salient, was the Second French Colonial Corps, and to the right of the French, along the southern face, the First, Forty-second, Eighty-ninth, Second, Fifth, Ninetieth and Eighty-second American Divisions. Six other divisions were in reserve or available if needed—the Third, Thirty-fifth, Ninety-first, Eightieth, Thirty-third, and Seventy-eighth. Here, altogether, were nearly half a million men—more than three times as many as Grant had commanded in the Army of the Potomac.

The operation was a romp rather than a battle—a statement which must not be interpreted to mean that the affair was not superbly executed. The salient was wiped out in twenty-four hours, and the sharpest fighting did not come until the First Army set about consolidating its new positions. The Germans had at least an inkling of the imminence of the attack, otherwise the quantity of prisoners and ma-

"A PLEASANT DREAM," BY WALLGREN

terial which might have fallen into American hands would have approached the fantastic—and the operation itself would have proved correspondingly more difficult. As it was the First Army captured more than 14,000 prisoners and 443 guns of all calibres, not to mention smaller arms and hundreds of tons of ammunition and supplies, including a hospital train complete with locomotive. This impressive victory—impressive not alone by reason of its statistical showing in captures and territory regained, but even more impressive as a blow to German morale and a boost for Allied morale and American prestige—was won at the comparatively low cost of 7,000 casualties in killed, wounded and prisoners.

The repercussion did not hit *The Stars and Stripes* office until September 16th. Our embattled staff representation, consisting of Lieutenant Rice, Sergeant Woollcott, Sergeant Bailey and Private Ross, penetrated to a depth of sixteen columns in the issue of September 20th, and mopping-up parties accounted for seven additional columns in the following issue. The front page of the September 20th issue, with the exception of two upstart rewrites of G. H. Q. bulletins, was devoted to the victory, and we offered to the world (for the first and last time in any newspaper, I hope) the amazing phenomenon of seven four-deck one-column heads standing, like Mistress Mary's pretty maids, all in a row.

Woollcott's comprehensive lead story included this eye-witness account of the artillery preparation and the jumpoff:

Shortly after one o'clock Thursday morning, the artillery preparation began. Suddenly out of the darkness, guns innumerable spoke. Spoke? They roared. They sang. They cursed. They filled the air with such a deafening and discordant salvo as soldiers seldom have heard since the world began. It was the tremendous overture of the score.

So it went for hours. Then, just before five, came the drum-fire, the steady, synchronized, harmonized barrage, the multitude of cannon firing as if a single hand were in control.

At its first notes, the spasmodic signals from the German lines changed suddenly in hue and quantity. Instead of the occasional inquisitive flares came rockets and star-shells, the lights that call for information giving way to all the fireworks known to the German signal corps, the fireworks that light up the whole countryside and mean "For God's sake, give us everything you have." They are a cry in the night for help.

The rain had stopped and dawn was streaking the east. The tanks were under way. The aircraft hummed in the skies. It was such a concourse of airplanes as Orville and Wilbur Wright must have beheld in their first little credited visions—and perhaps not even they.

And these, all these multitudinous arms and aids, were working with but a single purpose, working in a single service, the service of the doughboy, working to bring him food and ammunition and information, working to clear his path and simplify his job. And now the doughboy, on the stroke of five, rose out of his hated, water-soaked trench and went roaring over the top.

The Infantry swept across No Man's Land, across the trenches the Boches had been widening and deepening for four years, past dugouts whose none too hopeful occupants were still in hiding as a result of the artillery preparation.

They were advancing over a battlefield which, with its easy vistas and its gentle undulations, seemed made for maneuvres. The well-posted observer could sweep its operations for miles around. A movie man would have died of joy at the opportunity.

Indeed, it was a little like a movie war, that serene, unchecked advance, the Infantry waves mounting and disappearing over crest after crest, their ranks unbroken, their jaunty trot unslackened. Generals went by on white horses. Twenty minutes after five the first prisoners came trickling back. Had anyone seen it in the movies he would have choked with laughter at the ignorance of a director who thought a battle ever went as prettily as all that.

The great day drew to darkness—a darkness alert and alive with marching men, to be succeeded by the dawn of John J. Pershing's fifty-eighth birthday. In that dawn two outflung patrols of Americans came to a village, one from the west, the other from the south, caught sight of each other, and saw that each was clothed not in field gray but in olive drab. Their meeting signalized the erasure of the St. Mihiel salient.

Ross caught up with the First Division sergeant who had headed the patrol from the south which had met the Twenty-sixth Division patrol from the west and got his first-person story of that dramatic rencontre:

I started out Thursday with my squad to reach the first objective and then continue the patrol.

I think the first experience that brought any real thrill came when I reached Nonsard. Coming into this town, we heard singing down the street. When we went forward to investigate, we found a number of French girls in a bomb-proof dugout singing "The Rosary." They came out as we approached, and when they saw we were Americans—well, I don't think any of us ever got a finer reception.

Then we began to push along. It was tough going that night, as it was raining and bitter dark, and the woods through that part of the country are as thick as underbrush. But with the aid of a small compass we held our direction, worked our way carefully along, and reached each objective on time.

Here and there we'd run across a wagon and take it for a big gun. Here and there, too, we'd bump into a few loose Germans, round them up and start them to the rear.

I reached my last objective just before daylight, and then decided to push on to Hattonville in the hope of meeting an American patrol coming the other way.

I left the squad behind and took only Scotty with me. We left our rifles and packs and simply took our side arms, as it was long, hard marching, and we were pretty well worn out.

Hattonville rests down in a valley, and at dark is ordinarily hard to find, but Scotty and I had luck here. We suddenly saw a burst of flame and knew that Hattonville was burning, with the Boche in retreat. So, with this flame to guide us, we moved carefully on our way, on the lookout for any surprise.

I cut in by a graveyard back of the town and then went on in. About the first people I saw were five Austrians under an Austrian lieutenant. They didn't feel much like fighting, because they surrendered at once. So we took them in tow and then kept on moving to see what might be ahead.

Just at the edge of the town I saw two Yanks coming in from the other direction. Then I knew that we had the salient nipped off, that our lines had been joined up.

It was a wonderful sight to see these two men, for I understood what it meant. They had come from another outfit and were even more tired than we were, as they had been marching with full equipment. We both probably thought the others were Boches at first, but it didn't take us long to find out the difference.

It was still pouring rain, just faintly light, and we had been on the go for about 16 hours, so we didn't have an awful lot of conversation to spare. But we passed the time of day, shook hands to complete the last link and took another look around to see that no Boche had been overlooked.

These patrols also reported a number of prisoners they had rounded up and had started back to the rear, where they went with great willingness. One of them had run into a German colonel. But instead of coming out to surrender, he sent his man out to announce that he was willing to be taken prisoner, so they went in and got him.

After meeting the first patrol, I started back with my Austrian outfit. It was then I met the other patrol, for there were three sets working, and that was complete evidence that all of us had reached our final objectives and that the entire salient was in American hands.

The hardest part of the work was the long night march through the woods, where we never knew at just what minute we'd run across Boches looking for battle or stumble on a machine gun nest. I have never seen a darker night or thicker woods.

After I had met the two patrols and knew the line was joined up, I went on back a kilometer and a half to the place where I had left my squad, taking the Austrian detachment along. I then sent word back that the meeting had been effected and that the line across the salient was intact.

American cavalry fought at St. Mihiel—it was that kind of a battle. What a lark Jeb Stuart would have had! There were not many of them, but there were enough to be effective and to bring back the flavor of Balaklava and Waterloo and Poitiers. Ross filed this report of their activities:

A band of American Cavalry, riding as if to uphold the traditions of the service made when it used to number among its officers Captain John J. Pershing, had its share of honor in the redemption of the St. Mihiel salient.

There were many reports circulating about the exploits of the Cavalry after the fall of the salient. The most common was that "the Cavalry took 1700 prisoners and lost one man." The total of prisoners may be correct, but it is not confirmed by the Cavalry. The horsemen didn't stop to compute their captures, but turned them over to the Infantry to be added to the general total of prisoners without distinction.

The principal resistance the Cavalrymen met was from isolated German machine gun nests. These were usually encircled and put out of commission with pistol fire. On one occasion Cavalrymen came upon two Germans holding forth in a shell hole with a machine gun. One was accounted for with a pistol bullet in the head. The second crouched out of sight in the hole. The Cavalrymen took shelter and waited to see whether he would show fight or surrender.

They waited five minutes and nothing happened. A lieutenant had just started to give orders for the encircling of the hole when Mr. Boche appeared. He appeared suddenly, coatless and in his stocking feet, and started to do a Marathon towards Berlin. He was overtaken before he had gone 50 yards.

He had decided to make a run for it and had taken off his boots and stripped to his shirtsleeves to make better time, he explained.

The horsemen, riding into one little town, found that a German general had departed an hour before. Also they found a mounted major departing in the wake of his chief. The major surrendered gracefully to an American captain, who overtook him going up the main street. He relinquished his horse, ornate saddle, padded stirrups and all, and went rearward afoot. The horse was kept with the troop. They call him "Kaiser Bill."

In another town the Cavalrymen overtook a squad of Germans with a whole pushcart full of German pistols. There was a souvenir revolver for every American present.

Probably the most exciting episode of the Cavalry's advance was a fight with a Boche ammunition and supply train. The Americans had brought with them, strapped to their saddles, several light machine guns, and these, when the train was encountered in a wood, were unslung and set up. The Germans replied with machine guns hastily mounted on their wagons.

For 20 minutes a running fight was waged until the Boche gained the security of a position defended by machine gun nests and the Americans were forced to pause. The wagon train got away, but only after its members had suffered casualties and it had abandoned a couple of wagons.

Deep in the core of the salient the scattered clusters of French farmers and villagers and their families had for four years known only so much of what was going on as the German tenants had chosen to tell them. Seth Bailey's account of one such family's experience was typical of what hundreds had endured:

Marie Rose was nine years old in 1914. At that time her family consisted of her father, mother, brother and herself, and it was a happy family until the war clouds rolled up and the German storm broke across Belgium and into France. For days the battle was heard in the distance; then, one night, the Germans swept forward past the farm, the St. Mihiel salient was formed and the once happy family was shut in.

It was then, after the Germans came, that Marie Rose bid goodbye to her brother one morning, as the Germans took him away with some other boys who, so the Germans said, were going to do some work not far away. Just how far away they took her brother Marie Rose does not know, for she has never seen him since.

Marie Rose's story, as told to the Yanks who liberated her and her mother, is the same story as told by many others who were caught in the German advance four years ago. Some German transportation officers occupied the spare rooms of the farm house, and from time to time new officers came to take their places. The officers were not harsh, but they were strict. None of the family was allowed away from the farm. Once when Marie Rose became very sick a German doctor was brought in to care for her.

Marie Rose's father worked on the farm, while her mother did the housework and cooked for the officers. There was no school, of course, so Marie studied German, and often a German officer devoted his evenings to giving her instruction. She was told that the German language was very pretty, and that in a few years the entire world would speak German.

So the months rolled by, and Marie Rose learned to speak German. She did errands for the German officers, and sometimes they brought her candy and cookies. Occasionally she visited another little girl who lived only a few kilometers away, but this chance did not come often, as she had to be escorted by a German officer or soldier.

The day they buried her little girl friend in a nearby graveyard was a sad day for Marie Rose. There were no more playmates in miles and miles. She cried for two days and nights; then, so her mother says, she asked if there were any other little girls in the world. Her mother told her there were; that some day when the Germans were beaten back, they would go away from there to where there were lots of little girls and boys and a school.

This encouraged Marie Rose, but her courage was shattered when in 1916 her father died out in the field where he had gone to work. Her mother lapsed into a long sick spell soon after. Those were sadder and lonesomer days for little Marie Rose.

As the months rolled by and Marie Rose grew older, her mother often called her aside and told her of the great day coming when the Germans would be swept back. Marie Rose listened with much interest. One day she approached a German officer about it. He told her that there would soon be no French Army and everything would be German. Marie Rose returned to her mother with the news.

"Don't you believe them," her mother told her. "There will come a day."

During the early morning of September 12, 1918, Marie Rose and her mother heard the booming of distant cannon. As daylight broke the booming became louder and louder, and at noon the Germans hurriedly packed their belongings and left without even a word to Marie Rose and her mother.

Heavy shells were soon bursting in the neighborhood, and German soldiers began to pass in wagons, automobiles, on horses. Some—a great many—were passing on foot.

Marie Rose's mother almost cried with joy as she dragged Marie Rose after her down into the cellar, where they would be safe from the bursting shells. One shell hit the house and tore its way through the chimney.

Toward evening the bombardment passed on; only now and then did a shell explode near the farm. The mother and daughter had decided to come out of their shelter when someone scratched on the cellar door and a voice—not

"The Boches have Gone!"

ALMOST ANYWHERE IN THE HEART OF THE SALIENT—A BALDRIDGE SKETCH FROM
THE ST. MIHIEL FRONT

French, not German—spoke to them. The voice spoke some more—very gruff this time—and both Marie Rose and her mother crept nearer each other.

Finally, there came a heavy pounding at the door and it opened with a bang.

An American private slipped down the stairs, his bayonet pointed straight at the two huddled figures in the corner. "Oh!" said the voice. "Pardon moi."

When Marie Rose and her mother learned the truth, they insisted on kissing the American's hands. And, if the truth be known, the big American private, who hails from Kentucky, admits with a grin that he was really kissed smack on the cheek in spite of the protection his whiskers afforded him.

The most unusual adventure experienced by any member of the staff during the St. Mihiel operation was certainly that of Lieutenant Grantland Rice. Late that drizzly first night he had looked about him for a place to snatch an hour's sleep, and behold, at the roadside appeared a pile of rubble that, considering the time and place, matched the luxury of the Waldorf. Discerning a point at which the debris had not quite closed together, Rice crawled in, to find what passed for a floor and above it, more miraculously, what could pass for a rather sketchy roof. He lay down and slept. Toward dawn he half awoke and immediately went back to sleep with the vaguest sort of semi-idea that somebody was sharing his quarters.

A sound brought him back to full consciousness. It was by now nearly daylight. A yard from him a Frenchman and a German seemed to be engaged in a playful wrestling match. The Frenchman was winning, because he was pulling off the German's nice leather boots. A final tug and the Frenchman departed in triumph. Then Rice noticed that one of the German's legs remained extended in air at an odd angle. He was dead—had been dead several hours before Rice went to bed.

St. Mihiel produced its quota of absorbing little sidelights—dozens of them—to which the whole *Stars and Stripes* delegation contributed:

The Boche left the St. Mihiel salient so abruptly that he didn't have time to destroy the bridges, plant his usual number of booby traps, or render railroads, military and otherwise, temporarily useless, so the work of the Engineers wasn't as varied, on the whole, as it has been in some actions.

But many Engineer detachments distinguished themselves by going over the top with the doughboys for wire-cutting and the like, and some of these remained with the Infantry and romped on to the finish.

In one case two Engineers and an Infantryman pushed down a road, rounded a hill at the edge of a sizeable town, fired upon a quartet of Germans, who hastily departed, and then marched into the town and proclaimed to the joyful, enthusiastic natives that they took the village in the name of President Wilson. They announced that the town would be turned back to the natives as soon as an officer arrived to take charge of the ceremony.

At sundown on September 12, when a lull came in the business of examining prisoners at one divisional headquarters, the American officer in charge sat down to a bite of supper, and, thinking they might expand under such hospitality, invited two German artillery officers to share it with him. Two passing French artillery officers horned in on the hot coffee and well-plastered white bread.

In the slowly started conversation, **it** was discovered that the French officers had directed the very fire which silenced the battery these prisoners had commanded. They got to swapping memories of the battle, criticizing each other's work and pointing out just which shots had been effective and which were misses. The debate became warm and affable. A passerby, after studying the scene from his side of the cage wire, observed loudly:

"Well, I'll be damned! Sounds for all the world like one of those violent post mortems on the veranda of the Englewood Golf Club."

One unit, in the forward push, had been without cigarettes for two days. About this time it ran on to a German headquarters and about all it landed there was 25,000 gold tipped Turkish cigarettes of excellent quality.

The familiar looking and familiarly spelt French word "saint" is pronounced by at least 89 Yanks out of a hundred as though it were its English counterpart. There is one glorious exception. St. Mihiel is called "San Mihiel," not "Saint Mihiel," by everybody in O. D. who had anything to do with reducing the salient. It is not only pronounced San Mihiel. It has even achieved the distinction of being written that way on division bulletin boards—probably by old campaigners with Philippine, Cuban and Mexican memories cluttering up their orthography.

During the German's four year occupation of one tiny hamlet in the St. Mihiel salient, the French population was forced to work for the German officers, prepare their meals, wash their clothes, clean their dirty boots and do various other tasks that were imposed upon them, just as it did in the other towns.

One toiler was an old woman, much bent with years and suffering with rheumatism. Her daily task was to care for five rooms, wash and scrub the floors, change the linen and look after the officers' many petty wants. She was not allowed out after 7:30 in the evening or permitted to visit her neighbors without first obtaining permission.

During all those four years this old woman kept, hidden away in a secret trunk, a silk waist and tailored skirt, hoping against hope that a brighter day would dawn for her.

The bright day dawned when the Americans swept forward on the early morning of the 13th of September, driving the Germans before them. After the barrage had passed on and the streets had filled with Yanks, she dusted off the trunk, unlocked it, dressed up in her best, carefully smoothed out the wrinkles, asked a doughboy if it was bon, then went calling on her neighbors and even paid a visit to the American commander.

Two privates were jogging through one town on the seat of a ration cart last Friday morning when one of them spied a gray-green, handsomely braided overcoat hanging out to air in front of what had been a German P. C. a few hours before.

"I saw it first," said the large one, sternly. "Now, Buddy, while I keep my hand on these mares, you hike over there and cut off them sleeves for me. I'll bet Eliza Jane can make something pretty doggone nifty out of them."

The other, nothing loath, got out his pen knife and had just hacked off the second sleeve when out of the house swarmed a staff of junior officers. He felt his legs give way beneath him. He knew by their faces what he had done. He had ruined the overcoat which had been tailored and adorned in America to shelter the general commanding the brigade then in possession of the town.

The general was asleep below. His lieutenants, with ill-concealed relish, woke him up so that the show might start at once. The general said several things about the vandalism evidently taught in the rival brigade. He spoke of firing squads, years and years in Fort Leavenworth, pay detained for the duration of the war and so on. Then, after a struggle, he burst out laughing, and that's all there is to that story.

You may measure the instant success of the attack on the St. Mihiel salient by the fact that by sunset of the third day Jewish soldiers were leaving the line for the observance of Yom Kippur. One of them went off to the celebration in particularly uplifted mood. His "breeches, 1 pr., wool, O. D." had been scandalously dirty and, noting that fact, his captain had cheerfully lent him his own very best.

A Slovak butcher, working at some German headquarters in the St. Mihiel salient and blissfully unconscious of impending doom, had breezed into Thiaucourt, where there was the equivalent of a depot quartermaster, to buy him some supplies when he found himself gazing upon three Yankee sharpshooters.

"I was mighty scared at first," he said, "but they had no sooner spoken than I found they were Slovaks, too. You must have all nationalities in your Army. Well, they gave me an orange, they gave me a piece of chocolate, they gave me a cigarette and here I am."

———

Every big American gun has a name of its own, bestowed upon it by the men of the battery. One of the big ones that pounded away at the German communications behind St. Mihiel was named "Wilson's Answer."

You could hear Wilson's answer all over Lorraine.

———

Of course in every army the telephone stations have odd and frequently changed code names. For example, Parsnips may be Vladivostok tomorrow. It might be a boy's name one day or a flower's name the next.

In one P. C. that played a big part in the St. Mihiel battle, a skilful but rather effeminate young captain had to endure the titters in the dugout whenever he went to the telephone and was there obliged to say:

"Yes, this is Annabelle."

———

There are few braver, more hopeless deeds in the annals of this war than that of one 48-year-old German soldier who, deserted by his comrades and without food and water, stuck to his machine gun post in the tower of a shell-gutted church for three days after the Americans entered and took possession of one little town northeast of St. Mihiel.

The German, with a non-com and another soldier, had been stationed in the tower and told to stick to the last by a lieutenant who immediately left for the north. When the American Artillery got too hot, the non-com and the second private sought shelter in a cellar, and there they were found when the Americans entered the town.

The Boche shelled the same town a few hours after the Americans got through and continued his shelling intermittently during the next three days, but undeterred, the grizzled German stuck to his sniping post.

He fired only when an airplane was in sight overhead, and the spasmodic sputterings of his gun were put down to airplane fire.

Fortunately for the Americans, his post did not command any important points. A headquarters had been established in the shadow of the church tower, but the pitch was too great for him to negotiate with his gun.

At the end of the third day he was seen by a doughboy, who climbed up and captured him. He was feeble from lack of nourishment and thirst, or he might not have surrendered so easily.

"For Germany and the Kaiser," was his explanation as to why he had stuck it out.

"The master ill befits the servant," said the officer who examined him. "Give him a big feed and a package of cigarettes."

Residents of the freed towns got a real example of the American soldier's buying power. Stores and shops which had full stocks, enough to last for weeks or months with the desultory buying of the civilian population and the modestly paid German soldiers, were all sold out within two or three hours after the Americans arrived.

The hasty evacuation of certain towns by the Germans resulted in many curious finds by policing, mopping-up and salvage parties. One German brigadier who had departed with more speed than grace had apparently kept a complete file of all orders from German general headquarters and a thorough file of all confidential data and correspondence. An intelligence officer, called to the scene, started to go through it, but the task was too much for him. He shipped all the papers off to headquarters.

The collection exactly filled one Quartermaster's truck.

St. Mihiel did not tax unduly the A. E. F.'s hospital facilities—the big strain would come and the hospitals would be ready. But there were still plenty of Yanks abed to keep doctors and nurses busy as a result of the summer fighting, and *The Stars and Stripes* was hearing from them regularly. One who signed himself merely Harv pointed the contrast between line and hospital in free and effective verse. It was indubitably this same Harv who later offered a not practicable (and I am afraid not too sincere) scheme for the enforcement of prohibition, and the qualifications which he submitted with this document may help someone to identify him:

Holder of the following records:
1914—Winner of the Yale-Princeton Stone Ale Championship.

1915—Winner of the Pan-American Mixed Drinks Championship.
1916—Member of the Intercollegiate Schooner Crew at Poughkeepsie.
1917-18—Official tester of all liquors left behind by the Boche.

Harv's verses were entitled "Black and White":

> I was like the child
> Who believed there was
> A Santa Claus
> But had never seen him,
> Only

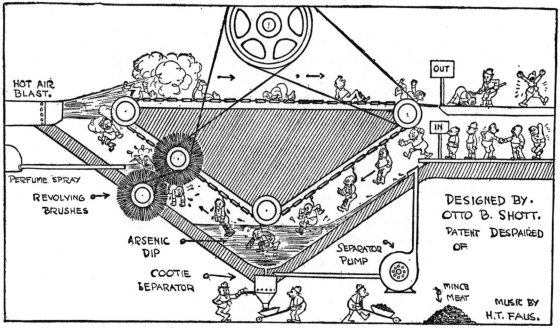

DECOOTIEIZING DEVICE (SOUTHERN EXPOSURE) DRAWN BY WALLGREN FROM A ROUGH SKETCH
SENT IN BY A FIELD WORKER

> I have seen another world
> And know it exists.
>
> I used to think that
> There was only one world—
> A world of
> Mud
> And bursting shells
> Which killed and wounded
> Me and my pals;
> A world of

Hizzing bullets
And mustard gas,
And cold, sleepless nights,)
And no food for days,
And Huns who cried
"Kamerad!"
(When their ammunition was gone),
And filthy clothes,
And cooties
And cooties
And cooties.

But now I know that there is also
A world of—
Clean sheets and pajamas,
And good food
And plenty of it,
And kind, gentle women
In white
Who give you cocoa and soup.
And doctors who give you more than "C.C." pills.
And peaceful days
Without a single shell,
And peaceful nights,
And officers who wear white collars
And have only *heard* of cooties,
And visitors who sit on your bed
And murmur "How thrilling,"
And street cars and taxis,
And buildings without
A single shell hole in them,
And everything
I only dreamed of before.
Gosh! but it's a wonderful war—
BACK HERE.

A patient with nothing to do but listen and get well used his ears to good
purpose:

To the Editor of *The Stars and Stripes*:

A few remarks heard at one of our new Base Hospitals:

Patient: "Nurse, tell me what these pills 'll do; that salmon we had yesterday 's goner poison us all."

Nurse: "Huh! I had salmon too. I got up at 6 a. m. and I'm feeling fine; get up out of bed and you'll feel better."

Patient No. 2: "I'm goner see the C. O. about the grub they dish out here and we're supposed to be sick men too. I ain't ate nothin' in three days now; if they'd gimme my clothes back, I'd get out of here."

Patient who is able to go for his chow: "There wuz four flies in the plate handed to me, and when I tried to wash it the mess sergeant said 'Whaddye

"AS THE POET REMARKED," FROM THE DRAWING BY LIEUTENANT PERCY L. CROSBY

mean by holdin' up the line?' What that guy needs is promotion near the front."

Patient No. 4: "What's that the Cap'n said? No patient allowed to go fifteen feet from the ward? I see 'm keepin' me tied up in this place!"

Sick Soldier: "Yep, it's the only place God made complete—New York!"

Nurse from near Chi: "You've never been to Chicago; I can see that!" (and then they rag one another for the next 'steen minutes).

Patient: "I'm goner ask for a transfer to the brig. I might have a little freedom there."

Patient No. 7: "If they keep us here much longer, they'll have to send us to a hospital." (Cheers.)

Patient No. 8: "Nurse, what's good for pains in the heart?"

Nurse: "A furlough home."

Patient No. 8: "You win."

Patient No. 9: "I know a doctor who would make a fine horseshoer."

Patient minus some toes: "I'd like to see 'em try to dress it without givin' me a shot. I ain't goner stand for it."

Patient No. 10: "The first three nights I was here I couldn't sleep. I kept beggin' 'em to give me a shot, but nothing doing. The fourth night I fell asleep from sheer exhaustion, and fifteen minutes later the wardmaster wakes me up and says, 'Here's a sumphin' that'll put yer to sleep!' And some folks say 'Don't cuss! be the man your mother thinks you are.'"

Nurse: "Who'll help me carry this mattress outside?"

Patient minus leg: "I will."

Another person in pajamas: "Nurse, what class 'm I in, D, C, B, or A?"

Nurse: "What are you trying to do, gold-brick it?"

A blue patient: "Here I am dyin', and I'll bet that Jane of mine is doin' Broadway with some slacker! I don't wish him any hard luck, but ——"

Patient No. 20: "Here comes that —— sweepin' detail again." Bugle sounds in the distance. "And listen at the bugle calls. I thought we had graduated from that kind of war."

Still another patient: "I see they're gettin' 'em from 18 to 45 now; they ought to send them over toot sweet; learnin' squads east and west ain't goner do 'em a dam bit o' good."

Patient minus arm, in severe pain most of the time: Nothing.

We've been through beaucoup hell, and now we're spending a short vacation in heaven; yet a soldier must grumble. He always longs to be where he ain't and when he gets there, it's "Where do we go from here, boys?"

The gift edition was received yesterday. We thank you, all of us.

SGT. SOLL MONSKY,
M. G. Co., — Inf.

Here is a pathetic plea with the germ of a good short story:

To the Editor of *The Stars and Stripes:*

Some time ago, knowing that I couldn't carry it much longer, I gave my violin to an ambulance driver in the Château-Thierry district. I told him to take it to a hospital for whoever could use it.

As I am now in the hospital myself, I would like to correspond with whoever has it, with the idea of getting it again.

My old address is on the bottom of the case: Pvt. Harold A. Kirk, Co. L., —
Inf. My present address is:

Pvt. Harold A. Kirk,
Base Hospital 3, A. P. O. 705.

Let it be hoped that the hero of the following incident soon came among his own:

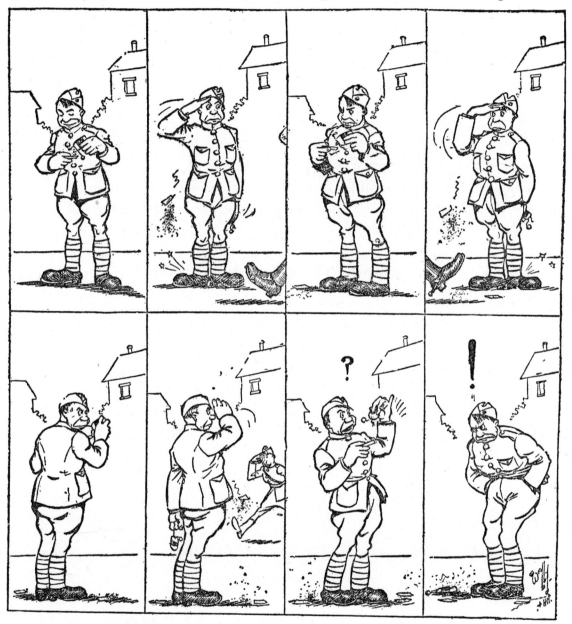

"YES, AND YOU'D HAVE SAID IT, TOO," BY WALLGREN

To the Editor of *The Stars and Stripes:*

    While going through a French hospital in Lyon some time ago, I ran across
a poor, lone negro soldier who had been wounded and sent there for treatment

—the only American in the large ward in which I found him. Over his bed, on the bottom of a soap box, scrawled in heavy, black pencil, appeared these words: "English spoken here."

THOS. B. SHINE, Capt. Q. M. C.

The great German offensive of March 21st was only six months back in history, but what a six months it had been! The week that saw the victory of St. Mihiel also saw British and French continue the attack north and south of the Somme that had got off to a magnificent start in August and regain at some points the positions they had abandoned at the beginning of the disastrous spring retreat. The German line along the Chemin des Dames, whence the enemy had lunged forward to create the Marne salient, was in definite danger owing to the persistence of French pressure above Soissons. Far away in Macedonia French and Serbians had initiated an attack against the Bulgarians that would soon result in the first of four armistices—the snapping of the weakest link. Since the opening of the Foch counter-offensive on July 18th Germany and her allies had lost some two hundred thousand prisoners at a time when the frantic cry from every front was for men, men, and still more men.

But the war was not quite over. The A. E. F. had yet to fight the greatest battle in American history.

CHAPTER TEN

THE MUD OF THE ARGONNE

OUT of the wealth of his wanderings Ross once told us a story of that lively summer of 1912 when Senator Charles Warren Fairbanks, who had been Vice-President under Roosevelt, was campaigning for the Republican ticket, on which he was a candidate for election to his former office. The Senator's train, east bound, had just passed out of Arizona and had stopped at the first station across the line. The Senator rose to his feet on his rear-platform rostrum and greeted the little company of townsfolk who had assembled to listen.

"My dear Arizona friends," he began, when an alert aide tugged at his coattails and whispered that he was now in New Mexico.

"Ah, yes," laughed the Senator, turning to his audience again. "Well, you know back East all these States out here look alike to us."

The doughboy who slithered through the sodden stretches of some hapless farmer's battle-riven acres between the mist-hung valley of the Meuse and the scrubby tangles of the Argonne Forest at any time from September 26th to November 11th, 1918, who inched his way forward when the inching was good, and held his ground —held it as tight as his sucked-in belly would let him—when it wasn't, who lay down to sleep in green pastures—too green, and much, much too damp—and was not grateful to his Lord for the privilege, and who stood erect at the last in the heart of a silence his prowess had imposed and of a peace his valor had wrought—that doughboy, when he had finally won his way to the incredible miracle of home, took a reasonable dislike to people who inquired of him eagerly if he had been at Château-Thierry and who became mildly patronizing when he answered, "No, I wasn't."

What, not at Château-Thierry? That, to many a civilian mind at home, meant that such a soldier, so-called, had merely stood at the land end of a gangplank at Brest or St. Nazaire and collected the tickets of the real fighting troops as they came up out of the transports. Back home all battles looked alike, and they were all Château-Thierry.

The two million men in uniform in the home camps knew better. Trained to a pitch that most A. E. F. divisions who were war-worn by the fall of 1918 had never known before the swift seasoning of battle, they constituted what a great English student of war, the late Lieutenant-Colonel Charles A'Court Repington, was to call "the last great reserve army of civilization". They were in the war. Every move that was made in France in those final flaming months, no matter who made it, was predicated on them. The German High Command held them in the highest respect, too well aware of the fact that a German victory must be achieved, if achieved at all, before this great reservoir of fresh and ready manpower was sluiced into what must inevitably become the final fight.

The Battle of the Meuse-Argonne owes some of its submergence in the lay mind to its very magnitude. In numbers of men engaged, in quantity of armament employed and ammunition expended, in extent of territory fought over and time consumed in the fighting, it was a grand-scale war in itself. It was too much to grasp —something too vast and too involved to be spectacular. He who sought the spectacular must select from the whole broad panorama such dramatic details as the exploits of a Sergeant York or a Captain Woodfill.

The Meuse-Argonne was not a swift, clean, comprehensible stroke like St. Mihiel, not a vivid counter against a victory-swollen opponent like Château-Thierry— it was a dogged, relentless wearing down of an enemy who must fight and die, a concentrated campaign of attrition.

The fireside spectator of the far-flung tumult of that lurid autumn found it superficially much more profitable and entertaining to trace the rapid progress of Allied arms almost anywhere else on the map. In Palestine, in the Balkans, along the upswing of the Western Front, where the enemy was hourly being dislodged from points in a defense system on which he had expended the pains and ingenuity of years, the line was moving resistlessly forward.

Nothing like that in the Argonne. But the fireside spectator failed to appreciate that it was precisely because there was nothing like that in the Argonne that there was something like it everywhere else. The enemy could yield five, ten kilometres in the north and count the loss cheap if he could thereby save one in the Argonne.

Behind the German front in the west the essential lateral line of communication was the railroad from Lille through Mézières and Sedan to Metz. At Sedan, city of evil memories to the French, this railroad was only some thirty-five miles from the front line. Thirty-five miles was a lot of kilometres to fight over, but the Germans were hardly foolish enough to reject the possibility that somebody some day might try to fight over it. They had accordingly converted the region between the Meuse and the Argonne into a virtual fortress twenty miles in breadth and from ten to twelve miles, on an average, in depth.

Whatever Prussian evolved the motto "Gott mit uns" must have been thinking of the topography of the Meuse-Argonne. To the east was the winding valley of the Meuse, flanked by highlands or by marshes of equal and powerful defensive value. Stretching hence toward the Argonne was a region of alternate slopes and depressions that were not of notable scenic impressiveness but were of great tactical significance. Running from east to west, these successive slopes lent themselves admirably to the security of any force that held them. The dominating height of this area was the crest of Montfaucon. It was hardly a peak to require the use of rope and alpenstock; today the motorist can readily win its summit without shifting gears. But in wartime it was a formidable natural stronghold—a tower of strength to him who possessed it, a prize worth vast sacrifice to him who would gain it and go beyond. At the western edge of the rolling plateau of the Meuse was the redoubt of the Argonne—more effective as a barrier than if the Great Wall of China had been reared on the German flank. The Argonne, too, was nothing to lure the pre-war tourist. Not grandly dominant in elevation, not particularly dignified in its ruggedness, it was more to be avoided than explored. It was just a piece of no-account, topsy-turvy country.

All these elements went to compose the doughty barrier against which the divisions of the A. E. F. were to be flung in the Battle of the Meuse-Argonne. The battle divides naturally into three phases: the initial lunge, the ghastly month-long grind of October, and the surge to victory that began on November 1st. The First and Second American Armies can be likened to a swimmer preparing to cross a wide, shallow river through whose center runs a deep and powerful current. He dashes in until the water is well above his waist, struggles long and grimly against the force in midstream that would sweep him away, finally puts foot to bottom, and gaily, breathlessly runs ashore. The phases of the Argonne are readily understandable when one considers the simple statistics of time involved and gains made. In the first four days of the battle the Americans penetrated on an average some seven miles. In the last eleven days they swept ahead to an average depth of twenty miles. In the thirty-one days between they gained seven miles.

A roster of A. E. F. combat divisions which participated as integral units in the Argonne fury is almost a roster of A. E. F. combat divisions. They were the First, Second, Third, Fourth, Fifth, Twenty-sixth, Twenty-eighth, Twenty-ninth, Thirty-second, Thirty-third, Thirty-fifth, Thirty-seventh, Forty-second, Seventy-seventh, Seventy-eighth, Seventy-ninth, Eightieth, Eighty-first, Eighty-second, Eighty-ninth, Ninetieth and Ninety-first. First and last, including auxiliary troops in the zone of combat, nearly a million and a quarter Americans took part in the operation. The

"THE NONCOMBATANT," BY BALDRIDGE

cost was 120,000 casualties. More than fifteen hundred square kilometres, over which were scattered one hundred and fifty towns and villages, were won back for France. The railroad passing through Sedan was cut, and with the cutting the German armies in France were divided, and an army divided against itself cannot fight.

On November 8th, with the Armistice only three days away (though nobody knew it was quite as close as that), *The Stars and Stripes* printed what was many times over the longest editorial that ever appeared in the paper. It was called "The Post of Honor", and it was a comprehensive summary of what the Meuse-Argonne campaign was signifying in the grand plan of victory:

> Since the morning of September 26 the American Army has been engaged in an offensive between the Meuse and the Argonne on a front of 32 kilometers. During the same period the French, British and Belgian armies holding the Western battle line from the Argonne northwest to the sea have waged offensives of their own which have liberated generous slices of France after four years of German tyranny and been heralded throughout the Allied world with joyful acclaim.
>
> Until this week, the American offensive, on the other hand, had received, in Europe at least, but scant notice compared with that given the offensives of our gallant Allies. Quite naturally, there has grown up here and there throughout the American Army some curiosity over this differentiation as to publicity of military accomplishments. The answer is not that the press of our Allies does not appreciate the meaning of the American offensive and its influence along the whole Western battle front, but that it is human nature—in the publishing world as in any other line of human activity—to give heed to the spectacular. It cannot be gainsaid that the advances of the Allied armies to the northwest of the Argonne have been far more spectacular than the dogged foot-after-foot battle which the American Army waged between the Meuse and the Argonne from September 26 until this week's swift advance began.
>
> But if the part assigned to the American Army in the present offensive operations has not been spectacular, it is, nevertheless, one of extremely great importance. Indeed, it will not sound boastful to those who know to say that in the present grand offensive of the Western Front the American Army, since September 26, has been at the post of honor. Let us see what are the facts that warrant this assertion.
>
> First, the German enforced withdrawal from France and a very large part of Belgium is pivoted upon the region where our First Army is operating. A penetration of the German positions to a considerable distance in this region

(which is now threatened, November 6) would seriously endanger the withdrawal of the enemy's forces between the Argonne and the sea.

Second, the German "voie de rocage" (a line of railway communication for the rapid shift of troops from one portion of the line to another) passes through Mézières. An advance of a few kilometers by our First Army from its present positions would actually interrupt communications along this line. With such an interruption effected, the German would be placed at an enormous disadvantage on account of the fact that a shift of troops from the north to Alsace would then have to be made by routing these troops through Belgium. In other words, the enemy would have to work on an outside line of communications instead of being able to shift his troops along a line approximately parallel to the front. To all intents and purposes, the German army defending the Western Front would be divided in two.

Third, the lines on which the Boche is fighting at the present time between the Meuse and the Argonne are really the outer defenses of the Briey basin. This basin is one of the great prizes of the whole world; it contains four-fifths of the iron supply of Europe. When it is considered that the remaining one-fifth of the European iron supply is located in Norway, Sweden and Russia, and other points more or less inaccessible to the Boche, it is clear how vital to him is the continued possession of this area. With the Briey basin wrested from him, he would be at an enormous disadvantage in the manufacture of munitions of war.

The American offensive, then, strikes at the vitals of the enemy on the Western Front—and the Western is the war's decisive front. That the German High Command is keenly alive to the seriousness of the situation is indicated by the fact that since September 26 more than one-sixth of the entire German force on the Western Front has been thrown against our First Army, and this on a front which is slightly more than one-twentieth of the whole line from Switzerland to the sea.

Many of the numerous divisions that the Boche has hurriedly brought against us are the very best he possesses, and included in the number are several Guard divisions, rightly ranked as the cream of all he has. The great majority of these divisions the German High Command has been compelled to withdraw from that portion of the line stretching northwest from the Argonne to the sea. In other words, the A. E. F.'s First Army, fighting between the Meuse and the Argonne, has compelled the Boche to mass there the flower of his fighting forces in great disproportion to the strength of his dispositions elsewhere on the Western Front, and this is one very important factor in the success of the French, British and Belgian armies fighting to the northwest of the First Army clear to the northernmost tip of the Western battle line. We have American divisions operating with these Allied armies. These American divisions have participated in the brilliant and spectacular successes of these armies. We can justly feel that their task has been rendered more easy of accomplishment on account of the pressure that, since September 26, our First Army has brought to bear upon the enemy between the Meuse and the Argonne.

Fighting over a most difficult terrain, opposed by so great a proportion of the German army, the very flower of it, every foot of France that our doughboys reclaimed between the Meuse and the Argonne up to November 1 became ours only after fighting, the intensity of which has not been surpassed during the entire four years of the war. Since the 1st we have advanced rapidly. There will be other advances. Our confidence is that we shall in good time pierce the vitals of the German line. But even if our First Army had made no considerable advance on its present front, it would, nevertheless, by engaging the pick of the German army in such great number, be serving a most useful part in the execution of the whole scheme of the Allied campaign against the most formidable of our enemies.

Not only in intensity, but in sustained effort and number of men engaged, the battle we are waging between the Meuse and the Argonne is the greatest in the 142 years and more of American history. It is one of the most important in direct and contributory results already obtained, and in the promise it holds.

The reduction of the St. Mihiel salient, the first offensive of our First Army, began on September 12. Exactly two weeks later, the First Army's offensive between the Meuse and the Argonne, involving hundreds of thousands of men, was launched. This necessitated the shift in the meantime of an enormous number of troops from the St. Mihiel salient to the region of the new attack, and was an accomplishment of which any army might well be proud. We have equally good reason to be proud of the fact that the Allied High Command selected American troops for the post of honor, between the Meuse and the Argonne, in the present grand offensive of the Western Front, and of the great influence our attack there has already played in recent events on that front.

Out of the turmoil of the Argonne came, inevitably, a bulk of copy for *The Stars and Stripes* supplied by Woollcott, Bailey, Ross, Von Blon and Rice that paralleled the dimensions of the battle itself. In the issue for October 11th appeared on page one a story headed: "Whole Battalion, Boche Encircled, Relieved at Last." It was Woollcott's first account of the plight and relief of the famous Lost Battalion of the 308th Infantry (along with elements of the 307th Infantry and of the 306th Machine Gun Battalion) of the Seventy-seventh Division. The following week he presented the story in more elaborate and more circumstantial detail, but I select the earlier account because of its very nearness to the event itself. Here was battle news of vivid moment:

One of the great adventures of this war reached a happy ending in the early hours of Monday evening when relief came through rain and darkness to a battalion of American soldiers that for six unforgettable nights had been surrounded by German forces in that blighted jungle which is known as the Forest of the Argonne.

The story of that siege, the story of the dreadful suffering borne with a high and undaunted spirit, the story of the defense and rescue when it can be told

"JUST OUT," FROM THE SKETCH BY BALDRIDGE

in full, will take its place in history alongside the relief of Lucknow and will quicken American heartbeats for centuries to come.

From the night of Wednesday, October 2, to the night of Monday, October 7, that battalion was isolated on the northern slope of a bleak, unsheltered ravine with the German army on a cliff above them and with a powerful German detachment deeply entrenched on the other side of the ravine, so close that the doughboys burrowed into the hillside could hear the calls and orders of their enemy, could be reached by German machine guns and German rifles if they showed themselves in the open.

When night settled over the forest on Monday last their situation was desperate. What little food they had had with them was spent on the second day. For three days they had been eating plugs of tobacco and chewing on leaves of the underbrush. For water they had to depend on a muddy stream at the bottom of the ravine and on one clear, grateful spring that bubbled there invitingly; but each trip to it meant exposure to snipers. More than one doughboy fell in fetching water. What few blankets and overcoats had not been discarded in the first, fine rush which carried the ravine had long since gone to wrap around the wounded. For their dead and wounded lay with them on the hillside.

They were drenched to the skin and weak from hunger and long exposure to the chill October wind. They had fought off three savage attacks—fought them off with their own machine guns, their own rifles and bayonets, their own hand grenades—but by the sixth night their store had so dwindled that there was little chance of their resisting successfully another attack.

They knew in their hearts and knew by their senses that the rest of the Americans, not more than 1,200 meters below them in the forest, were trying to reach them. They had seen planes come looking for them in the interminable fog. They had seen planes shot down in the effort to reach them. They had heard from time to time the sound of heavy firing nearby. They knew that the effort to reach them had been and would be unremitting, but there had come to the stoutest heart there doubt that relief would come in time. Yet in all that besieged battalion there was none who thought for one moment of surrendering to the encircling enemy.

The battalion waited its fourth attack without much hope, for its stock of ammunition had run low and the men were so weak they could hardly drag themselves to their feet. Some had written little letters of farewell to their folks and in these last hours each was entrusting his to some pal on the chance that the pal might get through alive. There were some thanks whispered shyly for little unchronicled deeds of kindness the week had witnessed. Here and there men promised to kill each other if it came to a question of capture.

Then suddenly out of the darkness voices could be heard calling, "Major Whittlesey!"

The boys along the line could hear him answering from his hole in the ground.

"Major, we've got here!" The whispers were exultant. "We're up on your right. We're here!" Then a pause. "And—and we've brought some rations for the boys."

There was a moment of absolute silence, and then all along the side of the ravine could be heard gusts of hysterical laughter. Relief had come.

The besieged battalion had gone forward on the night of the 2nd and taken up its position with orders to hold it. Into some strongly fortified German trenches just to the rear there filtered a powerful German force, how powerful can be guessed from the fact that when that trench was finally carried, a colonel, two majors, and their entire staffs were among the prisoners.

Major Whittlesey, when the dawn of October 3 showed that he was cut off, sent back runners with a report on his position. The runners fell in their courses. He sent up pigeons, and it was these couriers of the air who carried the tidings to the other Yanks in the forest.

Attack after attack was then made by companion regiments. Relief and instructions were rushed through the air. Airplanes went over again and again to drop munitions, bandages and, that best of all iron rations, chocolate.

Such was the lay of the wooded ravine, such was the fog that the airmen had to work as though blindfolded. One great package of supplies did come near its mark, but the doughboys who tried to crawl out and get it were killed by watching snipers from across the ravine. Several planes were brought down, one pilot was killed and two observers were wounded in the effort to carry aid through the air to the surrounded battalion.

Not once did that battalion try to fight its way back. It had been ordered to take the position and hold it. The battalion obeyed orders.

Afterwards, when the men had been relieved and had come out white, emaciated, unrecognizable in their black growths of beard, the talk among them was all of Major Whittlesey. Sixty-nine officers and men had been left dead on the hillside, and of the 394 soldiers to leave the ravine alive, 156 were wounded. Those too badly hurt or too weak were carried eventually to a sorting station on the edge of the forest, a beautiful abbey reared by pious hands 900 years ago.

There, huddled in blankets under a candle-lit statue of Jesus of the Sacred Heart, they looked like figures in some immemorial pageant of suffering. But their proud talk was all of their Major. How he had kept up their spirits by his hourly message of "Keep cool, men" and still more by his unfailing serenity. How the very sight of him shaving himself regularly each day was a calming spectacle. How, though it was perilous to move along the ravine, he managed somehow to see each man each day. That was the story the wounded told. One doughboy, cradling a bandaged arm, put it this way: "We held out because he did. We was all right if we could see him once a day."

There was more food at ten o'clock Monday night, and corned willy never tasted so wonderful.

The next morning the major's orderly—he was in the dressmaking business on Fifth Avenue before the war—was trying with his wounded hand to comb the mud out of a newly acquired beard when he heard a gruff voice demanding, "Major!"

"Everybody wants him; who is it now?" he answered wearily, and then scrambled to his feet when he saw that the inquirer wore two stars on his shoulders.

"Oh, sir, he's down the line handing out food with his own hands. I'll bring him to you."

"Bring him nothing," said the general. "I'll go to him."

In the shadow of Montfaucon (which is still a fighting word to the men of the Thirty-seventh and Seventy-ninth Divisions) Von Blon found the P. C. of Brigadier-General Charles X. Zimmerman of the 73rd Infantry Brigade, the hero (or at least the first assistant hero) of this battle drama:

There were German machine gun nests ahead on the left and German anti-tank guns ahead on the right, and German high explosive and gas shells were pouring into Montfaucon wood, but every once in a while the Ohio brigadier general in his P. C. among the trees found himself forgetting the battle ahead while he mused:

"I wonder how the boy is making out over there on the other side of the hill? The machine guns among those walls are hitting it pretty lively on the other side, too, and Carl is somewhere in the valley that leads up to them."

Meanwhile, above a little stream that curved away toward the Meuse at the right of the height of Montfaucon, a doughboy stumbled on through the bramble of barb wire and the wilderness of blasted trees and dead horses while the machine gun bullets from the hill swept among the cratered slopes. And as he broke his way forward, with his comrades dropping behind him, he still had time to think:

"I wonder how dad is getting along on the other side of the hill. That artillery over there sounds as if his brigade must be right in it by this time."

That is the way father and son, general and doughboy, fought their way past Montfaucon the second day of the Argonne-Meuse battle. But there were no messages over Signal Corps wires to tell the general that his son, a private in an Ohio Infantry regiment under another brigade commander, was thinking about him. It wasn't like the old days when Carl might drop into a telegraph office, anywhere, dash off a message on a blank form and sit down to wait until father wired the money.

Here, ahead of both father and son, was a stone city on a hill that had been considered one vast redoubt impregnable to assault by foot troops. The tide of battle, while they were thinking of each other, was carrying the general by that hill fortress on the left, while his son was being swept by on the right, with miles between them—and those miles a stretch of death and fire-swept woods, valleys and hills.

Prior to all this there had been the farewell before they went into battle. That farewell was also their first meeting in France. The general did not know until a few hours before the attack that his son was near him. The boy—he is scarcely over 21—had walked into his father's headquarters and saluted. There were the usual greetings. Then the general had turned to his maps and his runners. And Carl had hurried back to his company.

As they said goodby, the general called to the boy:

"Remember, son, you're where I was, and I'm prouder of you than I can tell. We'll tell mother all about this when it's over."

When the boy had passed behind the blanket that curtained the arched doorway of the half ruined house where the general's post was, the general told his staff the story of his son.

"I didn't know he had joined up until he walked into my office back home in June a year ago and said: 'Dad, I've hooked up with the Umpty-Seventh.' He said he was going in on his own merits, and damned if he wanted any one to hand him anything because his old man was a general.

"I patted him on the back and told him: 'Son, I'm with you all the way.' I gave him some advice on things he ought to know—you see, I was a private myself before the Spanish-American war. This has been a busy year, but Carl's letters have told me much—soldier's letters, you know, very short, with nothing loose or sentimental in them. It wasn't until they shoved the brigades up for this push that we came near each other."

.   .   .   .

Montfaucon was held by doughboys. The stone towers that had stood out boldly among the ruined walls were flattened in the wreckage that lay over the whole height. American artillery was firing over Montfaucon to the enemy lines in the woods beyond. German shells were bursting among the American positions over the dugouts full of dead German soldiers. The American lines lay up toward Cierges and all the way in front of Montfaucon to the right.

The Ohio brigadier general's P. C. now was miles ahead of where it had been. It was in a former German dugout under a clump of trees.

A private with bandaged head slipped over the muddy roadway to the P. C. and father met son again. There was the usual salute, then—

"Just had to find you before they sent me back, Dad," said the private. "They got me, but nothing bad, I guess. So I slipped over from the dressing station after they fixed me up a little. And I caught my Boche prisoner before they got me."

"You've got me beaten, son," said the general. "Wonder what your mother would think of us? I told you a few hours ago we'd tell her everything. Well, we won't. I fell off my horse a little while ago and got a strained shoulder—and that after two days of close-up work without a scratch. And your mother always said I couldn't ride. There's one thing we won't tell about the battle, will we, boy?"

Lieutenant Grantland Rice of *The Stars and Stripes* staff served two masters during the Argonne offensive. This former private, sergeant and shavetail in the Tennessee National Guard was doubly severed from his outfit. His ancient and original organization, the 115th Field Artillery, was mathematically affianced to the Thirtieth Division, but the Thirtieth and the Twenty-seventh Divisions, forming the Second American Corps, were doing nicely on the British front, where they were supported by British artillery. The 115th shared the fury of the Argonne by operating with the Thirty-second Division, and Lieutenant Rice so arranged matters that when his battery was in action he was in action with it, and when it was not he was a reporter for *The Stars and Stripes*.

During the course of the battle from a column to a page of *The Stars and Stripes* was regularly devoted to those little fragments of history which were from first to last such a distinctive feature of the paper's method of news-handling:

An American private spied a rooster prowling around a farm house in No Man's Land just after the Americans had captured Very. Being hungry, and having an appetite for roast chicken, this American private decided to crawl up on the rooster and trap him in the building.

The American was about to lay his hands on the astonished rooster when a German entered the rear door of the building bent on the same mission. Both were so surprised that they stood for a moment and glared at each other, then the American motioned for the German to do a right flank on the prey they were after and both closed in on him. The rooster was captured by the American, who later returned to the American lines with both rooster and German in tow.

Later, at the regimental P. C., the German roasted the chicken for his captor, who shared it with him.

———————

The following letter was written by an American soldier to his mother in California a few hours before the beginning of the Argonne drive:

"Dear Mother: We are going in to battle the Boche tonight. It is our first time in, as you know, so of course I am thinking of you more or less. But don't forget, Mother, my thoughts are of you.

"I am taking advantage of a few hours' rest and writing to you, as I know you are always wanting to hear from me. But don't worry one bit, Mother dear. If the Boches get me I will get ten of them while they are about it.

"This will be all until next time.

"Lovingly,
"Bennie."

The "next time" never came for Bennie. When the burial squad found this letter in his shirt pocket he was lying with his face toward Germany, his right front finger pressing the trigger of his rifle. A few yards in front of him was a German machine gun nest. There were nine dead Germans in the pit.

———————

A lieutenant of Engineers was scouting a few days ago along the road which forks on a hill-crest, one branch mounting toward Montfaucon, one branch dipping into the valley that cradles Cuisy. As to this latter road, he would have to do some prospecting to see how much stone and how many men would be needed to make it bear all the big trucks and ponderous tractors that would have to pass along it in the wake of the Infantry.

Along came a doughboy, rifle on shoulder, a doughboy taking very seriously his new responsibility, which was the escort to the rear of three German prisoners. However, though thus engrossed, he might possibly have noticed the condition of the road.

"Hey, Buddie, are you from Cuisy?"

The doughboy halted and saluted.

"No, sir," he said, "from Philadelphia."

He and his prisoners were both many meters on their way before the lieutenant recovered sufficiently to go on with his inquiry.

———————

One group of 18 disconsolate Boches had a hard time persuading any one to lock them up.

This little knot of 18 decided that, so far as they were concerned, the time had come for a separate peace, so they slipped through their own lines the other night and headed for America.

They rather expected that their arrival would cause something of a stir, but they found everybody busy as bees, and, anyway, the sight of a line of Boches filing to the rear of our lines is such a common sight these days that no one would give them a second glance.

So, considerably bewildered, the 18 got as far back as the headquarters of a division in support before they could induce any one to listen to their story. A division which is not even in the line feels scarcely called upon to be bothered with prisoners. The division telephoned the corps. Would the corps please send up right away and rid them of these unpaying guests? Certainly not, said corps coldly. Corps was too busy. Corps would consent to receive the prisoners, but division would have to deliver them at the corps cage.

In despair, the officer on whose neck the 18 were hanging rushed out to the crossroads and intimidated an M. P. into going without his lunch so that he might escort the captives into captivity.

Hermann Schmidt, late of Forty-second Street, New York, where he tended bar, and more recently of Yonkers, where he ran a little café of his own, has been taken prisoner. He is now in durance not noticeably vile, and doesn't seem to mind. It should be explained at this point that Hermann was taken prisoner by the Americans, not by the Germans.

For, just before the war broke loose, Hermann, who had an old sweetheart of his in Germany, went back to get her, and, though he had taken out his second naturalization papers in New York, he was grabbed and clapped into the German Army.

For four years he has served the Kaiser's purposes, and when it came his turn to be captured, it was just his luck that the opposing troops were from his old home town and numbered among them, without doubt, some of his thirstiest customers. Hermann's status has not yet been decided.

An American liaison officer who knew little French and a French Artillery officer who knew little English had important business together during the height of the recent fighting.

"Henri," said the commandant to a young sergeant, "I have seen you talking to Americans several times. Can you speak English?"

"No, mon commandant," answered Henri simply.

For all that, Henri and the American officer were soon engaged in vivacious conversation. At its conclusion the commandant turned to Henri.

"But you speak English very well," he said.

"No, mon commandant," Henri still insisted. "We were talking in German."

A shell landed in the exact spot where a platoon sergeant had told Private Lewis to go and pick off a German sniper who was holding up the advance.

"Got him, all right," said one of the doughboys.

But their fears vanished when two more shots were heard from the hill top.

A few moments later the sergeant himself went up to see what had been done with the sniper. Private Lewis was still lying in firing position and was watching a mound of earth two hundred yards away for the appearance of a Boche helmet.

"I nearly got him that last time," said Lewis. "I'll get him next shot or know the reason why."

The shell burst had shot away Private Lewis' right foot and had wounded him severely in the hip, but he was still after his Boche.

Almost 20 years ago, in a little village in Kansas, Wesley R. Childs looked with sorrow upon the closed shutters of a little brown house just across the street. He called his wife to his side and consulted her about adopting the Dillon children—a boy and a girl, the elder scarcely five years old. Mrs. Dillon had died that morning, and the two children were to be sent away to an orphans' home.

"Yes," said Mrs. Childs, "we can take them. And we must raise them as though they were of our own flesh and blood."

So the Dillon children were adopted by Mr. and Mrs. Childs.

One day last week, on a hillside near Very, France, a gray haired man was seen wandering about from shell hole to shell hole, crawling over the barbed wire entanglements as he made his way from one object to another.

The man continued to walk about. Shells were exploding on the hillside, and the machine guns rattled not far away.

Presently the searcher stopped and knelt down beside a still object. Wesley R. Childs of Kansas, a Y. M. C. A. worker in the A. E. F., had found the body of Sergeant Joseph A. Dillon, his adopted son.

To a sheltered spot over which whining shells passed at irregular intervals, to a graveyard on the hillside where several crosses were stuck in the ground, the father, although he had been severely gassed while conducting the search, summoned the aid of a chaplain and two men and buried his son.

An ambulance had just discharged its load at a dressing station, and the quartet of wounded were lying on stretchers on the ground.

One of the patients was a youth, very much of a youth. Even the bandages which concealed four-fifths of his face did not conceal that. While he waited his turn on the operating table his one available eye twinkled as he related to a line of walking wounded how it had happened.

Suddenly he paused in his conversation, having spotted a doughboy trudging down the road, a doughboy from his own home town and his own regiment.

"Hey, Joe!" he shouted, and when Joe reached his side he said, "Say, I'll bet you don't know who I am, Joe."

———————

A shell dropped in a horse transport train on a winding hillside road in Very, and two horses fell floundering to the ditch. A doughboy who had been standing by the roadside ran for an arched passage shelter, his right hand spurting blood where a shell fragment had torn away two fingers. Another soldier bandaged the wound, while several other shells burst near.

Then the doughboy looked out and saw one of the wounded horses struggling in the ditch. Although the shells had been falling regularly at intervals of a few minutes, the doughboy walked out from his shelter, drew his automatic pistol with his left hand and shot the horse. Walking calmly back to the shelter, he said he was sorry he had to use four shots on the horse, but he never had been able to use his left hand very well.

———————

One Infantry sergeant, badly wounded in action in the Argonne, did not really come to till he woke one morning in a snowy bed in a distant hospital. The nurse, a benevolent vision, was bending over him.

"Are you feeling better, Lieutenant Johnson?" she asked.

He thought that over for a while and then decided the voice was not part of the strange dream that had been haunting him.

"You've got me wrong, miss," he said, "I'm Sergeant Johnson."

"Oh, no, you're not," said the nurse, "you were promoted while you were asleep."

———————

On October 15, in the midst of the advance beyond Romagne in Argonne, a pigeon arrived breathless at one corps headquarters with the news that the Infantry was holding the line at Nantillois, a point several kilometers behind that from which the new advance has been launched. There was some bewildered and anxious telephoning before any one noticed that the date of the message was October 6. The bird had been AWOL for nine days.

The officer, bent over the candle-lit task of censoring letters written from the Argonne battlefield, burst into a sweat and prayed for strength to resist a great temptation.

There before him were two letters written by one soldier. One was to a girl in Brittany, begging her to be true to him and murmuring sweet prophecies of the day when he would come for her and take her back as his bride to America.

The other letter was to his real fiancée in Ohio. And into the mind of the censoring officer had crept the mischievous notion that it would not be a bad idea to swap envelopes.

At last accounts, he was still struggling with the temptation.

There are all gradations of thoroughness in the varying manners which different outfits show when they turn over their sector to their relief. Some turn over every stick and stone, every fact and every suspicion. Some are more casual about it.

The record instance for dispatch is told of a French captain who needed only six words and three gestures to turn over his sector to the American captain relieving him. The words were:

"Nous ici. Boches là. Au revoir."

He is the interpreter attached to a roaming brigade of Field Artillery, a little French soldier named Bouchette. You have just one guess as to what the Yankees call him.

Their regard for him, however, grew mightily the other night on the eve of the brigade's entry into the fight up Montfaucon way. They had noticed that he had a genius for knowing which kitchen in the outfit would serve the best dinner on any given night and for dropping in there casually at mess time.

They suspected him of an instinct for nourishment, but how great his talents were in that respect they never discovered until this particular night, when eight of the officers appealed to him to use his French to get them a decent meal. At the word, he collected seven francs from each man, vanished into the countryside, came back with a basket full of supplies, and with his own hands prepared such a luscious and wonderful six-course dinner as they had never encountered in all their days.

Fish with a celestial sauce, eggs transformed past recognition, a salad for the gods—it was a feast unbelievable. There were inquiries, and, when cornered, M. Bouchette admitted that, prior to the war, he had been head chef for the late Alfred Vanderbilt. Now he is trying desperately hard to retain his rank and status as an interpreter.

———

Not long ago a German field kitchen loaded with slum, coffee, cigars and cigarettes for a hundred men, and making a slight and quite pardonable error as to the whereabouts of the somewhat jumpy German line, drove up in the darkness to a battalion P. C. of the 28th Infantry and there started to unload before the delighted Yanks discovered them.

The captors were about to pitch in when a lieutenant rushed out of the dim-lit dugout and, with uplifted hand, postponed the feast, hissing out as he did so that there might be arsenic in the slum and that anyway the whole thing was probably a plot.

This turn of events dejected the German cook, who was fatter than any one in Germany is supposed to be in the fifth year of the war and who had just been congratulating himself that even the fiendish Americans could not be so very cruel to one who had brought them such unexpected refreshments. The cook brightened up, however, when it occurred to him that he and his drivers might disarm suspicion by themselves sampling all the rations on hand. They weren't allowed to do more than sample them when the bunch joined in, and in five minutes, 25 Americans had cleaned up a meal which had been prepared for a hundred Germans. The cook was still a bit worried about his scout, who had gone on ahead to feel the way and of whom nothing had been heard since. He was told that he would probably meet him before morning. Sure enough, at dawn, in the prison cage far behind, the stray ration detail all met face to face.

"Oh, Johann!" "Oh, Gottlieb!" It was a great reunion.

———

Because Adam Patercity was of German birth his colonel wanted to discharge him while his regiment was still in America.

"I don't want a discharge," Patercity told the colonel. "I want to go to France and fight with the rest of the boys."

So Patercity crossed the Atlantic with his regiment.

The other day, north of Verdun, Pvt. Patercity, although severely wounded, advanced straight into a machine gun nest which was holding up his company's advance. Four of the gun crew surrendered to Patercity. Five more were left dead in the pit.

————————

When a certain Field Artillery P. C. moved into its new quarters west of Verdun the Artillerymen discovered a pussy cat and four kittens in a wood-box.

"A CHECK FROM HOME," BY BALDRIDGE. OVERSUBSCRIPTION OF THE FOURTH LIBERTY LOAN
WAS ANNOUNCED WHILE THE ARGONNE FIGHTING WAS AT ITS FIERCEST

But the Artillery P. C. could not remain stationary for long. One day it moved forward two kilometers, and the Artillerymen decided that Polly and her family would do better if they were left behind.

The next morning, when the cook came down to his new quarters to start the breakfast fire, he discovered Polly's four kittens romping over his kitchen floor, while Polly herself lay stretched out in a corner. Polly had moved P. C. during the night, too.

Before participating in the final phases of the Meuse-Argonne the Second Division had operated effectively with the French along the Champagne front, and the Thirty-sixth Division had there its first and last taste of front-line service—the sector was sufficiently active to make the occasion memorable, for the Champagne operation was definitely linked with the Argonne campaign, since pressure against the enemy here inevitably must (and did) expose the flank of the Argonne massif. The Forty-second Division had already fought in Champagne, forming a powerful element in General Gouraud's famous "defense in depth" that met and checked the final German offensive of July 15th.

On the British front two American divisions, the Twenty-seventh and the Thirtieth, as effectively severed from the rest of the A. E. F. as if they had been in Siberia, battled throughout the summer and fall in the unrelenting attack that broke the Hindenburg Line and brought the victorious British-Yankee alliance into territory that had not been fought over since 1914. The part that had already been fought over looked it. West of Amiens to the St. Quentin-Cambrai line the rolling plain of the Somme uplands resembled nothing so much as a brown, sticky ocean that had been set aside to liquefy at the creation. The only sentimental tie between these forlorn Americans and the rest of the A. E. F. was *The Stars and Stripes*, and staff representatives brought back to a not uninterested Army long and short accounts of their discomforts and their triumphs. Here are a few of the short ones:

The Yanks with the British show the effects of their environment. They have acquired all the British slang, colloquialisms, and military terminology. They will tell you a certain place is near the R. E. D. and when you ask what the deuce the R. E. D. is, they will explain, paternally, that it is a Royal Engineers' Dump. They talk a lot in initials, say "right-o" with a persistency and consistency which convinces you that it is natural and habitual, and they call Fritz Jerry.

General Sir Douglas Haig, British commander in chief, called at an American headquarters, and around this headquarters they still talk much of his visit. They like him.

The headquarters was in the edge of a wood. It had been raining. A sergeant found the General trying to keep his footing on slippery duckboards while he endeavored to ascertain the whereabouts of the American commander's hut from the signboards. The sergeant led him to the place he sought, but the

American commander and most of his staff, following his troops, had left for a more advanced P. C. Two second lieutenants and two sergeants were holding down the recently vacated office.

"I'm Haig," said the General in such an "I'm Bill Jones" tone of voice that the Americans didn't realize who their visitor was for a full half minute. When they did they explained that their commander had gone up ahead.

"Just wanted to wish him luck," said the General. Then he shook hands with the two lieutenants and the two sergeants and left.

Bad news may travel quicker than good in some places, but it doesn't along the German front. Maybe it's because the German officers see that it does not.

Many of the Germans captured by the Americans north of St. Quentin had maps in their possession, printed maps of the whole battle line which they evidently kept for their own information and use. None of their maps showed the German retreat from the St. Mihiel salient.

That protuberance into France, recently effaced by the Americans, was outlined as prominently as of old. Questioned, none of these Germans had heard of the St. Mihiel defeat. All of them, however, knew of the British victories between St. Quentin and Arras, probably because most of them had participated in the retreat out of the Picardy salient.

He was 40 years old and a cook, and he harbored a constant grouch because the skipper, under pretense of his age, would not bust him and let him go forward with the doughboys when his company went in the trenches. He had brought many a wrinkle from the Fourth Avenue chop house which he abandoned the third day after the United States declared war, and he did a hundred different things to army rations which made his own company enthusiastic and every other company in the regiment jealous.

His company, fighting on the British front, had been in the line four days, and this day it was coming out. He didn't know how much of the food which he had toiled to prepare and dispatch forward in those four days had actually reached the men. He figured that it wasn't much.

So he had prepared a meal for them, a meal which excelled even all his previous efforts. The principal feature was hash, a wonderful variety of hash which he had been able to make only after obtaining half a dozen unusual ingredients in two days of argument and near-fist fights with various representatives of the commissary.

He had timed the cooking of this hash for the arrival of his company from the line, and as a K. P., detailed as observer, signaled its approach, he watched his hash brown with the tender eye of a true artist. As the men came up the road, hungry, tattered, muddy, exhausted, happy, he went forward to meet them. He stood beside the road waiting paternally for them to approach.

As they got near enough for him to make out individual faces in the line a shell struck within a few feet of him. It tore one foot off and inflicted a dozen other wounds. He died a minute later. His dying words were an order to the K. P. who had run to his side.

"Don't mind me, Harry. You run back and see that the hash don't burn."

Among the vast quantity of material which the Germans left in their wake where the Yanks attacked on the British front was a tombstone of large dimensions intended for the grave of a German colonel. On it was chiseled the replica of an iron cross of the first order and the familiar inscription, "Gott Mit Uns."

Subsequently, the grave of the colonel was found. The Americans finished the work the Germans had left undone. A detail of eight men carried the stone to the grave and, as they set it in place, a bugler sounded Taps over the grave.

This fact might be construed as likely to give aid and comfort to the enemy, but here it is, anyway. The Americans with the British are fed on British rations, and British rations mean tea.

The other day a quantity of coffee arrived in the mess shack of one American unit. The report that seven army corps had been detailed to stand guard over that coffee is exaggerated, but only slightly.

The Tommy is a fine scout, individually and collectively; his M. P.'s, for instance, are the soul of courtesy to a brother soldier, whatever his flag and his uniform. But the Tommy has one shortcoming in which, through no lack of good will or politeness, he still persists. He calls the American soldier a Sammy.

Sometimes he shortens it to Sam, which is at least not quite so feminine. Sometimes, never having experienced the delights of a minstrel show, he distorts it into Sambo.

You may not like it, but you haven't the heart to tell him so. He uses it in utter friendliness, and as a mark of friendliness the Yank receives it.

There are a few tolerably intact houses in the Somme region, but there ought to be a reward for anyone who can locate a whole window pane. The windows in a division C. O.'s office, if the room is fortunate enough to have a whole sash left, will probably be covered with oiled paper, which lets in the light, but keeps out the cold and the scenery. Anyway, there is not much scenery left thereabouts.

———————

The Allied juggernaut rolled on and stopped, for there was no more rolling to be done. Private Cyrus LeRoy Baldridge, Infantry, unattached (most remarkably unattached), viewing the shifting scene much as he chose, likely to pop up on any given front at any time, reared a nostril to windward like the old Illinois warhorse he was and detected the scent of the approaching end. The day before the Armistice found him in Belgium, where the Thirty-seventh and Ninety-first American Divisions were crowding into fresh A. E. F. country. There was undoubtedly a slight element of the vindictive in Baldridge's desire to see the war out in this sector, for it was hereabouts that the Germans, four years earlier, had arrested him and taken from him his drawings and his bicycle. They had returned the drawings, but this did not appease him, because he could make more drawings but did not know how to assemble a bicycle.

Abandoning the crayon in favor of the typewriter, Private Baldridge wrote a story for *The Stars and Stripes*. The writing American to whom he alludes is, of course, Mr. Baldridge:

In the fall of 1914 an American writing for American newspapers tramped through the slippery mud from Brussels to Roulers, marching with the victorious troops of the German Kaiser. Four years later he tramped over these same cobble stones once more; but this time as a doughboy of the United States Army. Never was there presented to anyone a contrast more dramatic.

The first time these roads were packed with field-gray men; an endless, machine-made, irresistible, moving mass, singing as it went. Like water, this torrent flowed down every channel toward the French border.

By the roadside and in the fields the browns and purples of autumn were splotched here and there with flaming red, the red pantaloons of fallen poilus. Right at the border roadside where the singing army brushed by him there was one. His hand almost touched the stone marking the frontier line.

Watching this scene were groups of huddled peasants, scared, stupefied. They listened to the booming guns and tried to guess whether the sound was getting further from them or was being driven back.

And as one looked about the countryside he saw from the windows of almost every house a white cloth of some sort tied to a stick—pathetic attempts of the peasants to save their homes. There were no other flags in Belgium.

"THEN WE WILL HAVE PEACE," BY BALDRIDGE. THIS SINGULARLY PROPHETIC CARTOON, WHICH
FIRST APPEARED ON OCTOBER 18, 1918, WAS REPRINTED FOUR WEEKS LATER IN THE ISSUE OF
THE STARS AND STRIPES IMMEDIATELY FOLLOWING THE ARMISTICE

In 1918, on November 10, an outpost of the 91st American Division, fighting in Flanders, rode into Hoorebeke St. Corneille at eight in the morning. It saw just disappearing over a hill two German field kitchens doing a Ben Hur, cans and lids bumping about and flashing in the early sunlight.

A captain of a headquarters company of a California outfit followed immediately and knocked on a door of the village to ask for quarters.

At once he was fairly suffocated in the embrace of a Flemish grandmother.

"You ask for a room!" she cried. "For four years the vaches have been taking all without asking!"

She flung open the door. "Here, Amerikaan, the house is yours."

He seemed cold. From somewhere they dug him up a stove, and built a fire. He seemed hungry. Soon he dined on Belgian hare. The old man of the farm, who could think of nothing else, insisted upon presenting mon capitaine with his heavy home-made cane. And by that same miracle which was being enacted in thousands of liberated homes a big five foot black, yellow, and red flag was found flapping over the doorway.

The next morning, at six, an American attack was planned at this place. Crisp with a biting mist, the day began to clear. Through the purple haze hanging over the hill opposite, now and then a Boche shape could be seen lurking for an instant. Behind a stone wall five hundred yards from a German machine gun nest Lieut. Crawford, eyeing his watch, sat with his battery. His minenwerfer (once of the German army and now doing duty as a Yankee Stokes mortar) was in position by the gate ready to romp out on the minute, down the road and up a hill and straight ahead.

It was to be a divisional attack. Everybody knew the part he was to play, and only waited for the chance. The harassing fire from the artillery had begun.

Then comes news to delay the attack until nine.

Rumors. Messages. More waiting. Yanks all in position.

A quarter of an hour before the time for the barrage to start, and the artillerymen stand by their guns.

From the temporary trench of an advance post a major looks through his glasses. Certain movements in the turnip fields across the valley appear strange to him: people running and jumping about.

"Belgians," he comments. "There can't be many Germans there now with all that excitement going on."

Then at that moment came that famous order from Marshal Foch which everyone has now read so many times that he knows it by heart. The attack of the All-Western division was never to take place.

And from where the German lines had been came little groups. They were Belgians with a sagging wheelbarrow load of household goods—coming home.

The doughboy who had been twice in Belgium under such different circumstances walked back to the headquarters mess for breakfast. There was no excitement, little comment. A cook was toasting bread on the top of the kitchen stove. A top sergeant came by, called attention and read the order suspending hostilities. Two Yanks sitting in the stone courtyard near at hand cleaning their rifles never stopped work.

"What'd he say?" asked someone in the rear as the top walked away.

"Didn't get all of it," answered his buddy.

"Oh, damn!" said the cook. "This toast got all burned."

CHAPTER ELEVEN

UP WITH THE RATIONS

ALMOST at the identical instant that Private Baldridge was seeing the war out from a front-line foxhole in Belgium, Sergeant William Hale and Corporal B. C. Warlick were congratulating each other on the fine stretch of road they were encountering on the edge of what was supposed to be a battle-field. Their Ford truck bounced along with an abandon it had not been able to exhibit in weeks—the seven weeks in which the gruelling test of the Meuse-Argonne was exacting from every inch of highway all that the traffic would bear. It had been a miscellaneous traffic but an insistent—guns and caissons, ammunition trucks, supply wagons, tanks big and little, ambulances, staff cars, motorcycle orderlies, rolling kitchens, motorized machine-gunners, troops coming out, troops going up, replacements, replacements, replacements. Along those muck-filled streaks that led into battle one measured one's rate of speed not by mileage but by yardage.

How different now! Sergeant Hale and Corporal Warlick chanted the song of the open road.

A dip, a rise, a curve, then an unsuspected and unsuspecting village. Sergeant Hale and Corporal Warlick stopped just in time to avoid running down a group that wore the field gray of the German Army.

Technically they were prisoners of war. But there was barely half an hour of war left to be a prisoner in, and the Germans had already lost interest in it. Their curiosity, however, was definitely aroused. What priceless cargo was it these two Americans were bent on carrying into the very heart of Germany? Hope ran high —here, clearly, was some unusual trove to be borne back to the wives and kiddies beyond the Rhine. Eager hands were laid on the bulky sacks in the truck.

Out fell several hundred copies of *The Stars and Stripes* for November 8th intended for the Ninetieth Division. A little late, unfortunately, but then the American Army had been on the loose for the past ten days, the railhead was some thirty miles back, and the intervening territory was a barely navigable and freshly fought-over battlefield.

The Germans shook their heads and smiled. It was, after all, comforting to know that everybody, and not merely themselves, was going crazy.

"Go peddle your papers," said the Germans, and Sergeant Hale and Corporal Warlick departed in peace—a real peace.

The Hale-Warlick episode was a fitting climax to a chapter in the history of newspaper circulation that can hardly be matched again save in a bigger and better war. When the A. E. F. was young and *The Stars and Stripes* much younger Lieutenant-Colonel Frederick Palmer of the General Staff had gone over to London and had a talk with Captain Richard H. Waldo, who had become well acquainted with the complexities and subtleties of circulation through his experiences as an executive with *Cosmopolitan*, the Butterick Company, *Good Housekeeping* and the *New York Tribune*, and who was now in charge of the London office of the Bureau of War Risk Insurance. When Colonel Palmer alluded somewhat casually to *The Stars and Stripes* Waldo assumed he was talking about flag ceremonials—wasn't there something in a sentry's General Orders about saluting all colors and standards not cased? Such was the extent of our repute in those days. Colonel Palmer went back to Chaumont, and soon thereafter an order came through transferring Captain Waldo to *The Stars and Stripes* as business manager.

It was hardly the assignment he had expected to draw in the fantastic lottery of war. Well before Colonel Palmer's visit Waldo had put in for a transfer to an Infantry company, from which task nothing could be further than this novel tour of duty to which destiny had shunted him. But G. H. Q. was accustomed both to propose and to dispose, and Waldo crossed the Channel.

The small and select committee which then comprised the staff of *The Stars and Stripes* was delighted to learn that a circulation manager had definitely been sighted. Up to then the editorial personnel had been reporters every day except Thursday and had then regularly turned into distributors. Visk and the rest of us would drag sackfuls of papers aboard taxicabs, direct the cabs to the required railroad terminal, dump them on the platform and inform delegations of voluble and inflammatory French baggagemen that the stuff was now their worry. Visk's resolute refusal to learn French stood him in excellent stead, and the baggagemen would finally give up expostulating and get to work.

What happened to the bundles thereafter was somebody else's concern, except that very often it became nobody's. For the cutting of a string involved an assumption of responsibility, and who shall blame a colonel or a major or a captain or a lieutenant for fighting shy of any fresh responsibility when he already had too many, and was looking forward with manly foreboding to the moment when he would command the arbitrament of life and death? Monkey with a mysterious couple of hundredweight consigned vaguely to the Blanks? No, thank you. Bucks unaccepted did not have to be passed.

Waldo reported to Colonel Walter C. Sweeney, Chief of the Press Section, at Chaumont and was asked if he had any suggestions for a plan to distribute *The Stars and Stripes*. He had by now caught up with his reading and liked the paper. He asked for time and he produced a plan. It required, first of all, vehicles. Colonel Sweeney directed him to Colonel (now Major General) George Van Horn Mosely of the General Staff, in charge of transportation. Waldo explained his status and then modestly requested fifty Ford trucks. Colonel Mosely smiled the smile of the father to the child who demands the moon.

"Fifty Ford trucks," he mused. "I could just as easily let you have fifty angels, captain, and I've never seen an angel in any army yet. Why, do you realize that we can mount a machine gun in a Ford truck?"

"Yes, sir," replied Waldo, "and you can transport five thousand copies of *The Stars and Stripes* in a Ford truck, and five thousand copies of *The Stars and Stripes* are more important to the success of this war than a machine gun."

Colonel Mosely was silent. He had read the first few issues of *The Stars and Stripes* and he must have liked them.

"All right," he said. "You can have your fifty trucks."

Had it not been strictly unmilitary, Captain Waldo would have gasped. He had bid fifty in the hope of making twenty-five.

Established in Paris, Waldo set about assembling a circulation staff. Now that he had the trucks, it would be a simple matter to fill the drivers' seats. Manpower is the least of a belligerent nation's troubles—a nation, at least, as newly in the war as the United States was early in 1918. For his right-hand man he requested, and got, Lieutenant Milton C. Ayers, whom he had met and whose initiative he had learned to admire when they were both candidates for commissions at Plattsburg. Ayers, who died a few years after the war, was a pre-bellum broker who had gone to camp with the full expectation of becoming a combat officer, and who would have certainly given odds of better than a million to one that he would never become a co-executive in the business department of an army newspaper.

It was a comparatively simple matter to select from the army qualification cards a group of enlisted men about whom a circulation and business staff could be constructed, and who would themselves constitute that staff while the construction was in process. In theory, and to a large degree in practise, it would have been possible to select from those cards, if anyone had wanted him, a red-headed tinsmith twenty-three years old and weighing one hundred and forty-seven pounds who had been born in Tonopah and had a cousin in Juneau. Waldo soon had a skeleton organization of a dozen soldiers—some of them circulation men, but more of them advertising and editorial men and printers. Not least worthy of respect among the dozen was Sergeant Joseph G. Daly, who was not alone an old soldier but also an old employee of the Fifth Avenue Coach Company of New York, and who got into the war to find that he was enjoying a busman's holiday. Joe had known cars from the day when the really sporting driver wore goggles and a linen duster and when folks still peered out of windows to watch a gasoline carriage go by.

This nucleus had barely been assembled when word came from G. H. Q. that if *The Stars and Stripes* really wanted those fifty Ford trucks it had better collect them at Issoudun, a hundred and fifty kilometres south of Paris, within the next three days. The nucleus immediately set out for Issoudun. It was not a day in which everybody knew how to drive; if the dozen men who made up the expedition had all known, it then might have been possible, one would surmise, for them to make off with a dozen trucks.

Under the circumstances they did fairly well. They drove out of Issoudun with thirty-eight trucks. The feat required prodigies of hitching on the part of Sergeant Daly; inexpertness and eagerness landed a couple of trucks temporarily in a ditch; still another pleasantly punctured the monotony of Issoudunian existence by catching fire. This oddest cavalcade of the war moved slowly and awfully back to Paris with Lieutenant Ayers at the wheel of the leading truck with four others chained behind it.

It was during this same exciting and hysteric era that Lieutenant Ochs, the treasurer without a treasury, stepped into Captain Waldo's office and asked: "Captain, I wonder if you'd mind giving me a hand with my books?"

"Not a bit," said Waldo. "Let's see them."

"No, you don't understand, captain," said Ochs. "I mean with *some* books. I think we ought to have books, and I'd like to have you help me start them."

"You have something, of course?"

"Oh, yes," and Ochs excused himself, to return an instant later carrying a cigar box. He opened it and poured out an assortment of French paper, silver and copper that totalled around five hundred francs. It was the working capital of *The Stars and Stripes*.

When *The Stars and Stripes* was launched Visk had skilfully wangled a loan of twenty-five thousand francs from the General Staff. It was not much in a war that was costing the United States a million dollars an hour and would soon be costing her two million, but it was one of the finest witnesses to faith in an idea that the war would produce. The money had been spent to the best possible purpose; it had not alone paid the pre-natal expenses of *The Stars and Stripes* but had carried it well through its earliest infancy.

Additional cash trickled in occasionally. When the first bundles of the first issue

"THE OWNER OF THE STARS AND STRIPES," BY BALDRIDGE

of *The Stars and Stripes* reached Chaumont there was some perplexity as to what was supposed to be done with them. Army Field Clerk Dan Sowers had a suggestion. Sowers had enlisted in an ambulance section in which his presence soon became definitely embarrassing. It occurred suddenly to his commanding officer that when the moment arrived for the unit to move up to the front its usefulness would be seriously impaired by the attendance of Private Sowers, since the ambulance to which he was assigned would hardly be able to return any patients unless Private Sowers himself dismounted and walked back. Private Sowers weighed three hundred pounds. His subsequent transfer to the status of field clerk was therefore hailed with joy by the Medical Department. Hawley christened him the largest body of troops in the A. E. F.

Sowers had been assigned to the Press Section at G. H. Q., and when the first bundles of *The Stars and Stripes* were dropped on its doorstep he volunteered to act as newsboy. Tucking as many as he could carry under his arm, he went out into the gravelled quadrangle that was the Army's official front yard and disposed of copies without discrimination to generals, privates, and grades between. There was only one qualification to be met—everybody, general or private, must pay the stipulated price of fifty centimes. He sold a thousand copies, but, more important even than that, he introduced the A. E. F.'s own paper to the A. E. F.'s capital city.

Lieutenant Ochs had something more than the cigar box. Despite his lack of books, he had evidence to show that some 24,500 francs of accounts receivable were outstanding. Waldo decided that the best way to handle this situation temporarily was to resort to the fine old civilian practise of dunning the debtor. He was somewhat dubious as to what the results would be, but the duns could go out and meanwhile he would try to devise something else.

The duns went out, and the Army Postal Service speedily returned 28,000 francs. Waldo had had plenty of collecting experience in civil life, but he was compelled to admit that his persuasiveness had never produced results quite like this. It was due, he saw, to no special cogency in his appeal. The unit commanders who had accepted and distributed copies of early issues of *The Stars and Stripes* had a war to fight, or would one day have it; paper-work, particularly if it involved finance, was their especial bane; they lived in a nightmare of mental stress occasioned by the formidable quantities of ordnance and Q. M. material for which their jobs compelled them to assume full responsibility, and they were properly more afraid of G. H. Q. than of the combined German and Austrian Armies. When *The Stars and Stripes* suggested that they please remit they remitted. Better be broke than busted.

The 28,000 francs helped, but the thriving child was requiring more and more sustenance. The need happened to mortise in neatly with another idea of Waldo's. For *The Stars and Stripes* to collect individual cash payments issue by issue would be something like operating a five-and-ten cent store exclusively on a delivery system. The thing was gorgeously impracticable.

I have noted earlier, and it is worth noting again, that the editorial problem of *The Stars and Stripes* was hardly unique save for the accident of location and the more distressing accident of war. For the rest, granting some technical acquaintance with the assembling and presentation of the contents of a newspaper, the editorial task was comparatively simple. This statement is offered not as a display of sham modesty. All of us who served on the editorial staff are intensely proud of what we did, and believe with equal intensity that we did a whale of a good job. We were, we admit, so good that we were able to appreciate the fact that the circulation task was a hundred times more involved than ours.

When *The Stars and Stripes* was a year old and the war three months over we issued an anniversary number of which more will be said. In that number appeared a succinct exposition of the work of the circulation department which included this brief and accurate statement of the circulation puzzle and of the principal factor in its solution:

> Put the problem up to any first-rate circulation expert in any American city. Ask him how he would get a paper, issued Friday morning, to 550,000 members of a moving, fighting army, and get most of them there before Friday night and the rest before Saturday night, with no regular means of communication, and see what he says. Figuring on a peace-time basis, it couldn't be done. But figuring "as is," it was done, and if it wasn't done perfectly—ah, well—if everyone were perfect we wouldn't have an Army. . . .
>
> One little difficulty encountered by the business office was that, while lots of subscribers wanted the paper, none of them had permanent addresses. They just kept moving and moving.
>
> Coupled with this circumstance was the additional complication caused by the censorship. For several reasons, some obvious and some more military, *The Stars and Stripes* did not possess and did not want to possess any secret information about the location of troops. Hence, if Subscriber Bill Smith moved from A. P. O. 701 to A. P. O. 717, the S. & S. was merely able to chuck the paper in the mail and let the postoffice department do the rest. If you remember anything about the speed with which second-class mail was moving around the A. E. F. in those days, you have some idea of why the distribution of *The Stars and Stripes* was not exactly a howling success. More howling, anyhow, than success.
>
> And still the business was growing by leaps and bounds, until one day in mid-spring there were 50,000 subscribers. And about that time the "coupon-

ticket" idea was born. It originated with Capt. Richard H. Waldo, a circulation expert in civil life, who had come to *The Stars and Stripes* as business manager. And Captain Waldo admitted that he got the idea from the humble and pestiferous bread ticket. "If bread can be rationed," said Waldo, "why can't *The Stars and Stripes*?"

It could and it was.

The bread ticket, in case any member of the A. E. F. has forgotten it, was a stiff paper checkerboard whereof each square (though it wasn't exactly a square) was good for a certain amount of bread in any restaurant. The amount was a stated fraction of a kilogramme that sounded like a lot but looked like a little. Waldo copied the idea so exactly that he used the same printer who made the bread tickets.

Each leaf of *Stars and Stripes* tickets was good for six months—twenty-six issues. (This was in a day when it seemed absurd to think that the war could possibly last longer than six months.) The ticket cost the soldier subscriber eight francs, of which one and a half francs went to his company fund and the remaining six and a half francs came to the paper. This reduced the cost of the paper to the subscriber fifty per cent—in theory. But Waldo appreciated the fact that the trading-stamp companies back home reaped a neat harvest annually from the stamps that were never presented for redemption, that banks profited regularly from the casual destruction of considerable amounts in banknotes, that the United States Government throve on the pennies that people dropped through gratings. Thousands of *The Stars and Stripes* coupons would never be redeemed—and *The Stars and Stripes* did not purpose to take advantage of the man who fell in battle or was dropped on a stretcher in tatters by assessing him for his unredeemed coupons.

Once the Ford trucks were assembled and the tickets printed the circulation machine was ready to go. The rest would be just a tolerably simple mathematical exercise—more men, more trucks, more tickets. Before the paper's career was over the number of field agents had reached around one hundred and fifty, and probably a hundred more soldiers had been engaged in circulation work in the home office. Many of the field agents had never driven in their lives. Their instruction was simple. When the increments of personnel were not too large Sergeant Daly could give a rough individual supervision. But when newcomers came in large contingents about all he could do was to guide his charges to whatever M. T. C. center was supplying the cars and say: "These are Fords. Follow me to Paris." It was an effective method. By the time the contingent reached Paris every man in it could drive. It is remarkable that despite this necessarily casual instruction and the omission of even the most primitive driving tests, only a single office Ford was so badly damaged during the paper's whole career as to send it to the scrap heap.

This mobile army within an army could hardly be managed from a desk in Paris. Two capable field supervisors were early acquired in the persons of Sergeant Richard Seelye Jones and Private Melvin Ryder, both subsequently elevated ser-

"TWENTY YEARS AFTER," BY WALLGREN

geants major. It was their job to rove over France and keep the far-flung circulation machine oiled and in good repair—to see that every field representative with a combat division got his papers to his subscribers by noon of the Friday of issue. If a doughboy fell in battle after Friday noon he should have a *Stars and Stripes* on his body, and many a blood-smeared copy was so found. The man in the line came first. The rest of the Army could wait, but they never had to wait long. And with the exception of an allotment that was reserved for free distribution to men in hospital, every copy of every issue was paid for by the man who got it.

Dick Jones wrote a brief account of the circulation task in the anniversary issue, a portion of which has just been quoted. He should be inveigled into the compilation of a history of the circulation staff to which every field agent would contribute his most exciting adventure. For there is the story of *The Stars and Stripes*. The editorial staff's share was to chronicle the adventures of others; the circulation staff had adventures on its own. The Hale-Warlick incident (blandly lifted from Dick Jones's memoirs) has already been told, and there is the story of Private Alden H. Kenyon, field agent with the First Division, who delivered his papers in the particularly hot sector below Soissons in July, 1918, and brought back a load of wounded under fire, an achievement for which he was cited.

His pockets bulging with detached coupons, the field agent would return from his outfit to a point where he could unload the coupons and forward them to Paris. By the time the paper's circulation got up toward a quarter of a million it became manifestly out of the question to count the coupons individually, so Lieutenant Ayers and his staff would weigh them. The results were accurate—they do the same thing with gold in the Bank of England.

The machine was functioning smoothly and efficiently well before Captain Waldo was reassigned to duty in London. Not long before his transfer a serious crisis developed in the paper situation, which was already serious enough, and Waldo was informed that only Clemenceau himself could straighten out the difficulty. It seemed a trivial matter to put up to that doughty old walrus, but from the point of view of *The Stars and Stripes* and the A. E. F. it wasn't so trivial after all. Waldo decided to risk it. He was greeted jovially, not in English but in bonafide American. Why not?—the Tiger, in his cub days, had taught French in a young ladies' finishing school in Stamford, Connecticut, and had sent dispatches to our neighbor *Le Temps* telling all about that grandest exemplification of petty politics in American history, the impeachment of Andrew Johnson. Paper? Certainly. Would the captain please go and see So-and-so and explain the business to him, and Monsieur le Président du Conseil would send a representative on his own, and it would be attended to. It was.

We depended on the French for more than our paper. About a third of the total of each issue printed (which third, at the peak, exceeded 150,000 copies) was handled by Hachette et Cie., most powerful of the world's periodical distributing agencies, whose perfected machinery, put at *The Stars and Stripes'* disposal under the supervision of M. Louis Teyssou, transported the bundled copies to virtually every news kiosk in France—to every one, at least, which a Yankee customer might pass. Not all of the A. E. F. was mobile, or at any rate the A. E. F. population in large S. O. S. centers remained tolerably constant, and the firm of Hachette kept such centers—as Bordeaux, Tours, and Nevers—regularly supplied with papers. As the combat divisions began to go home Hachette et Cie. assumed more and more of the responsibility of distribution.

Fifty thousand copies of each issue went home to the States at the paper's maximum circulation point. How many copies were read by soldier subscribers and then neatly folded into envelopes for dispatch to America there is no means of knowing. Dick Jones estimated that the total was probably in the neighborhood of 200,000 at a maximum average.

The men who got *The Stars and Stripes* out to its intended audience were more than mere crude circulation persons. Ryder devoted some of his spare time (or the company's) to lyrical exercises and was a frequent contributor to "The Army's Poets" column—take "Letters":

> My buddy reads his letters to me, and, say, he sure can write!
> I have to sit and chew my pen and even then
> The way it reads when I get through I know it's pretty sad
> As far as composition goes; the grammar, too, is bad.
> But talk about—gee, he can sling the ink to beat the band,
> And picture everything he's seen a way that sure is grand.
>
> I got him to write a note to my gal and, golly, it was fine!
> I copied it and signed my name, but, all the same,
> It didn't seem to please her, for she wrote in her reply
> She'd read it several times and it didn't sound like I
> Was sayin' exactly what I meant, and was I feelin' good;
> I'm kind of glad she took it so—in fact, I hoped she would.

Jones, I believe, erupted into meter only once, but the product made the paper—an average that many poets will envy. His contribution was called "Corporal's Call":

(American scientists have discovered a method of removing the bray from the Army mule. Mules in future wars will be unable to betray the location of ammunition trains, etc., by their raucous voices.—New Item.)

When first we came to foreign lands
    The native jackass yodeled for us,
So like the bugles and the bands
    We learned to love his daily chorus.
More keenly pitched than reveille,
    It shook the rafters of his stall
Or cross the sward rolled heavily—
    We knew it as the "Corporal's call."

Now as the days creep into weeks,
    December slowly drags toward June,
Back at the ports, each doughboy seeks
    That old familiar martial tune.
He only hears the distant sea
    Or clicking trans-Atlantic cable—
How dreadful lonesome he must be!
    No welcome bray from field or stable!

Science, that made great cannon roar,
    Noise belching from each mammoth gun,
A million dinning sounds that bore
    Disaster to the quavering Hun,
What ignominious works of peace
    Now claim you as a willing tool:
The brains that saved a world now cease
    To function—save to gag a mule.

The many friends of Sergeant Joseph G. Daly who have seen him spit through his teeth and make smoke come out of his ears will not, I hope, take it in bad part to learn that once, years ago, he courted the Muse and won her. He called his lyric flight "His Grief":

Well, Pal, the game's near over, and we need but one more run;
The Doughboy started batting and made second on the Hun;
A single from the gay Marines and Doughboy went to third

To rest there while the Big Guns hit a bunt that was a bird—
The bags are full, we're on our toes and rooting hard as hell
For Wilson and his clean-up hit, the blow that soon will tell
The dizzy world we've won the game, and played it bully well.

. . . .

But when I leave the grand stand, it's toot sweet home for me,
For I can't share the gate receipts—I'm in the Q. M. C.

CHAPTER TWELVE

THE TUMULT DIES BUT THE SHOUTING CONTINUES

O N THE morning of November 11, 1918, the battle-cry of the A. E. F. shifted from "When do we eat?" to "When do we go home?" Nearly two million men and several thousand women were caught in the grip of a delusion, reared in the face of a logic which they knew could not be gainsaid, that all that now remained to be done was to about face and double time to the nearest seashore, whence the chafing transports would depart with the expedition of a line of trolley cars leaving a back-home ball park at the end of the game. Everybody knew better, but who among us would forego the scenario on that account? It was too good to be true, but it was also too good to give up.

Not all of us, of course, were going home. Some seventy thousand of us lay scattered in shallow graves from the Belgian border to the Moselle and beyond. Woods and ravines were being searched for bodies that had fallen in grotesque and haphazard concealment—the task still goes on; the end is not yet nor may ever be.

On the Rhine we were to contrive an effective garrison whose stay, as we reckoned the heavy moments in those days, would be as good as permanent—it would be there many months anyway, and six months, according to our reckoning, equalled one eternity. The A. E. F. in Germany, soon to be officially designated the Army of Occupation (and unofficially, with somewhat palpable wit, the Army of Preoccupation and the Army of No Occupation), must maintain lines of communication and bases of supply. The stage was not yet quite set for the march up Main Street.

It was not that the Army was particularly anxious to keep us. In fact, so much of the going-home machinery as was in G. H. Q.'s and the War Department's hands was soon functioning with almost impeccable smoothness. Half of the A. E. F., however, had come over in British bottoms (very close to the bottoms usually), and a large share of this tonnage was no longer available—England had need of it. France, likewise, now that the war was won, wanted her railroads back to

223

aid in the restoration of that twelfth of her territory which had been a four-years' battleground. Moreover, while the A. E. F. would have been willing to go back

"THE REALLY HOMESICK," BY BALDRIDGE, A FRANK PROPAGANDA CARTOON, DRAWN FOR AND RECEIVED BY ITS CLIENTELE AS SUCH, AND NONE THE LESS EFFECTIVE ON THAT ACCOUNT

five in a bunk, or even without bunks, health considerations forbade any such glamorous concentration. Influenza was carrying on where shrapnel had left off—carrying on far more effectively in the home camps than in the A. E. F.—and G. H. Q.

was not anxious to invite its ravages by resorting to the sardine plan of passenger-handling.

Anything that had to do with home-going became the livest of live news to *The Stars and Stripes* audience. If the data had been available it would probably have shown that Charles Kingsley had become the A. E. F.'s favorite author and Horace Greeley its chosen epigrammatist. It was not until well after the Armistice that for the first time in Europe I heard the strains of "Home, Sweet Home" scratched out of a war-weary Y. M. C. A. phonograph. Anyone who had attempted to play it or sing it a few weeks earlier would have been shot without waiting for sunrise.

The Stars and Stripes printed as early as December 6th a detailed account of the departure of the luckiest of the lucky—the return to a dreamland called America of certain unfortunate (as they had previously regarded themselves) Yanks who had almost but not quite reached France:

> Twenty thousand American soldiers have sailed from England for the United States since the armistice. The exodus began November 22, when 6,700 men boarded the transports at the rate of 3,000 per hour per ship.
>
> Some of these, the first Americans outside of sick, wounded and men on special missions to give up their membership cards in the A. E. F., had been in England eight months. Some had been in England only nine days. None, with the exception of some flying officers who have seen active service in France and Italy, had ever been in France as members of the American Army.
>
> The first to go were assembled at Camp Knotty Ash, near Liverpool—Knotty Ash of unsavory memory; Knotty Ash, where some thousands of Americans spent their first nights on foreign soil and did not like it. It is not the same Knotty Ash now. Huts capable of housing 4,000 men during their two or three days' stay at the camp have been erected, replacing a good share of the dirty white tents that used to keep most of the water out at the top, but let in enough to make up for it underneath. There are streets, too, and sidewalks, and an adequate drainage system, but there is still mud when it rains.
>
> Here the 20,000 spent their last nights on English soil as American soldiers; here they underwent the twice-a-day tests that make it certain that not a case of flu shall get back to America unless it reaches the transport by wireless, that not a single cootie shall enter the port of New York through the ruse of concealing himself in the undershirt of some member of the American Air Service.
>
> Knotty Ash, before the war a brewery surrounded by scattered clusters of semi-detached cottages, a development project of the kind that makes west-

ern Long Island what it is today, is one of the boom towns of the A. E. F. just now. Queen's Drive, its main thoroughfare, is one Army truck after another, and every truck is piled high with those blue or O. D. protuberances known as barrack bags, and many of the barrack bag strings are drawn tight over O. D. helmets—issued, but never used.

The drive itself, too, is piled with barrack bags—whole piles of them surmounted by a guarding detail that passes the time in barbershopping the same paeans of victory with which the conquering doughboys greeted a certain hour on a recent November 11: "There's a Long, Long Trail A-Winding" or "My Little Girl," with especial emphasis and gusto on that last line, "And I'm coming back to you!"

They are coming back to her as fast as the debarkation officer can get the ships into Liverpool and the men aboard. They are going on at the rate of 25 per minute per gangplank, which means that there is no standing in line—the line is always moving.

Charles Jones, Pvt., A.S., steps up to the little table on the wharf right behind Timothy Johnson.

"Jones!" calls the checking officer.

"Charles!" answers Private Jones, and precious time is saved.

Special details, trained several hours beforehand, take care of the homeward bound soldier when he steps on deck and steer him straight to his bunk. The guides are not sailors—they are soldiers picked from the departing squadrons, and one of them stands at every turn, if necessary no more than a yard from the guide ahead of him, to see that no one strays from his appointed destination.

Arrived in their bunking spaces, the men are kept there for as long as need be, with a sentry at the door, and are not allowed to leave the compartment until the passengers are all aboard. This is not much of a hardship, as only on a big boat could they be kept confined for more than an hour. On the biggest transport that has thus far gone back, 96 guides were at the turns to direct men to their quarters.

They are going home with good United States money in their pockets, too, these men who have never seen France. One group, by the way, nearly did see France. They went down through England and were on another transport at Southampton ready to leave when word came that they were not going in that direction. Back to Knotty Ash they went. That was the day after November 11.

The American Red Cross, which is operating a dollar exchange under government orders, paid out nearly $124,000 in return for the equivalent in pounds, shillings and pence in the first five days of embarkation preparations alone. The average per man was $20 to $25. The lowest amount cashed was three shillings, and there were probably a lot of deadbeats who didn't even show up at all.

Life at Knotty Ash is more than just cashing money and waiting for the boat, however. And what hardships there are sit just as heavy on the heads of the officers as they do on those of the enlisted men. Nobody can leave the company street except on duty, and anyone reported as being in Liverpool without proper authority is held for disciplinary action. Equipment C must be in the hands of each man before he can hope to pass final inspection, and his identification tag must be properly marked and in the proper place.

Carloads of O. D. blouses and trousers have been distributed at the camp, and if any man goes back looking like six months of K. P. he will have to find some dirty clothes on the boat to do it. And in this fresh equipment there appears an old friend, if it really was a friend—the canvas leggin. Wrap leggins are not available, and as every man must have two pairs of some kind of leggins, the chances are that only one pair will be issue spirals.

Troops arriving at Knotty Ash are paraded twice a day for medical inspection as a precaution against shipping any infectious cases, particularly influenza sufferers. Every man's temperature is taken at one of these inspections, and suspicious cases have theirs taken twice. No one who shows any degree of fever on the day of embarkation is allowed to embark. The transports, as a health precaution, are carrying only two-thirds of capacity.

But the Atlantic Ocean, even now, was not a one-way street. The most distinguished member of the A. E. F. was yet to come among us to do battle—as doughty a battle as any of the two million had waged, and one from which he was to emerge not unscathed, to become at the last as literal a war casualty as any doughboy who fell in an Argonne thicket with his face toward the enemy. On Friday, December 13th, President Wilson disembarked from the *George Washington* at Brest, and *The Stars and Stripes* of that date hailed him with this comment:

The A. E. F. will welcome President Wilson on his arrival as its partner and backer in the long scrap now ended, as well as welcoming him formally as its Commander-in-Chief. It will not only turn out the guard for him; it will turn itself inside out, for in the person of the President are represented all of the millions of backers and co-workers of the A. E. F. at home.

This Army has not forgotten how the President said, after St. Mihiel, "The boys have done just what we expected of them," nor how he declared in his message of last week that he was "proud to be the fellow-countryman of such stuff and valor." It knows that the President has had faith in it and has supported it through thick and thin, lending the powerful aid of his high office to the furtherance of all the works that would help it to carry out its appointed task. It is glad that the President is coming to review the Army in all its activities in France, to see for himself how the mission intrusted to it by America has been fulfilled.

The French and the other Allied Governments will welcome and acclaim the President as the official representative of the United States. The A. E. F. welcomes and acclaims him as something more—as the representative and embodiment of the home folks.

The President's visit and the impending peace negotiations lent special emphasis to the lure of Paris, but the lure would have operated anyway. Thanks to the establishment of the wise policy of three-day leaves to the capital thousands of men were eventually able to gain a bird's-eye view of it, but there were other thousands who, seeing no immediate prospect of a legitimate entry, were willing to risk an invasion on their own responsibility. Additional thousands were astute enough to betake themselves otherwhither than to an M. P.-infested metropolis.

To the soldier appertains the God-given privilege of protest, and only the most fatuous and fat-headed of commanders would think of attempting to deny him this hereditary and inalienable right. In time of war most of his dissatisfaction with the scheme of things can be worked off on the enemy, or, which is almost as good, on the divisions to right and to left (especially, for some reason, the division on the left) and there results that quality of belligerent cockiness which goes by the name of esprit de corps. In the aftermath of war this restiveness continues to clamor for an outlet. It is nothing to be concerned about—at least it is nothing to be concerned about when the clamorers are Americans. Some of our better people at home, to be sure, became tremendously concerned. An army out of work—there were the analogies of Russia and Germany to prove it—invariably went haywire, linked hands with a risen proletariat, and turned life into a perpetual May Day. Just where the American Army in France was going to collect its proletariat was not divulged. No such grandiose scheme for remolding the universe entered the hearts and minds of Privates A, E and F. They simply wanted to get out of uniform and back on the old job. Things might have gone better if a certain proportion of their officers—quite as distraught at the cessation of gunfire, quite as confused as to what one was supposed to do now, and quite as anxious to get home—had not conceived the idea that the perfect way to maintain discipline in their charges was to drill the feet off them.

Thereupon large quantities of soldiery decided that if they must use their feet, they would use them by going away from there.

"SO THIS IS PARIS!" BY BALDRIDGE

The problem of the AWOL—the absentee without leave—thereupon became one of the major worries of a harried G. H. Q. It seems to have worried the French even more than it did G. H. Q. Stories of alleged American depredations circulated far and wide and won their way into the fictitious authenticity of print. The fulcrum and pivot of A. E. F. transgression was Paris, according to these accounts, and one otherwise responsible French journal, commenting on what it considered the inadequate American policing of the capital (and *that* was a good joke), declared: "The incapacity of this police organization was shown lately. A statistical officer gives, in fact, for the month of December last, a total of 34 murders, 220 day and night attacks and nearly 500 bloody combats caused by American soldiers in the Department of the Seine alone."

Despite the fact that the statistical officer quoted was obviously Baron Munchausen, Headquarters of the District of Paris took the charge seriously enough to offer in rebuttal a formal denial bolstered with statistics assembled by the French authorities:

> Cases of crime of all sorts in which Americans were concerned, reported by Prefect of Police, Paris, January 4, 1918, to November 18, 1918—39.
> Shooting affrays from June 24, 1918, to December 18, 1918—6.
> Cases during December, 1918—Assault and battery, 2; housebreaking, 3; disorderly conduct, 7.
> Cases during January, 1919—Attempted murder, 3; manslaughter, 1; assault and battery, 13; robbery, 6; auto thefts, 7.

G. H. Q. pronounced, threatened and fulminated against the AWOL, and then played its ace of trumps, fired its silver bullet. The man absent without leave would not, when apprehended, be hung, drawn, quartered, doused in boiling oil and tossed to the wolves. No such mild fate for him. He would merely be assigned to one of various specially organized labor battalions (with the accent on the labor) which would be the last units in the A. E. F. to go home. General Order Number Ten said so. How many wandering Yanks would ever have heard of G. O. 10 had there been no *Stars and Stripes* no one may say. No AWOL was going to sneak inside a military post or billeting area in the dead of night to inspect the bulletin board. But somewhere, somehow—in an obscure just-out-of-bounds café, in a Y. M. C. A. canteen where his very uniform equipped him with the finest disguise in the world, in the hands of a friendly and righteous fellow-tourist amply protected by travel orders—he could see a copy of *The Stars and Stripes*. On page one of the issue for January 24th he would undoubtedly note this heading: "G. O. Hands Jolt to AWOL's; Last Home, Lots of Hard Work." And two weeks later, if he were able to hold out that long, he could read, also on page one: "More Grease on Skids for AWOL's; G. O. 10 Working." *The Stars and Stripes'* statement of the case was brief and to the point:

Going AWOL is on to the way to becoming a lost art. Following the announcement two weeks ago of a plan whereby wilful absentees are to be transferred to Labor Battalions which will be the last A. E. F. outfits to leave for home there comes the following further discouraging—for them—news:

"WAITING: THE HARDEST FIGHT OF THE WAR," BY BALDRIDGE

An M. P. motorcycle corps will comb the country districts all over France for soldiers who have made themselves at home in small villages off the A. E. F. map without letting their C. O.'s know about it.

A new scheme of co-operation between all the American police agencies and the French secret police will help to make the AWOL's lot harder in the big cities, particularly Paris.

A new Division of Criminal Investigation has been created in the office of the Provost Marshal General to which hundreds of former detectives and investigators now in the service are being sent. They will wear O. D. or civilian dress, as suits their purpose. Men of French and other nationalities will also be incorporated into the division.

On top of this, the Q. M. C. has gone in for detective work on its own account by organizing the Protective Branch of the Inspection Division of the Chief Quartermaster's Office, which will safeguard Q. M. C. supplies against loss or damage, particularly at the hands of thieves. Principal sources of losses at present, it is stated, in addition to improper loading of supplies and improper protection of supplies from weather, are the use of unprotected cars which are somewhat too open both to the weather and to the chance pilferer, and looting of goods in Q. M. C. depots, railroad yards and sidings, and from cars in transit.

Meanwhile G. O. 10, which announced the establishment of the last-to-go Labor Battalions, is already having its effect. The ink had hardly had time to dry on the original draft of the order before droves of penitent AWOL's began to flock back to their outfits and put the roll call back on its feet. Divisions which had thought nothing of a few absent platoons are waking up to find themselves back at wartime strength.

Within two weeks of the publication of this story the problem of the AWOL was eighty percent solved. Four out of every five absentees, with or without pyorrhea, were back with their outfits.

The A. E. F. had all the right in the world to know just what the low-down was on the going-home situation. Moreover rumor (and rumor has marched with every soldier since armies began) had it that the A. E. F. was soon to be bustling back at such speed that it behooved every soldier to keep his pack rolled tightly lest he be caught napping at the critical instant and be compelled to wait for the afternoon boat. This report of an incredible rapidity of return somehow got itself invested with what were taken for official trappings, and Heaven knows what ill might have befallen if *The Stars and Stripes* had not gone to the fountain head of sailing knowledge and got the facts. Von Blon interviewed General Harbord and presented an authentic picture of the situation. Publication of this interview (it appeared in the issue for February 21st) would alone have been sufficient excuse for the establishment and maintenance of a *Stars and Stripes*:

A warning against exaggerated hopes of a too speedy return of the A. E. F. was given this week by Maj.-Gen. James G. Harbord, Commanding General, S. O. S. He pointed out that both the War Department and the heads of the A. E. F. had refrained from indulging in over-optimistic estimates because the transport problem from one month to the next is affected by so many influ-

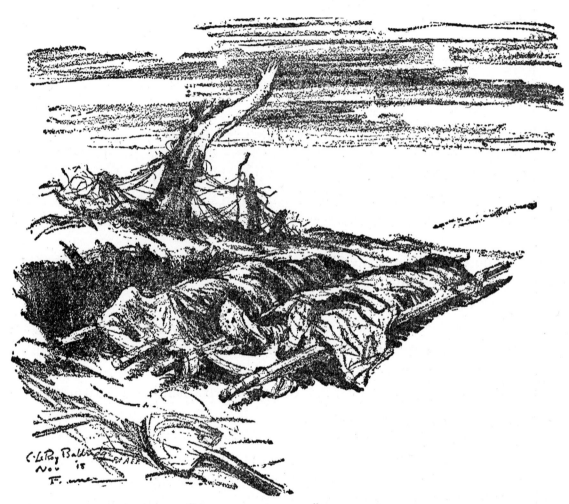

"THE FIRST TO GO HOME," BY BALDRIDGE

ences that no person may predict accurately how many troops can be transported in any given month.

Some optimistic estimates, without particular foundation in fact, made in unofficial quarters, have aroused hopes which cannot be realized at the present time, General Harbord pointed out.

"The War Department has never said that we would be transporting 300,000 men a month back home at this time, and all talk of that sort is nonsense," said General Harbord. "Give us the ships and the monthly sailing records will take care of themselves. We can fill the vessels with soldiers no matter how fast they come. We have received all the shipping we have been promised by the War Department and our sailings have been as heavy as anyone who appreciates the present state of the world's shipping could expect.

"We confidently expect to have 175,000 embarkations in February. That is about the average for January, allowing for the fewer days in February. We expect not only to maintain this average, but gradually to better it until the middle of spring, when we look for a substantial increase in shipping, both from foreign sources and from United States cargo boats which are now being fitted out to carry passengers.

"An immediate increase in the number of passenger vessels available from foreign sources is not looked for. We have secured a certain amount of German shipping, and in March we expect to carry 17,000 troops back to the States in these boats. These ships will remain in the United States for several weeks, however, to be repaired and refitted with increased carrying accommodations and then put into transport service again. That will increase our troop carrying facilities.

"I cannot say how many boats we have engaged in carrying troops at the present time because all of the shipping is furnished us from the United States and varies from month to month. For example, we may have four ships carrying troops at the present time which will be withdrawn from the service on their arrival in the United States and other ships of different capacities put on in their places by the War Department. Ships are in constant need of repairs, and when a ship breaks down it is difficult to tell when it will be ready for sea again.

"One must realize that when the United States was rushing troops to France at the rate of 300,000 a month last summer, more than half of the shipping engaged in that work was furnished by the British Government. Great Britain, France and Italy were going on short rations to make that diversion of shipping possible and get our troops over here where they could fight.

"After the Armistice, naturally enough, Great Britain set about the work of getting in a supply of food and material and transporting home her Colonial troops to India, Australia, New Zealand, Canada and South Africa, troops that have been over here for several years.

"When that task has been completed Great Britain will turn over to us a number of additional transports which will increase our troop carrying capacity greatly. At the present time we are utilizing a number of British boats. Every month we are told how many men we can figure on transporting home in British boats the next month. So far the British have exceeded their estimates very liberally.

"We are already using French, Italian and other vessels, and are adding new ones as opportunity offers.

"The return of the A. E. F., therefore, is almost wholly a question of boats. At all times since the signing of the Armistice the Army has been prepared to load without undue delay all the transports available. At present there are 300,000 to 400,000 officers and men ready for quick movement to the gang-planks; and of these 5,183 officers and 139,211 enlisted men are actually at embarkation ports, the remainder being within easy traveling distance of the ports."

Let it not be assumed from what has gone before that at least every other company commander, rubbing the sleep from his eyes at the first frosty notes of Reveille some winter morning early in 1919, stepped out onto the parade ground to be confronted only by so much inanimate acreage. The great majority played the game. A lot of them took out their annoyance in writing letters to *The Stars and Stripes*—letters of protest, complaint, remonstrance, appeal; letters that breathed the spirit of irony, pity, indignation, cussedness; letters that in their sum portray this disembattled and impatient A. E. F. better than any quantity of *Stars and Stripes* staffs could have hoped to portray it. Somebody's error (not ours) announced the departure of the 144th Machine-Gun Battalion for the States, thereby bringing down on our sorrowing heads this eminently sustainable objection:

To the Editor of *The Stars and Stripes*:

Sometime ago we read in your wonderful paper of the famous Lost Battalion. We reveled in the account. Now we think we have reason to advance a claim to similar recognition and publicity. We want to be known as the Lost Machine Gun Battalion. Our reasons are as follows: In *The Stars and Stripes* of March 21 under the heading, "Recent Departures," we have discovered that we sailed from France on the good ship Rijndam, ostensibly bound for the United States.

Now, if the Rijndam arrives in the States without the 144th Machine Gun Battalion, there is only one conclusion to be drawn, and that is that we were lost in transit. The States papers will copy your announcement of our sailing; our people will read that we have sailed for home, but we'll never arrive.

Perhaps we did sail and we are only dreaming that we are sitting in the rain on the beach at Pauillac watching the transports come and go. It would be awfully jolly to wake up some sunny morning, pop our heads over the rail and see Miss Liberty proudly watching us come home. But we fear that it is no dream.

In that case, what is going to be done? Will searching parties scour the seven seas for years to come for some trace of us? Will there be an investigation into the system that allows an entire battalion to evaporate without leaving a trace? Such questions as the above vex us as we sit in the rain on the beach at Pauillac watching the transports come and go.

But the chief question of all—will our paper see that we are duly recognized as the Lost Machine Gun Battalion? We would appreciate any help you can be to us in this matter.

And now comes the San Francisco Examiner and says that the 144th Machine Gun Battalion has arrived in the United States and that California is very happy over the return of her troops.

> ENLISTED MEN OF 144TH M. G. BN.,
> A. P. O. 705-B, A. E. F., France.

There was some point to the following complaint, and the Twentieth Engineers (Forestry) eventually received their due, for theirs was the world's largest regiment, equal in size to two or three French divisions and not far below the size of a war-strength American division:

To the Editor of *The Stars and Stripes*:

We of the Engineers (Forestry) have read and enjoyed your excellent journal ever since its entrance into an all-balled-up world, and we have noted the achievements of other outfits with just pride, and we have read of the superb fighting qualities of the Yank doughboy, and we're glad. But never once have you mentioned the guys—unhonored and unsung—that have produced the lumber for all the docks, warehouses, hospitals, barracks, etc., that the other chaps have put up, and that have produced the ties that the Engineers (Railway) have laid down and strewn with steel.

So, in a moment of reckless abandon I sat me down and dashed off this melancholy fragment:

THE LAMENT OF THE FORESTRY ENGINEERS

Say!
You know it's a damn long war?
We got two service stripes and all that,
But
They don't make the grub
Any better. Mostly it's

Slum, and beans, and
Salmon.
God!
How I hate that fish.
We've been down here in the wilderness for
A whole year,
Making slabs and sawdust and
Sometimes boards
Out of
Logs.
We've worked all day and fought
Fire all night. That's all the
Fighting we've seen—and we had
Beaucoup of that.
But
What I mean,
We have cut some lumber—
Yeah, and we've had
Generals
And other ginks
Come down and give us
The Once Over.
The dear General,
He said
Our stables weren't so
Sanitary
As he liked. And he wanted to know what
Slum was. A Colonel said
We were
Roses
Born to blush unseen.
We don't get no
Medals
But we work like hell.
We've had a lot of brand new lieuts.
For skippers. We taught
Them how to saw-mill; and one
Wept
Because we didn't bow down before him
And give thanks
Because he bought us cabbages and tomatoes
Out of our own mess fund.
Say!

Ain't this man's Army
A queer proposition?
But at that we've had a heap of fun
And lapped up our share of
This foolish French booze—
Lord! but I wish I had one bottle
Of real American
Beer.
Say, guy—
What would you give to see
That big old Statue
There in the bay
And all them high buildings
Shining white in the sun?
And to slap your old feet
Down on that same
Broadway
We used to know?
Gee, guy,
That would be hard to take.
Damn the Germans
Anyway.

PVT. RICHARD W. BATTEN,
Engrs. (Forestry).

What O. D. typewriter could match the pathos of this appeal?

To the Editor of *The Stars and Stripes*:

We read the article entitled, "The Last of the M. P.'s," and as we happen to be la même chose, we can fully appreciate their position.

Incidentally, we happen to be the nurses of Base Hospital No. 12, of Chicago. We arrived in France June 11, 1917, and we have three service stripes each. Perhaps they want us to have four, and, while we appreciate their possible interest, yet we are quite satisfied with three.

Our officers and men sailed the 27th for the U. S., leaving us behind, and, you may take our word for it, we don't like being left. And, too, we are wondering why nurses who have had only six months' or one year's service should be sent on, while we wait—not patiently, if we must be honest—as we have been playing that waiting game for just three months.

We are wondering if there is any way in which you can give us any publicity. Some people tell us that we are lost, others that we are casuals, and still others that we are supposed to have sailed.

Anything you can do for us will be greatly appreciated by the

NURSES OF BASE HOSPITAL NO. 12.

This stone-cast must have produced several scattering casualties and an abundance of loud cheers:

To the Editor of *The Stars and Stripes*:

Being a member of the S. O. S., I have keenly enjoyed the running comments and quips made at the expense of that branch of the service. I have listened the longest and laughed the loudest, from the fact that the folks who brayed the loudest were combatant officers who never saw front line service.

Recently I was entertained by a group of aviators, dressed in regulation "swank," who sang a barber shop chord entitled, "Mother, Pull Down Your Service Flag, Your Son's in the S. O. S." This was sung in a public place.

After inquiring as to how long they had been in France, I received the reply that they had arrived in October, and had not made any flights at the front.

The reason this is entertainment for me is that, until October 20, I had been a member of the 3rd Division and had seen front line service until being commissioned in the Q. M. C. I have seen Q. M. officers work day and night, while under severe fire, in order to keep their division in the line. The 3rd Division Q. M., for instance, kept a ration dump just outside of Montfaucon, directly in the rear of the Infantry reserve trenches, and had casualties every day.

The one and only branch of the service that has any right to swank for enduring the most hardships is the doughboys—and they don't say anything.

Q. M. OFFICER.

The long-persecuted second looey found time and occasion to rise in his own defense:

To the Editor of *The Stars and Stripes*.

Now, a word for the most picked-on, kidded, ranked-over and helpless victim of buck-passing in the A. E. F.—the second lieutenant.

Them's harsh words, I'll admit, but even if they don't rhyme there may be a little truth in prose as well as in poetry. The writer is stationed in a port in which, the papers say, the Y. M. C. A. conducts over 80 entertainments— minstrels, vaudeville, etc.—daily, and when he has had the opportunity to attend an occasional entertainment he has invariably had the exquisite pleasure of hearing at every one of these some threadbare joke pulled off at the expense of the helpless "second looeys," as we are familiarly called. And the tendency, although seasoned with a goodly portion of well meaning, is to hold this particular member of the commissioned personnel of the American Army in a position of ridicule, reflecting considerable disrespect upon his status as an officer.

I speak as a soldier who has seen service in the Army all the way from a buck to a second lieutenant, and who, during this military evolution, has worn three branch colors of hat cords before being commissioned. And with everybody in the A. E. F., including top sergeants and ham fatters, continuously trying to explode all the regulations and traditions of the service by using our status and rank as a joke before the screen of ridicule, I sometimes wonder why we were ever required, in the old school, to respect our superior officers. Certainly, the pride, glory and honor of being called a "shave" is another incentive to the enlisted man to become famous. First sergeants (except mine) are getting away with that of late, and I am in dread of the day when the M. P. on the corner hails me with a "Mornin', shave."

We don't expect General Pershing to come within a hemisphere of us when he "promotes to fill vacancies in the A. E. F.," but we would request that the poor, hard-working second lieutenant be spared from being the subject of jokes and ridicule **and** left to bear his cross alone.

ONE OF 'EM.

A comrade sprang to his side:

To the Editor of *The Stars and Stripes*:

In your last issue there is a letter from a second lieutenant, signed "One of 'Em," and I want to take this opportunity of pushing his point a little further.

I am a second lieutenant and have recently come back from the front, and I know a few things about it, so would like to ask a few questions of those who have been there and seen. Did anybody ever see a colonel lead a second lieutenant "over the top"? And in what battle was it that the generals drove the tanks? And when did the majors fly combat ships over the lines to engage in battle with the Hun? Have you ever read in the casualty list where it says, "Second lieutenants, unless otherwise stated?" The reason for that is plain. If the paper put the full title in front of every "shave's" name there would be no room left for the news.

So, please tell me, why do they kid the second lieutenant?

ANOTHER OF 'EM.

This assault on the higher ratings brought a sterling advocate into the lists:

To the Editor of *The Stars and Stripes*:

I noticed in your paper of March 21 a letter signed by "Another of 'Em," claiming that he recently came back from the front and knows a few things about what went on up on the line. He wants to know of any one who has been there and seen a colonel lead a second lieutenant over the top.

I want to say that I have been there and saw a colonel go over the top in a raiding party on the morning of November 10; also saw a general on the front line at Châtel-Chehery in the Argonne about October 8, when 77's, one-pounders and trench mortars were shelling the line, he being the only commissioned officer on the line at the time, picking out emplacements for machine guns.

We had this kind of colonels and generals in our division. I also want to state that I was a sergeant at the time, acting commander of my company. The first sergeant of my company was acting major of the battalion. I have seen the major in command of the regiment on the front line time and again, when liaison was poor, getting information and helping get the men straightened out, there being no commissioned officers in the companies, all being killed or wounded. The enlisted men of my regiment seeing these officers on the front lines regained their spirits and pushed ahead fighting.

About this raid on November 10, I want to state that I was one of the lieutenants second in command. The first lieutenant in command of the raid was recommended for a D. S. C., and personally I think that the colonel deserved a D. S. C. Furthermore, will say that I am not handshaking with generals, colonels or majors.

ANOTHER OF 'EM.

The most effective pleader of all for the second lieutenant was that wearer of the golden bar who conducted his defense with such surpassing good humor as this:

To the Editor of *The Stars and Stripes*:

Why is it that we second looies are the fall guys for all the bunk you fellows on *The Stars and Stripes* hand out to the A. E. F.? I've read your columns since *The Stars and Stripes* came into existence, and if I remember right you started the very first issue with a reference to "the poor looie."

I've even reached the point where I walk down the regimental street and salute sergeant majors. I'm even bawled out by corporals. Why not put us into squads and put a corporal over us?

A. L. Finch,
2nd Loot, Infantry.

Censored O.K. by
L. K. Johnson,
Corporal, Q. M. Corps.

In its early issues *The Stars and Stripes* printed, I think, too many comments telling how good it was. Happily these were soon crowded out, but I am glad we found room toward the end for this endorsement:

To the Editor of *The Stars and Stripes*:

Before leaving France I want to say "Goodbye and good luck" to *The Stars and Stripes*.

This seems only quite natural. Your little paper is something human; something one can shake hands with, slap on the back, borrow five francs from and offer to buy the drinks for.

And, strangely enough, this comes from a

2nd Loot.

The second lieutenant was by no means the sole butt of A. E. F. scorn:

To the Editor of *The Stars and Stripes*:

Our collective friend, Louis II, having aired his grievances before the High Court of *The Stars and Stripes* readers, I rise to defend that much slandered man who, with his sidekick, the supply sergeant, is popularly credited with enjoying mysterious and illegal sources of income at the company's expense. Why pick on the mess sergeant?

In the first place, who ever wanted to be a M. S. anyway? Very few, if any. After a few months' close association with beans and slumgullion in the making squads east sounds like a rare adventure. We don't even class with the M. P.'s—whoever heard of the query as to who won the war being answered, "The Mess Sergeants?"

The Q. M. C., in its infinite wisdom, issues macaroni, tin willie and goldfish. Not being an alchemist, the M. S. is unable to convert willie into fried chicken. But whom does the irate buck heap curses upon, when willie and beans arrive on his mess kit—the issuing Q. M., think you? Not by a deuce of a sight, as the Y song-book would put it. "Dang that blinked belly-robber to

Brest," he shouts, consigns W. and B. to the incinerator, and rushes out to spend his francs for pommes de terre in some vin rouge parlor.

They sigh for Mother's Cooking (capital letters and reverent voices), and lest the M. S. should fail to get the point, they hint that a nice mess of chicken, some sweet potatoes and ice cream sure would go good. Mother bought whatever the market offered, and cooked it for a family of, say six, assisted by Maggie, the female K. P.

In most cases the Q. M. plays the star and only part as market. It would be a poor compliment to mother under the circumstances if we could even approach her results.

But we try. We lose our appetites also upon the appearances of tin willie, so out of our sympathy comes the resolve to do a masterly job on that unloved commodity. We prepare it with onions, mould it, fry it—hamburger steak. (I almost wrote that humbugger steak.) Is the company fooled? Not so you could notice it. "What t'ell?" snorts the first buck in the line, "corn Billie again!"

So it goes, day after day, till even the hours from taps to reveille are filled with the ghosts of Willie and Goldie. Alone, friendless, cursed alike by the details under him and the company he serves, the mess sergeant passes his thankless days, belly-robber and camouflage artist being the mildest of the epitaphs he bears.

But he doesn't care. Like the martyrs of old, a power more than earthly sustains his drooping spirits. Lost in the rapt contemplation of the beauty and mystery of slum, his hours are passed in a state of exaltation that recks not of even a buck private.

ONE OF 'EM.

The outfit which thought it had never had proper recognition, either from *The Stars and Stripes* or from G. H. Q. or from anybody else, would frequently rise to expostulate:

To the Editor of *The Stars and Stripes*:

There is one big group of S. O. L.'s who have never been mentioned in your paper, as far as I have seen. I mean the Depot divisions and the divisions broken up as replacements. I personally know of several such—for example, the 41st, 76th and 83rd Divisions, which were doomed to function as Depots, and the 31st, 34th, 84th, 86th and probably others which as soon as they had disembarked were broken up as replacements, losing their identity as divisions.

Just think it over. These divisions were trained as combat units. They went through all the monotonous training back home, and at last came over, with all the esprit and enthusiasm that has marked the combat units. They expected to have their chance at the front, but the exigencies of the war made replacements more necessary than new combat units. They saw the units which they had learned to love and believe in broken up. They saw their comrades scattered from Bordeaux to Lorraine. And the vast majority of them did their work wherever their lot fell, and kept their mouths shut.

Then the Depot divisions have not had the easy life which the men at the front seem to credit to the S. O. S. I know of many men in the 2nd Depot (83rd) Division, for example, who worked almost literally night and day, week after week, month after month, receiving raw replacement troops from the States, giving them all possible instruction in rifle and gas in the ten days or two weeks allowed them, and then sending them on up to that front to which they themselves would give their very eyes to go.

I have known two officers and 50 enlisted men to have a company of from 800 to 1,000 replacement troops to billet, feed, instruct, discipline and father while giving them this brief preparation.

Replacements came and went at all hours, necessitating hours almost as fatiguing and irregular as those required of the combat units. Billets were in small villages no more luxurious than those near the firing line. Training was kept up regardless of weather. Day after day was spent on the muddy firing points or in the slimy pits, at the most monotonous of work, and half the night often was spent billeting new men or doing some of the thousand other things necessary in company administration.

The combat troops need not be afraid that the Depots will try to steal the glory of the fighting units. They are the first ones to give the men at the front all the credit. It was their pride to send the replacement troops forward just as well prepared as possible in order to help "up there where the boys are doing the real work."

Now, I am not pleading for glory for these Depot divisions. They know they don't deserve it and they don't want it. But something is needed for their self-respect. Why not print a line to let them know that they have done something commendable in the war, even if ill luck did deprive them of a chance to show their fighting qualities? None of them can go home with medals or souvenirs of battle or stories of the front. They do not deserve the same measure of gratitude that is the due of the men who have fought and died. But as long as praise is being passed around unstintedly, they do deserve just enough crumbs of it to prevent their feeling that somehow they have failed to do their bit.

JOHN F. HALL,
1st Lieut., Inf.

[The glory of the Depot Divisions is the glory of the men who went out from them to the front as replacements and were absorbed into combat outfits, sharing their ups and downs and helping to develop and maintain the esprit de corps of the foster division of which they became a part. But they would have been poor soldiers had not the Depots so rounded out their training that they knew just what to do the minute they reached the line—and did it.—EDITOR.]

Here is a communication pitched in a somewhat more resentful key:

To the Editor of *The Stars and Stripes*:

With no desire to start a divisional controversy, I beg of you not to mention the 82nd Division so often. It is quite embarrassing to the officers and men to receive such publicity. We want to be modest like some of the divisions that come from the large cities where large newspapers are published.

Next to the M. P.'s, I think we did the most to win the war. We arrived over here last and are going home first. We weren't in the lines long, only being in once for 26 days without relief, and our artillery stayed in for 37 days. We never had any lost battalions, because it isn't healthy to get lost at the front. Most of the casualties were caused from overeating and consuming the large quantities of chocolate, etc., the various welfare organizations who were at "the front" fed us upon.

Some day in the dim, damn distant future somebody will be pawing through the archives at Washington and discover there was an 82nd Division in the war, for won't the proof be there in black and white on the many memorandas and orders issued from G. H. Q.? Then let the bands play and the press agents get busy, for the 82nd will come into its own.

But perhaps, after all, there may be some truth in the old saying that silence is golden, for we are now at Bordeaux and on the way home. If we had had our press agent with us along in the Argonne and St. Mihiel we might now be in Germany.

PRIVATE PETE.

The theory that any Frenchman (and only a Frenchman) would walk a mile for a centime and then snake it out of an American pocket was slightly punctured with the publication of this bit of independent research:

To the Editor of *The Stars and Stripes*:

Here is what an Expeditionary Force member writing home to his father had to say about the money-grabbing natives among whom the troops had to make their way for a time:

"They fleece us pitilessly; the price of everything is exorbitant; in all the dealings that we have with them they treat us more like enemies than friends. Their cupidity is unequaled; money is their god; virtue, honor seem nothing to them compared to the precious metal. I do not mean that there are no estimable people whose character is equally noble and generous—there are many, but I speak of the nation in general. . . .

"Money is the prime mover of all their actions; they think only of means to gain it; each is for himself, and none is for the public good. The inhabitants along the coast, even the best Whigs, carry provisions of all kinds to the English fleet, which is anchored in Gardiner's bay, and that because the English pay them well."

That last is puzzling, isn't it? You see, the letter was written back in 1782. The writer was a Frenchman, Compte de Ferson, an officer attached to the F. E. F., which was then helping the colonies of America fight their fight for Independence. The "they" were the first Yanks.

ANTIQUARIAN.

It is always comforting to learn that somebody else's predicament is a little worse than yours. In the late summer of 1918 the 339th Infantry of the 85th Division, comprising troops from Wisconsin and Michigan, reached Archangel, in northern Russia, to form part of the Allied force—British, Canadian, and French—that was to help the loyal Russians suppress the Bolsheviks or something like that. With auxiliary troops, the American contingent comprised about five thousand men. Corporal Knight, I am certain, raised the morale of the A. E. F. in France and Germany a perceptible notch with this account of the 339th's life in the Arctic sector:

To the Editor of *The Stars and Stripes*:

Sometimes, about once or twice every now and then, copies of *The Stars and Stripes* find their way up here to No Woman's Land and are instantly devoured by the news-hungry gang, searching for information regarding their comrades and general conditions in France, where we belong, but through Fate were sent up to this part of the world to quell Bolshevism and guard the Northern Lights.

We are so far north that the doggone sun works only when it feels inclined to do so, and in that way it is like everything else in Russia. The moon isn't so particular, and comes up, usually backwards, at any time of the day or night, in any part of the sky, it having no set schedule, and often it will get lost and still be on the job at noon. Yes, we are so far north that 30 degrees below will soon be tropical weather to us, and they will have to build fires around both cows before they can milk them. Probably about next month at this time some one will come around and say we will be pulling out of here in a day or so, but then, the days will be six months long.

In one issue of your very popular paper we noticed a cartoon, "Pity the Boys in Siberia," but what about us, Ed? Now, up here in this tough town there are 269,831 inhabitants, of which 61,329 are human beings and 208,502 are dogs. Dogs of every description, from the poodle to the St. Bernard and from the wolfhound to the halfbreed dachshund, which is half German and half Bolshevik and looks the part.

The wind whistles across the Dvina river like the Twentieth Century Limited passing Podunk, and snowflakes are as numerous as retreating Germans were in France a few weeks ago. We have good quarters, when we are here, thank Fortune for that, and good food, when it comes up. If we can stand the winter we will be all jake, for a Yank can accustom himself to anything if he wants to. But just the same, we would like to see your artists busy on "The Boys in Northern Russia"—and tell them not to leave out the word "Northern."

We also read in *The Stars and Stripes* that the boys in Italy had some tongue twisters and brain worriers, but listen to this. Centimes and sous and francs may be hard to count, but did you ever hear of a rouble or a kopec? A kopec is worth a tenth of a cent and there are a hundred of them in a rouble. As you will see, that makes a rouble worth a dime, and to make matters worse all the money is paper, coins having gone out of circulation since the beginning of the mix-up. A kopec is the size of a postage stamp, a rouble looks like a United Cigar Store Certificate, a 25 rouble note resembles a porous plaster and a 100 rouble the Declaration of Independence.

When a soldier in search of a meal enters a restaurant, he says to the waitress, "Barishna, zakajreetyeh bifstek, pozhalysta," which means, "An order of beefsteak, lady, please." You see, you always say "barishna," which really means "girl," and until a young lady is married she is always a "barishna" and is always addressed in that manner. She will answer the hungry customer with "Yah ochen sojalaylu, shto unaus nyet yestnik prepasov syechas" (a simple home cure for lockjaw), meaning, "I am very sorry, but we are right out of food today." He will try several other places, and if he is lucky he is apt to stumble across a place where he can get something to eat, but when he looks at the bill of fare and learns that it will cost him about $7.50 for a sandwich and a cup of coffee, he beats it back to the barracks.

Every time you get on a street car ("dramvay") you have to count out 60 kopecs for your fare, and most of us would rather walk than be jammed in the two-by-four 'buses and fish for the money. Before boarding a car each passenger usually hunts up a couple of five gallon milk cans, a market basket or two, and a bag of smoked herring, so they will get their kopecs' worth out of the ride, besides making the atmosphere nice and pleasant for the rest of the passengers. If you should see a soldier walking down the street with his nose turned up and his mouth puckered in apparent contempt you would be wrong in thinking he was conceited, for if the truth be known he has probably just got his shirt back from the wash-woman, and she has used fish-oil instead of soap, and he is trying to escape the fumes.

When you take your clothes to have them laundered and tell the woman to please omit the odor, she'll tell you that she has no soap and if you want them washed to your satisfaction, please send in a cake. Anything in the world to keep your clothes from smelling of fish-oil, so you double time back and get her the soap, and then she gives the kids a bath, and that's the end of your soap.

When a Russian meets another man he knows on the street, both lift their hats and flirt with each other. If they stop to talk, they always shake hands, even if they haven't seen each other for fully 20 minutes. Then they simply must shake hands again when they leave. When a man meets a lady friend he usually kisses her hand and shows her how far he can bend over without breaking his suspenders. "Ah," he will say, "yah ochen rrad vasveedyet, kak vwi, pazhavaetye?" which in United States means, "How do you do?" to which she will reply, "Blogadaru vas, yah ochen korosho," or "Very well, thank you." It is the knockout. A fellow has to shake hands so much that some of them are getting the habit around the company.

And another thing, Ed, are they really holding a separate war up here for our benefit? Just because we weren't in on the big doings in France is no reason why they should run a post season series especially for us. We appreciate the kindness and honor and all that, but what we want to know is where everybody gets that stuff. Believe me, after all the dope we got on the trenches, about pianos and wooden floors, steam heat and other conveniences, when we see ourselves on outpost duty with one blanket and a poncho, sleeping (not on duty, of course) in 28 inches of pure ooooozy mud, which before we awaken turns into thin, fine ice, it makes us want to cry out and ask the universe what we have done to deserve this exile.

Now don't think, dear old Ed, that we are kicking—American soldiers never do. We just wanted to have something to write you about, to remind you that we ARE a part of the American E. F., although "isolated."

With best wishes to your paper and a Merry Christmas and a Happy New Year to all the boys, I'll close with the consoling assurance in my heart that we'll meet you back on Broadway, anyway.

C. B. KNIGHT,
Corp., Hq., 339th Inf., American E. F. Archangel, Russia.

Not all the Russians in the world were in Russia. Thousands of them, the toll of the disintegration of the Eastern Front, had been wandering in the wake of the German armies in the West up to the Armistice and had then tramped across the forsaken battlefields into France impelled by the understandable urge to get something to eat. They were the hoboes of war, and they presented a considerable problem. They gravitated inevitably to American camps (which was a noble tribute to the American commissary) and were harder to get rid of than the itch. Here is the story of one of them who fell among friends:

To the Editor of *The Stars and Stripes*:

The day before Christmas, a poor, shy, hungry, ill-clad Russian came into the vicinity of the 269th Aero Squadron. His main purpose was to get food. His figure was thin and his face wrinkled from the horrors of more than four years of war. During the early stages of the conflict he was made a prisoner. The tale of hardships, cruelties and persecutions at the hand of the Hun was indelibly written on his face in lines one would never forget.

His willingness and honest appearance made an impression on the 269th's mess sergeant, who set him to peeling spuds for the big event on Christmas Day. Not being able to communicate with him in English, German or French, we finally thought of one of our men, named Smokoska, who could speak some Polish, and who found that Pete, as he soon came to be called, could also speak Polish. Through Smok we learned his story.

After getting the consent of Lt. Hale, our commanding officer, Pete was initiated into the Grand Order of K. P.'s. We then began to investigate his clothing record and found that he was minus beaucoup clothes. Every man in the outfit became interested in Pete, so we soon had him all Yanked up.

Then came Christmas Day, with all the spirit that we always associate with that time. Every man was set in readiness to plant his feet under the mahogany and enjoy a real honest-to-goodness meal, and they did enjoy every bit of it, too. But there was something else to their Christmas joy. They gave physical comfort, ambition, confidence, hope for the future to a poor, crushed soul. The boys, being 100 per cent Americans, every one, shared their happiness and joy with Pete. He ate the same, drank the same. There was that big, kind-hearted feeling to help the other fellow along manifest in them all. Pete had more cigarettes and candy than any man in the squadron. On payday Pete received more than a private's pay in France from the boys.

As night came Pete lay down and slept as he had not since he was born; dreamed of a land far away that he had never known—a land of equality and freedom. He became a new man. A human being with a soul he showed himself—a man among men, who treated their fellowman "as they would have others do to them." What greater joy has life for either?

As time progressed Pete became a valuable worker around the kitchen. There never was a thing he saw to be done that he did not gladly do. He was almost immaculate about his person and his work in the kitchen. He would touch no food either for himself or to serve to the boys without carefully washing his hands. The first time he saw the cooks going for their bath he dropped his scrub brush and went along.

Though the men in the kitchen knew no Russian and Pete no English he picked up the lingo of the Army kitchen quickly. Several of the men took special pains to teach him English, and he showed himself an able student.

Pete was not much of a rounder. He had only two passes—issued by the mess sergeant to explain Pete to the M. P.'s. He was gone only for a few hours at a time, and always returned perfectly sober. We don't know whether Pete was a prohibitionist or an anti, but he never hit up any stronger drink than coffee.

Pete did not stand reveille, but he was always on the job in good time, the first man in the morning and the last at night. During this time he was picking up and becoming a full-fledged heavyweight.

Then, as a cloud from a clear sky, came the order from Headquarters. It was suspected that some of the Russians wandering about the post had caused serious trouble, and Pete had to suffer with the rest. Every one was determined that he should have an honorable discharge. We were sorry to see him go. He was such a royal fellow beneath his foreign tongue. Every officer in the squadron knew Pete and was interested in his welfare, but orders had come from above and must be carried out.

The heart of every man went out to him. They determined to send him off a better man than he was when he arrived in the squadron. In regular American style of brotherhood, Fred Hummel, our big top kicker, passed the hat around the mess hall, and all gave to insure Pete comfort until something definite could be done for his class.

When he was told that he must leave the next morning his eyes filled with tears. He was again a man without home or country. He was again to wander into nowhere. Yet it was not all nowhere, for he saw definitely a place—far off, 'tis true—where men lived together according to the spirit that he found in his hour of need with the 269th.

ENLISTED MEN, 269th Aero Sqdn.

There was an abundance of seekers after the bubble reputation, even after the cannon's mouth had ceased to belch. You boasted of what you could, as an individual or as spokesman for a group. Thus:

To the Editor of *The Stars and Stripes*:

Here's something for mess sergeants to work on.

My company of 160 men is fed in one large hall, heated. They have china plates, cups and saucers, no chow line, but breakfast, lunch and 5 o'clock dinner is served on the table by regular waiters—picked up at inspections.

We claim to be the only company in the Army of Occupation doing this. What?

Think of it—no mess-kits to wash!

MESS SERGEANT, Co. H, 356th Inf.

And then somebody went you one or two better:

To the Editor of *The Stars and Stripes*:

I notice in your *Stars and Stripes* a letter from a boastful mess sergeant about using chinaware instead of mess kits. Where does he get off at?

Why, we've broke more dishes here in Ehrenbreitstein already than they've got in their whole company.

And table waiters? Why, we had them things before he knew there was an Army. And if it were not for the Saturday inspections I would have forgotten I ever had a mess kit.

I pity the K. P.'s the day that certain mess sergeant reads this.

HERMAN FRANKEL,
Pvt., Troop K, 3rd Cav.

But the spirit of rivalry could rise above the vulgar concerns of the alimentary canal:

To the Editor of *The Stars and Stripes*:

In order to insert a little novelty into the competition which is going on between different individuals, divisions, etc., in the A. E. F., I wish to issue a challenge to any individual in the A. E. F. from the Chief of Staff down to the lowest
buck to meet me in a spelling contest at any time and place suitable to both
parties, the only rules governing the contest to be that each party shall be given
no less than one thousand and no more than ten thousand words to be chosen
by a committee of three disinterested parties.

Webster's Dictionary shall be the final authority in case of dispute, the party
misspelling the fewest number of words to be declared winner of the contest.

I also wish to issue a challenge to any man or men in the A. E. F. to meet me
in a reading contest, the material to be read being any piece of English prose,
and that participant being declared winner who reads with the best expression.
The piece of prose read shall be chosen by a committee of three distinterested
parties, from any source whatever, and shall be of such length as to consume
a minimum of 15 and a maximum of 45 minutes, figuring on a basis of 150
words to the minute.

HAROLD A. MACCALLUM,
Pvt., 310th Field Hospital.

Private MacCallum's challenge did not go unanswered:

To the Editor of *The Stars and Stripes*:

I seen in your issue of February 21 the challenge of Harold A. Maccallum
for a speling and reading compertition, and while far be it from me to uligize
myself (guess that word would sort of get him) I'm not the sort as hides a bushel
under the light—especially as most of the company knowes my qualerties and
gets me to help them out whenever they has serus letters to write and wants to
emperscutiously use big words.

It don't matter to me where and when we meet, and his rules is satisfactery
to me as promolgated—but if it's all the same to everybody, I'd like to make it
San Francisco sometime early next month. As to not less than one 1000 words or
more than ten 1000, all I can say is my spelling is just the same regardless of
quantity.

While I ain't so good maybe at reading, I'd just as leaf take him on for a bit
of that, and would name "Ivenhoe" or "Dinkie Merriwell to the Death" as suit-

8

able literchur—and since his nam's MacCallum "wa might gae on wit' a bit o' Bobby Burns."

THEODORE J. RILEY,
D. L. R., A. P. O. 703,
Care Adjutant, L. R. C. S.

P.S. My spelling is more on the fonetic style, but I can use either.

P.S.S. Could also enter a pie or doughnut eating contest, or could take on any man of the A. E. F. for a 1 mile dash. My record for the mile was established last October when the company arrived in the Argonne, and was executed under—that is, started under—severe shell fire.

The most remarkable series of examples of the flowering of the competitive spirit was set in motion by the publication of the following innocent communication while the Argonne fighting was at its bitterest:

To the Editor of *The Stars and Stripes*:

I would like to find out through your paper, if we made a record in hot cake making. During the big drive on the Toul sector, we started in at 7.30 a. m., and continued one steady fry until 3 o'clock the next morning, making hot cakes on a plate four by four feet, making 12 large cakes at a time, three plates every five minutes, or something like 8,000 cakes in one stretch, without stopping.

I have talked to several cooks and they all seem to think this is the record. If any one place has beaten us, kindly let us know.

This is a Salvation Army flap-jack place, and the originator and operator is Ensign Fred Anderson of Tacoma, Wash. I shall be glad to hear from any cook on this just for the fun of it, and will be willing to run a race on frying for a canteen, when and wherever it can be arranged.

Ensign FRED ANDERSON,
Salvation Army.

Not long afterward came this reply:

To the Editor of *The Stars and Stripes*:

I notice a challenge from Ensign Fred Anderson of the Salvation Army. I accept the challenge if the proper arrangements can be made. I agree with him that for a one griddle fry it was some fast work.

Although not a member of the Salvation Army I am the next thing to it—am, or rather was, a mess sergeant in a non-combatant unit. While in this line of duty I was placed in charge of one of the largest camps in France; I dare not tell the name of the place, for it would cause every soldier in the A. E. F. to go AWOL to see this wonderful kitchen; I won't tell you the number of men we fed there, for I don't want to give the impression that I am trying to kid someone.

Now for the kitchen: The kitchen range was 928 feet wide and 1,358 feet long. It took 18 firemen to keep it hot; we had 519 cooks and 700 K. P.'s. We mashed potatoes with a pile driver and ground coffee with a 350 h.p. Liberty motor. They hauled out dirty pans on railroad cars and the K. P.'s went on roller skates. As I was mess sergeant I rode up and down the kitchen on a motorcycle shouting orders through a megaphone.

Now for the flap jacks: We mixed batter with 12 concrete mixers; had a steam shovel moving egg shells away from the door and six K. P.'s with bacon rinds strapped on their feet skating over the griddle to keep it greased. When I tell you that on three occasions I was forced to fry all of the cakes myself you will agree with me in thinking I would have some show in a contest with Mr. Anderson.

I am willing to take on anyone in the Allied Forces under any conditions they wish to name: blindfolded, handcuffed, one eye closed, one foot on the floor, turn 'em with a shovel, toothpick—well, any old way they care to do it.

Pardon this letter, as I am not a writer—I am a pancake fryer and what it takes to make 'em, I've got.

CLARENCE D. BROOKS,
Air Service.

It was evident that nobody in the vicinity of the A. E. F. was going to be allowed to get away with anything. J. Gorman Strasler of the Field Artillery recalled a record output of hot cakes "in Luna City, the motion picture capital of the world and several hours' ride from Los Angeles, in the outskirts of that city's business district." It seems that "the greatest production in history was being filmed"—no fewer than 783 cameras were on the job simultaneously. To provide hot cakes for the participating host required apparatus that put Brooks's efforts to shame:

The grease was applied by a street sprinkler suspended on overhead rails. The batter was dropped at the proper intervals by an automatic sprinkler system remodeled by myself for this purpose. Six turbine engines forced the mixture through the pipes, and one turn of the operating lever started 20,000 hot cakes baking at once. These I turned by my own turners, modeled after a gang plow, and which I guided up and down the range by hand, I being suspended by a trolley wire in a basket. The number I turned out each morning may be imagined when I tell you that the salt alone used in the batter often ran over three tons.

Guido J. Freund of the Q. M. C. thereupon announced that while he had deliberately been keeping mum as long as the contest remained strictly an A. E. F. affair, the fact that Strasler had brought the home grounds into the enterprise ought to permit him to recall a scrap of experience from his days on the Minnesota iron range:

We had 2,000 compound locomotives and 160,000 cars at work hauling away the ore to the lake front. Sixty-five thousand steam shovels were on the job, and there were 9,800 miles of railroad track in the pits. A fleet of 22 five-ton trucks carried production reports to the offices, and the work was directed from airplanes. The battle of the Marne, if it had taken place in these mines, would have created no more disturbance than a canary perched on top of a stone crusher.

As the whole crew at these mines was fed under one roof, the kitchen was, of necessity, the ninth wonder of the world. The pantry consisted of a train-shed and warehouse where freight trains were unloading from six tracks day and night. Eleven hundred men worked in the pantry and kitchen proper. The hot cakes were baked in a separate room by special machinery designed and perfected by myself. The griddle consisted of 800 steel plates 15 by 30 feet linked together and run over a series of gas jets on the endless chain principle.

At the beginning of the run grease was automatically applied to the plates from a heavy brush 30 feet wide fed through the back by 60 one-inch pipes. The batter was applied as the plate assumed a level position by 1,800 nozzles geared to the rest of the machinery in such a manner that they automatically opened and emitted just sufficient batter for one cake at just the right time. As 400 plates were in operation at a time, there were constantly 720,000 cakes in various stages of completion. To turn them the chain of plates was carried over special pulleys half way down the line so as to drop the cakes from one plate to another and flip them over en route during the fall.

At the end of the run they automatically unloaded themselves on to a conveyor belt which ran down the entire length of the chow house. The length of this building may be computed from the fact that it took six paper mill whistles to relay the mess call from the kitchen to the farther end, and the curvature of the earth had to be considered in designing the machinery to carry the belt.

Owing to the perfection of the machinery, the only working force in the hot cake room consisted of a crew of 60 armed with gallon cans who kept the bearings oiled, and 100 machine tenders in the power house, the size of which may be estimated from the fact that six weeks were required for the building of the concrete foundations for the engines.

While the cakes were baking, I sat on a high platform, my eye constantly on a huge board before me which carried 76 indicators on which I read at all times the exact operation of every part of the machinery. This was rather an automatic way of baking hot cakes, but as no hand touched them from the time the batter was prepared in the beater room till the completed product was spread from the conveyor belt in the mess hall, I consider myself as being the one who did the baking, and wish to enter the contest.

This was by no means all. The controversy continued to flourish, and would doubtless be going yet if there were still an A. E. F. I shall leave it for some qualified specialist in American folk-lore to report the entire episode and assign it to its proper place in the Paul Bunyan legend.

If a wrong cried to be righted, what better way to air the grievance than to write your favorite newspaper a letter about it? *The Stars and Stripes* ironically entitled the following complaint "Sweets to the Sweet":

> To the Editor of *The Stars and Stripes*:
>
> Why is it that the commissary at Bourges sells chocolate candy to officers only? This question was asked me a hundred times at Bourges last week.
>
> G. T. R.
>
> [We bite. Why does it?—Editor.]

If it were so, it was a grievous fault. And if it wasn't so, the fault was all the more grievous. A few weeks later *The Stars and Stripes* printed this editorial under the title "The Candy Kids":

> Under the title of "Sweets to the Sweet" there was printed on this page some weeks ago a note from an indignant reader who asked why the commissary at Bourges sold candy only to officers. The answer, which has just come in via the Chief Quartermaster, A. E. F., shows that the sales at that station during the period from February 26 to March 10 were as follows:

	Officers.	Enlisted Men.
Chocolate bonbons, 1-lb. cans	277	1,520
Chocolate bonbons, ½-lb. cans	135	1,545
Chocolate bars	96	2,104

Not all letter-writers were special pleaders—there was always room for the company wit:

To the Editor of *The Stars and Stripes*:

For the information and guidance of all concerned, the following Matrimonial Drill Regulations for Military Weddings are forwarded:

1. The march of the bridal party up the aisle of the church will be at attention. A cadence of 80 steps to the minute will be maintained for the length of the march.

2. Unless otherwise announced, the guide is right as the party proceeds toward the altar.

3. The guests will execute eyes right or eyes left, as the case may be, as the bride, bridegroom and their respective staffs march toward their objective.

4. The father of the bride, after having given her in marriage, will right oblique and continue to march until he has deployed himself from the bridal party proper.

5. The bridal party, as it aligns itself in front of the altar, will dress on the best man.

6. Ring bearers, flower girls, pages, etc., will act as file closers.

7. During the ceremony the guests will remain at parade rest.

8. When the party has arranged itself in company front formation, the officiating clergyman will take his place two paces in front and will read the articles of matrimony.

9. Immediately after the ceremony the command at ease will be given. (Note: Bride and bridegroom are not expected to be at ease, however.)

10. The bridal party will execute an about face after the ceremony and will then countermarch.

11. On gaining the vestibule of the church, the manual of arms will be executed by the bride and groom as they receive the congratulatory handshakes of the reviewing party.

12. The waiting party and guests will fall out as soon as they leave the church.

BARNARD J. RICHARD,
Co. C., 21st M.G. Bn.

Let it not be assumed from the foregoing quotations that the only letter-writing which the A. E. F. did was to *The Stars and Stripes*. We were sending home such an abundance of mail as was never shipped before. Months earlier, centuries earlier (the preceding May, to be exact—the May that was to set in a blaze of blood at Cantigny and Château-Thierry), the A. E. F. had observed Mother's Day by sending home a whole shipload of mother's letters. How many went we could not say, for the figure would have just about disclosed how many of us were in France. In November *The Stars and Stripes* announced a similar campaign on behalf of Father, and as the Armistice happened to come along in the middle of it, the plan won great impetus from the fact that the letters could tell anything and everything —the story of the voyage over, the name of the ship, submarine scares, citation of specific locations in France, life and death at the front. The total of Father's Letters was well over two million—a little better than one letter per man.

The Mother's Letter campaign brought this tender descriptive tribute from a modest captain who took shelter under the anonymity of "The Old Man":

The worthy activity manifested by "Our Paper" that led to the sending of a shipload of Mothers' Letters across the sea to the ones waiting back home was, it struck the writer, about the last word among its collection of worthy stunts —even topping by a shade, in my humble opinion, the orphan movement.

In my capacity as commander of a company of 250 men, of whom 27 are white non-commissioned officers and 223 are drafted Texas negroes, I did my best to rise to the occasion at the pace you set. I plastered pages of "Our Paper" all over the bulletin board, talked "Mother" to the boys, and had the orderly room supply the stationery (envelopes stamped in vivid red—a violation of A. R. 822, amply justified by circumstances—as per your specifications) and the C. C. pass it out at Saturday inspection.

The results overwhelmed us. They all did it. Saturday night and Sunday morning everybody was doin' it. And Sunday we all worked. That night my mail orderly took a suitcase full of letters to the base censor headquarters, and some unknown captain just shutting up shop peeled off his raglan and sat him down then and there to affix the Great Seal of the B. S.

But this is the thing that will interest: Did you ever censor a letter from a Texas cotton-patch darky to his mother? I was irresistibly moved to make pencil extracts from three, anonymously, of course. They weren't ALL like these; but, no matter how high the education of their writers had progressed, those letters all breathed the same spirit—the spirit that makes the American soldier, by and large, a sort of nut that no victim of the Prussian iron heel can ever crack, much less crush. *Regardez:*

"Mother, when I stop to think what I am here for, and of the thousands that are here with me fighting for the same Cause, it makes me feel big and proud to know that the good Lord has given me health and strength to be one of the number. And, Mother, you must think often of your soldier boy, and pray that he may return to you, when our country is at peace, just as strong and healthy as when he left you."

That extract is verbatim—not edited in the least by myself. Its writer never had a college education. Had he been just *two weeks older* the draft would not have called him. He is married, and, as the allotment records show, a Class A provider. Also, he is what is termed a 100 per cent man—he is a confidential orderly and never forgets a detail of instructions or routine.

Here is another:

"I never shall forget what you and papa said to me before my leaving for Camp Travis—'My boy, in all your trials do not forget to be true to your country and your God; and, whatever you do, obey orders.' I have been trying to do this—not only while here, but I mean to keep that in my heart throughout my life; not that I may be praised, but that people may see *you* and your *raising* in me."

That chap, a full-blooded, dark-skinned, fine-looking negro, was an undergrad in a southern college for negroes when he was drafted. Like the writer of the first extract, he is a natural leader among his fellows—one of the sort we depend on as a nucleus for good discipline in a command. This extract is likewise verbatim.

And here's another bit, thrown in for good measure—from a letter by a youngster who has rambled over the face of God's earth and learned a few things in the Big School, but is not a college man:

"Mother, I am a long way away from you, but my thoughts are always with you. Every day is Mother's Day for me, for I think of you by day and dream of you at night. Don't worry about me, for I am getting along fine."

Pretty good doctrine for all of us of the A. E. F., enlisted men or officers though we may be, to "try on." And may I query: Was any letter to Mother, homeward bound on that famous ship, truer in its ring or tenderer in its sentiment than these three, picked at random from the outgoing mail of a 250-man company? Could any one of us do better than to trim his sails according to the second sentence of that last extract?

And remember: The writers of those letters were our southern darkies—many of them descendants of black men and women brought to America in the slave ships of the forties and the fifties for which the beautiful French river city of Nantes was noted. It is a romantic circumstance that many of these fellows are here as American soldiers on French soil, offering their lives for the country whence, in less enlightened times, came those who took them from their native Africa to enslave them in the sugar-lands of the very nation to which slavery in any form is today the most abhorrent.

The men who sanctioned my making anonymous extracts from those letters are all enlisted men in Company B, —— Engineers.

But all the A. E. F.'s tremendous capacity for sentiment was not expended on Mother. Quite a bit of it survived the stress of battle and was available for Father the following November. Through the hands of Second Lieutenant Charles H. Grasser of the Signal Corps passed a document which he thought "some other readers of *The Stars and Stripes* might enjoy—a letter from a boy of German parentage to his Dad. I secured permission to send it on to you." Here is the letter:

France, November 23, 1918.

Dear Dad:

This is the first letter that I have written to you in years. Seems that I always have only enough dope for one letter, and it was sort of right to send it to Mother. However, this is Father's Day in the A. E. F. and we all promised to write a letter to Dad. So here goes.

Do you know, I think the Old Gents back home instigated the whole affair for the purpose of receiving at least one letter from the boys over here. Guess it was rather tough to have to depend on the ladies to drop a few hints of the news such as they felt willing to hand out. A kind of crawling to pick up the crumbs dropped by the chosen few. Of course we never thought of it in that light, so don't blame you a bit for starting a little propaganda in your own favor.

Things have been going just fine with me, Dad. Lots of fun mixed in with our work, and lots of interesting work, too.

It seems the joke is on the folks back home. Understand that you celebrated the armistice several days before it was signed. To give you the dope straight it was signed at 5 o'clock in the morning of November 11. Of course I didn't hand the Kaiser the pen or anything like that. But you can bank on this being the straight dope. I didn't fire the last shot, either. But it was fired at 10:59 the same morning.

Dad, our friends sure did spoil this country plenty. You can't imagine just what it is like unless you could see it yourself. An acre or two of holes in the ground and a sign with the name of the village is about all there is left of many. Our friends sure didn't play the game square, Dad, and I sort of feel ashamed of them. You know, just like you would feel if your friend were caught cheating at pinochle at the club after you introduced him as a good fellow. I used to try to find excuses to offer myself for him, but I'm through with him, Dad. He's a bum fellow, this Fritz. Not at all like he used to be some 35 years ago. Guess all the good ones came to America in 1800, and that's why Germany went on the bum. No good fellows left to run her.

I never told you, Dad, but I sure felt proud of you back in '17 when I came home after being in the Army six months without your knowing it. Didn't know just how you would take it. But you sure were tickled to death after the first surprise of seeing me back in the United States. Guess you were sort of afraid that I and the rest would sort of leave you in the lurch as the Dutch father of a bunch of bum Americans. Guess now we didn't take the wind out of the sails of some of those birds who thought they were Yankees, and called us Dutchies. It sure made me laugh to see some of 'em digging for wives and the shipyards when the draft came around.

Well, Dad, la guerre est finie, and we are all coming back home toot sweet (French for "so bald wie möglich"). We'll have a good old fashioned blow-out when we all get together, and I hope you will see to it that we don't have to drink ice water, either.

Give my love to Mumsy and all the neighbors.

CHAPTER THIRTEEN

LOITERING LAUREATES

O N JANUARY 31, 1919, appeared Number 52 of Volume 1 of *The Stars and Stripes*.

It marked the end of such a year as the world could hardly hope to survive again. Exactly how the staff of *The Stars and Stripes* survived it is an affair of minor moment in view of the admittedly larger concerns which the war involved. We did not, we do not, expect the rest of the A. E. F. to be any more interested in our heartaches than we would expect it to be interested in our toothaches. Not long after the Armistice Visk became a major in the Army of Occupation; he reached home in time to take an active part in the campaign for the Victory Loan. We could soon discern the affable features of Captain (later Major) Mark S. Watson, once of the *Chicago Tribune* and now of G-2, G. H. Q., A. E. F., one pace to left and rear of whom strode Lieutenant (later Captain) Stephen T. Early, the young Lochinvar of the Old Dominion, courageously suppressing the rebel yell. They were about to become, respectively, Officer in Charge and Assistant Officer in Charge of *The Stars and Stripes*. With Captain Watson's installation the editorial destinies of the paper were placed virtually exclusively in the hands of the enlisted staff, under the direction of Private Ross as managing editor.

It might not be out of order at this point to show precisely how we were ligatured to this Army to which we properly made so much of belonging. We were a part, not perhaps of all that we had met, but certainly of G-2, the Intelligence Section of the General Staff, which section was presided over by Brigadier-General Dennis E. Nolan. Cadet Nolan of the United States Military Academy had been commissioned a second lieutenant not quite a month before William Jennings Bryan had objected to the crucifixion of mankind upon a cross of gold. Now, after twenty-two years as an officer in the United States Army, General Nolan found himself hitched to a desk across which, when the wind was right and the artillery moderately active, drifted the occasional rumble of guns fired in anger. He would cock his northeast ear, sigh, and pitch a couple of papers into the Out basket. In the fall of 1918, when the Twenty-eighth Division was battling its way up along the flank of the Argonne Forest, an emergency arose which demanded the instant despatch of a new commander to the Fifty-fifth Infantry Brigade. General Nolan was ordered to the post pending the appointment of a permanent commander. This took two weeks or so, at the end of which interval General Nolan was back at his desk in Chaumont superintending once more the destinies of G-2. But during his lively furlough at the front he had become one of the eleven general officers of the A. E. F. who would one day wear the Distinguished Service Cross for gallantry. His citation read: "For extraordinary heroism in action near Apremont, France, October 1, 1918. While the enemy was preparing a counter attack, which they preceded by a terrific barrage, General Nolan made his way into the town of Apremont and personally directed the movements of his tanks under a most harassing fire of enemy machine guns, rifles and artillery. His indomitable courage and coolness so inspired his forces that about four hundred of our troops repulsed an enemy attack of two German regiments."

Sundry subdivisions of G-2 were concerned with such romantic enterprises as espionage and counter espionage, by comparison with which the activities of G-2-D, the Press Section, seemed singularly prosaic. *The Stars and Stripes* was a segment of G-2-D, and for military convenience was listed on the books as the First Censor and Press Company. At the head of the Press Section was Colonel Walter C. Sweeney (who, by the way, was the vociferous objector to the phrase "officers and soldiers" who has already been anonymously referred to). When Colonel Sweeney became Chief of Staff of the Twenty-eighth Division his post at Chaumont was taken by Colonel E. R. Warner McCabe, who subsequently was reassigned to the fighting Army as C. O. of the Twelfth Field Artillery of the Second Division and after the Armistice overlooked half Europe from the lofty eminence of Ehrenbreitstein, opposite Coblenz. Colonel McCabe was succeeded by Major Alexander L. James, and Major James by Captain Donald L. Stone. Major Watson had been the most permanent feature in this shifting landscape, having been on the staff of G-2-D since before *The Stars and Stripes* came into being. He and Steve Early (whose ancient oufit was the 317th Infantry of the Eightieth Division) remained through to the not particularly bitter end.

On February 8, 1919, exactly a year after the appearance of the first number, the staff held an anniversary dinner within the secluded precincts of the Palais Royale. The Palais Royale had been sacked by roistering revolutionists in the grand hubbub of '48 and a good part of it had been burned by Communards in '71, so that it was able to come through the anniversary dinner in pretty good shape. For this occasion a special four-page issue of *The Stars and Stripes* was put together for exclusive distribution to the staff. I find it difficult to wax uproarious today over what were once, I am sure, telling local hits. An editorial entitled "We Give a Damn" which has all the earmarks of a production of Regimental Sergeant Major Augustus Edward Giegengack, one of the circulation wheel-horses, wears well after thirteen years though concerned strictly with intramural activities:

In the issue of *The Official Stars and Stripes* of February 7, 1919, there appeared a story on page five, first column, entitled "Editorial Staff Consists Wholly of Enlisted Men." What we want to know is, why wasn't the enlisted

PRIVATE WALLGREN AS SEEN BY PRIVATE BALDRIDGE, FROM A DRAWING MADE FOR THE PRIVATELY ISSUED ANNIVERSARY DINNER EDITION OF THE STARS AND STRIPES. THE POINT OF THE CARICATURE IS BLUNTED TODAY FOR ANY WHO HAVE FORGOTTEN OR NEVER KNEW THAT PRIVATE WALLGREN WAS ONCE SNARED IN THE INFAMOUS PARIS SALUTING TRAP

personnel of the Business Department mentioned? Far be it from us to take any credit away from the Editorial Staff, but, in the minds of some of the best printers in the United States, it seems only fair that we at least get our names in linotype. Since we are known as the First Collegemen's and Printers' Company we feel justified in making this kick, inasmuch as we are the better half of that company.

For example, we will say, suppose Hawley, Winterich, Ross and Woollcott and Wallgren did write 99 per cent of the editorials, what good would their editorials have been if Katz, Miller, Greenhaw, Marshall and Rigney had not been on the job every week to look after the wrapping and mailing of said editorials? We can go further and say that had not the work of the Addressograph Department been efficiently handled by Born, Healey and Dowd the wrappers also would have been S. O. L.

Now then, let us go back even further and mention the fact that Geschardt and his able-bodied corps of typists were the boys who prepared the lists that the addressograph plates were made from. The amount of complaints received, looked up and satisfied . . . were all handled by Hall, Howard and Winston, much to the satisfaction of all concerned.

Seth Bailey may have been a wizard with his Henry letters, but how could McDermott be forgotten with his 300 and odd Ginger Letters each week that he turns out on his multigraph—another printer? Nobody ever stops to think of the sixty-odd thousand individual subscription tickets that are filed and kept in perfect order by Forshay.

Another article on the same page tells of how the Field Agents just push out the papers to the boys in the O. D. Where would they get off if Patrey and

PRIVATE BALDRIDGE IN ACTION—A STUDY BY PRIVATE WALLGREN FOR THE DINNER EDITION

Rhodes did not see that their orders were filled and shipped to the proper place? Nobody ever thinks of Lammers, the red-headed chauffeur who gets the mail for all the boys—even the editorial department.

Modesty prevents us from signing this document, so our names will have to be concealed from the public, but believe us—

THE COMMITTEE.

The formation of a sub-committee to present a formal complaint to The Committee might well have been in order, for while The Committee exacted a tardy tribute of fame for some seventeen members out of the whole personnel, behind these seventeen, when the final rollcall was taken, stood ranged some twenty times their number. From Ackerman, Henry H., Pvt., to Zimmerman, Charles W., Cpl., we numbered from first to last some three hundred and fifty souls. Given this company (considerably better than a company militarywise), any publisher could get out—can still get out—a good newspaper, a good chain of newspapers, anywhere. Pressmen, stereotypers, compositors, photo-engravers, accountants, bookkeepers, reporters, copy-readers, advertising solicitors (and copy-writers and whatnot), circulation builders and circulation holders—in whatever department he required experts they could be had from among the three hundred and fifty. And if he wanted somebody (as he undoubtedly would) to shovel coal, run elevators and captain the head, company punishment would provide a steady reservoir of forced labor for these essential chores.

Much of the space in the first number of Volume II was devoted to celebrating the paper's anniversary. Hawley, in an unguarded moment, was left alone with a typewriter and before anyone could put out a hand to halt him had almost gained the last page. There was a message from Visk headed "What Our Old Boss Says":

It fell to my lot to propose *The Stars and Stripes*, to give the paper its name, to set forth its aims and its policies, to organize it, and then to manage it, as officer in charge, until some weeks after the armistice.

But (barring an officer or two, who had to be around to satisfy Army traditions) *The Stars and Stripes* has actually been produced by enlisted men, many of the lowly, or buck, variety.

A handful of enlisted men has written and illustrated the greater part of the paper—I believe, for its size, the most brilliant and—er—erratic editorial staff ever possessed by an American newspaper.

Enlisted men have helped compose and make up the paper. It has been distributed among the Army by enlisted men. The financial department has been managed by still others from the ranks—every line of its activities has been largely in the hands of enlisted men.

The glory of *The Stars and Stripes* is not any officer's. It belongs to the enlisted American soldier—specifically, not only to the writers and cartoonists on the staff, but also to such quiet, earnest, 18 hours a day workers as two privates, who, starting as orderlies, became mainstays of circulation; and, generally, to the great body of the rank and file at the front and in the S. O. S. who took *The Stars and Stripes* to their hearts, called it "our paper" and furnished the inspiration for those of their comrades detailed to the publication to fight the war in a sector that never knew a day without heavy casualties.

It has been said that *The Stars and Stripes* stands unique in the history of newspaper publication. Well, the American private is the greatest man in the world at fighting or writing or anything.

And there were other gratifying encomiums from our less immediate bosses:

May I not congratulate *The Stars and Stripes* on the completion of its first year of publication and express my gratification that it has rendered so interesting a service to the men under arms?

Cordially and sincerely yours,
WOODROW WILSON

PERSHING, AMEXFORCE

Paragraph 1. *Stars and Stripes*, the newspaper of the American Expeditionary Forces, is to publish an anniversary issue on the 7th of February. Please convey to its editor my hearty and grateful congratulations upon splendid service this paper has rendered. When I was abroad I realized that its successive issues were most eagerly welcomed by the soldiers in the trenches, camps, and in the hospitals. It has been not only a medium of communication, but a strong force in making for our Army abroad a united spirit, and the copies which have reached America have been the best evidence our home people have had of the spirit of the Army. In this anniversary issue I wish not only the above message to appear, but to send a word of greeting to the officers and soldiers of the American Expeditionary Forces through their newspaper. We are filled with high pride and satisfaction at their performances, and are bending every energy to provide increasing facilities for their speedy return to their homes and friends.

BAKER

On the anniversary of the foundation of *The Stars and Stripes*, it is my great pleasure, as Commander-in-Chief of the American Expeditionary Forces, to congratulate the editorial, business and producing staffs who have so successfully labored in the creation of this remarkable newspaper. It has, in my opinion, fulfilled the purposes for which it was conceived and has maintained all the best traditions of journalism. It has been an important factor in creating and supporting the excellent morale which has at all times characterized the American Expeditionary Forces.

PERSHING

On the occasion of your first anniversary let me congratulate you on your brilliant accomplishment. You have successfully carried through an undertaking unique in the history of journalism and warfare. You have gained, as you have merited, the confidence of the entire American E. F. as the official newspaper of our Army. Through your agency the Army has been kept in touch with events back home and has been made aware of the work being done by its several elements in France. You have instructed, inspired and amused. *The Stars and Stripes* has played an important part in the highly organized business we have carried on to defeat Germany.

With best wishes,

J. G. HARBORD,
Major General, Commanding S. O. S.

Secretary Baker and General Pershing were the two most distinguished visitors we ever had. They came to see us (not in collaboration, but some weeks apart)

PRIVATE BALDRIDGE, TIRED OF DRAWING CHERUBS IN SUPPORT OF PRIVATE ROSS'S ORPHAN CAM-
PAIGN, RELEASES A PENT-UP EMOTION IN THE DINNER EDITION

in our newest and last headquarters at 32 Rue Taitbout, whence we had moved from what had early grown to be very cramped quarters at 1 Rue des Italiens. Tip Bliss had adopted a dog, whom, as he resembled an animated mop (the dog rather more than Bliss), he had christened Rags. A campaign to rename Rags Verdun Belle as a tribute to Woollcott was scotched in its infancy. Rags became the office mascot and it was most amusing to see him chewing somebody else's package of cigarettes to pieces or eating the lining out of Captain Parker's hat.

Secretary Baker's entrance was accompanied by such a lack of alarums and excursions that there was no time to remove Rags from the premises and barely time to anchor him securely under a double desk. The entire staff assembled to listen to Mr. Baker, who paid us the finest impromptu tribute we had ever listened to, at the end of which, probably contrary to all known regulations, we applauded tumultuously. This was too much for Rags, who was all for tearing the desk apart in his eagerness to get at Mr. Baker's unfettered trousers. As Rags's frantic barking rose above the racket Mr. Baker looked at him in pardonable bewilderment and then burst out laughing.

The identical little comedy was re-staged when Pershing came among us. Rags was hitched under the same desk, the same applause woke him to action, he received the same puzzled stare, evoked the same hearty laugh. Captain Watson happened to be out of Paris when the General came to town and Steve Early did the honors and did them handsomely. He introduced each of us to the General, and I believe Hawley's fifth and sixth vertebrae have never quite settled back into place after the strain to which he thereupon subjected them in coming to a surpassing attention. Ross, Woollcott, Baldridge, Mel Ryder and I had just got our discharges but were still in uniform, and in introducing the biographer of Verdun Belle to the General Steve Early said:

THE STARS AND STRIPES PERSONNEL (AS MANY AS WALLGREN COULD CROWD INTO ONE STRIP), FROM THE ANNIVERSARY ISSUE—VOLUME II, NUMBER I—OF FEBRUARY 7, 1919

"Here, General, is Sergeant Woollcott—or rather Mr. Woollcott, since he's a civilian now."

"H'm," murmured the General. "Doesn't look much like a civilian to me."

Woollcott was unbearable, or I might better say unusually unbearable, for weeks thereafter, and began to devote his evenings to reading lives of Napoleon, Frederick the Great, Hannibal and Zachary Taylor.

Garrulity increases with advancing years—this chapter set out to present a few extracts from "The Army's Poets" column of post-Armistice days and to preface the extracts with a brief summary of prosodic statistics gleaned from this same issue of February 7, 1919. The staff estimator computed that we had received some eighteen thousand poems in our year of existence—many more in the second half of that year than in the first. We had already printed 384 poems, he declared, exclusive of verse in such departments as F. P. A.'s "Listening Post" and Grantland Rice's "Chow" and Stuart Carroll's "Star Shells". Probably three or four thousand more poems were submitted in the remaining four and half months of the paper's existence, and enough of these saw print to bring the grand published total to more than five hundred.

The post-bellum school of poetry had several sharply-defined characteristics. There was a dearth of paeans of victory. Such recollections of desperate days that had been as became the stuff of lyricism had to do in the main with those momentous trifles that make up a war as they make up a peace. A vivid little snapshot of transport days survived in "It's the Little Things That Count":

> Everywhere wetness and chill,
> And light fog and grayness,
> And Private Samarski, slicker adrip,
> His rifle aslant beside him,
> Sags against the rail.
>
> Truly no martial figure—
> A sodden cap,
> A swarthy face,
> His figure blurred by a slicker,
> With rain trickling down
> Through a week-old beard.
>
> With the tender care
> And the reverence due
> His mother's picture,
> Or a lover's amulet,
> Private Samarski, soldier and human,
> Puts his hand in his slicker
> And draws out a cracker.
>
> A soda cracker,
> Of war quality,
> With the darker cast of Hoover flour—
> The simple soda cracker,
> Fallen on evil days;
> And Private Samarski,
> Soldier of fortune,

Bound for France,
Falls to munching it—
To rolling it under his tongue.

It is a gray day,
And a wet day,
And the ocean is full of subs—
And a cracker, of course,
Is only a cracker;
But the way he shields that cracker,
Tenderly, clumsily,
And toys with its eating,
And rolls it under his tongue,
Makes you know,
Somehow, and surely,
That a simple soda cracker,
Dark with the flour of evil days,
Is lifting the fog in Private Samarski's soul.
                    JOHN P. ROCHE, Lt., Q. M. C.

"Buddies o' Mine" was hardly without its undercurrent of sentiment:

You were right, Mister William T. Sherman,
    When you uttered that message divine,
For only today I have laid them away—
    Those two little buddies of mine.

We had crossed in a transport from Gotham
    To the land that the papers call France;
We had buddied together in any old weather,
    Together we'd taken our chance.

And many a time in our hiking
    When I was unable to crawl,
They carried the pack that was slung on my back—
    With never a kick at it all.

Rugged, they were, tough and sturdy—
    Though maybe they never would shine

In a high-brow café on the rue de Broadway,
  They were genuine buddies of mine.

And now that their duty is finished
  The thought that is left to console
Is: though they were rough, they were made of real stuff
  And each of them harbored a sole.

So thus, when the snow fell this morning
  And keen as a whip was the air,
My buddies checked in—to a fat sergeant's grin,
  Who issued me then a new pair.

                              PVT. JOHN P. E. BRIGGS,
                                       A. P. O. 795.

Neither was "Bon Camarade":

  We both were tramping the same way
  And both were glad of the golden weather.
  He spoke no English; I could say
  Ten words of French. We walked together.

  We both were proud that we fought for France,
  And called each other "Camarade."
  He left at length with a gay "Bon chance,"
  And all the cigarettes I had.

                              RALPH LINTON, Cpl., 149th F. A.

There is a touch of the artlessness that betrays art in "Albert in the Argonne, or, Over the Top With a Bookcase," which was preceded by this explanatory note:

(Delivered with pathos upon presentation to Sgt. Albert Dietrich, 138th Personnel Section, of a tin medal in recognition of his great services in the recent Argonne offensive, when he went over the top with a book-case on his back, service records and field desk in one hand and a bottle of ink and a pen in the other.)

  Listen, my friends, and I will tell
  How Albert Dietrich went through hell.
  'Twas up in the Argonne, where we put on our drive
  That Albert went through hell and came out alive.

It was early on the morn of September two-six
That we started out the Germans to fix,
Some had Eddystones and some a Chauchay,
But Albert, he carried a book-case that day.

The cry of the boys was "On to Berlin!"
Still some were in doubt about Albert getting in.
Jack Davis, he said, "It's Berlin or Bust,"
And Dietrich's book-case fell in the dust.

'Tis said that the shrapnel then filled the air;
We were calling for help from the boys back there.
Albert shouted, "I'm doing all that I can—
My little son Otto says I'm a brave man."

We battled the Hun for the next five days
Going over the top wave after wave—
Cheppy, Very and Charpentry fell—
And then we came back our story to tell.

Many asked Albert just what he did,
He was smeared with mud and had lost his tin lid.
Then Albert told of his part in the fight,
How he carried his book-case and records day and night.

The question is asked in the Personnel
"What would have happened if Albert had fell?
Would the Germans have whipped us and pushed us back
If Albert hadn't been there with his book-case on his back?"

There were many tender threnodies to buddies who had gone. The anonymous writer of "Goodbye, Old Pal" even left his comrade nameless:

Goodbye, old Pal.
I've been to hell and back again;
There's where you fell, in mud, and blood, and rain.
Sure, we won—you paid the bill;
You swapped your life for that green hill;
Goodbye, old Pal.

> Goodbye, old Pal.
> We're sailing home, our job is done;
> But still your grave's a trench against the Hun.
> Call us back; we'll make our stand
> Where you keep guard in No Man's Land.
> Goodbye, old Pal.   SOLDIER.

The Rainbow Division went home to most of America and the 165th Infantry, the old 69th New York, marched up its own Main Street—Fifth Avenue. *The Stars and Stripes* received this tribute to Sergeant Joyce Kilmer:

> Today the Sixty-ninth parades—
> I cannot see them through the trees.
>
> The trees who lift their arms in thanks
> That those they love have wandered back,
> And call a benediction down
> Upon the ones who stayed behind
> To guard the trees of France.
>
> The trees who through the winter days
> Unbendingly present their arms.
> The trees who stand so firmly there,
> The thin line of eternity.
> Not snow nor rain can wash from them
> Their certain immortality.
>
> The Sixty-ninth parades today—
> I cannot see them through the trees.
>   H. J. M.

But the theme of themes was home. The writer of the following lines frankly entitled them "Homesickness" and goaded his Pegasus to a lively gait perhaps to keep the mist from his eyes:

> Gotta be a soldier. Gotta stick t' biz—
> Gotta keep on marchin' while the marchin' is;
>   Gotta keep salutin';
>   Gotta keep in trim;
>   Bugle keeps on tootin',
>   Home looks mighty dim.

Gotta keep on stitchin',
  Gotta foller like a lamb—
But, boy, my feet am itchin'
  For th' feel of Alabam'.

Gotta answer reveille. Gotta stand retreat;
Gotta be K. P. sometimes—soldiers has t' eat;
  Gotta keep a-workin'
    Jes' like there was war;
  Ain't no time for shirkin'
    Lots o' jobs in store;
  Ain't no time for switchin'
    Er lettin' things go slam—
But, boy, my feet am itchin'
    Fer the feel of Alabam'.

Mammy writes she's "waitin' with a possum pie,"
My doggone mouth keeps waterin' till my throat is dry.
  "Watermelon's handy—
    Sugar cake am hot—
  Enclosin' love from Mandy—"
    An' yet a feller's got
  T' sweat here in a kitchen—
    It's all fer Uncle Sam,
  But, boy, my feet's sure itchin'
    Fer the feel of Alabam'.
  Sometimes, my lips get twitchin'—
    Baby that I am—
  But, boy, my feet's done itchin'
    Fer the feel of Alabam'.

E. RUTHERFORD, JR., Corp., Tours.

Here is "The Song of St. Nazaire," from the typewriter of a *Stars and Stripes* alumnus:

Hurry on, you doughboys, with your rifle and your pack;
Bring along your cooties with your junk upon your back;
We'll house you and delouse you and we'll douse you in a bath,
And when the boat is ready you can take the Western Path.

For it's home, kid, home—when you slip away from here—
No more slum or reveille, pounding in your ear;
Back on clean, wide streets again—
Back between the sheets again
Where a guy can lay in bed and sleep for half a year.

Hurry on, you lousy buck, for your last advance;
You are on your final hike through the mud of France;
Somewhere in the Good Old Town, you can shift the load,
Where you'll never see again an M. P. down the road.

For it's home, boy, home, with the old ship headed west;
No more cooties wandering across your manly chest;
No more M. P.'s grabbing you—
No more majors crabbing you—
Nothing for a guy to do except to eat and rest.

Move along, you Army, while the tides are on the swell.
Where a guy can get away and not be S. O. L.
Where the gold fish passes and the last corned willy's through,
And no top sergeant's waiting with another job to do.

For it's home, kid, home—when the breakers rise and fall—
Where the khaki's hanging from a nail against the wall—
Clean again and cheerful there—
Handing out an ear full there—
Where you never have to jump at the bugle's call.

GRANTLAND RICE.

And let it not be forgotten that there were ladies in waiting:

I got a letter
Yesterday,
An' it said
That she (She's my girl)—
An' it said
That she just heard
That I was in the hospital,

An' both
My arms were shot off.
An' she (She's my girl)—
An' she said
She was prostrated
And that she'd
Take care of me
When I got back,
Dearest.
An' it was signed
Helen,
An' she's my girl,
An' I ain't
In the hospital,
An' both my arms
Are on.
But she
Can take care of me
When I get back.
An' besides,
I'll show her
That my arms
Ain't shot off
When I
Get home.

                    G. A. C.

A good-natured lament from a stay-at-home could awake our sympathy for those whose lot it had been to remain on "The Other Side":

HE
Darling, here's your hero bold;
Silver stripes instead of gold
Shine upon my sleeve today,
'Cause I couldn't sail away.

SHE
But, my darling, don't you bleat.
No one thinks you had cold feet;

You had to do as you were told—
Silver stripes instead of gold.
      David M. MacQuarrie,
      Chaplain, Camp Merritt, N. J.

Those who had come safely through shot and shell must continue to live, contended the author of "Endorsing an Appeal":

In a letter to President Wilson, the Prince of Bosnia asks the President to watch over the interests of Bosnia and Herzegovina. He desires only the possession of his estate usurped by the Hapsburgs. He says that he is obliged to work in order to eat.—News Dispatch.

Wilson! Thou judge of all disputes
    Within this world's arena,
Take pity on a hungry prince
    Who daily groweth leaner,
Him who was Prince of Bosnia
    And of Herzegovina.

Ere Bosnia became a pawn
    In war's colossal gambit
The Prince he had a cushy job,
    As near as I can lamp it:
And work (that low and menial thing)—
    He never did a dambit.

But read his piteous story in
    The Paris New York Herald!
The haughty Hapsburg sits upon
    The throne his flight imperiled;
The Hohenzollern gets on edge
    On beer the Bosnians barrelled!

Wilson! Give ear to this appeal
    And do not lightly flout it;
Hunt up a well-fed workless job
    And give this grand old scout it;
And—I'm a casual, too, so make
    It two while you're about it.
      Morris G. Bishop, 1st Lt., Inf.

Former Lieutenant Bishop is now an instructor in French at Cornell, which situation, for the sake of students and faculty alike, is not, I trust, the workless job he had in mind.

There were a multitude of parodists among us:

A. E. F. MOTHER GOOSE

Peter, Peter, pumpkin eater,
    Had a wife and couldn't keep her.
Went to France as his country's guest
    And Uncle Sammy did the rest.

Simple Simon met a pieman
    On the way to chow.
Said Simple Simon to the pieman,
    "This is luck, I vow."
The pieman made a clearance sale
    And Si spent all his pay,
And lost his well-earned rep of being
    Such a simp that day.

Jack and Jill went up the hill
    To get a pail of l'eau.
Jack fell down and broke his crown.
    (Too much vin rouge, you know.)

Little Jack Horner sat in a corner
    Eating his Christmas pie.
But it came in a nine by four by three,
    So most of it was shy.

Little Bo Peep, she lost her sheep,
    And thought she'd find them soon.
But she made a poor guess, for the officers' mess
    Had mutton chops that noon.

Old King Cole is a merry old soul,
    Oh, a merry old soul is he,

For he's on his way to the U. S. A.
Across the deep blue sea.

                                                A. J. M.

The "nine by four by three" allusion above demands a footnote for the sake of the uninitiate reader. For Christmas of 1918 each of us could receive from home only a single package nine inches long, four wide, and three deep. Probably it had to be, but the ruling was responsible for more profanity than any other indignity which the A. E. F. endured.

A SOLDIER'S GARDEN OF VERSES

The world is so full of a number of Huns
I'm sure we should all take good care of our guns.

. . . .

Oh, a tent is a wonderful place
    When the smoke blows all about
And the rain comes down in little drops
    And puts the fire out!

. . . .

The pen beneath our billet floor
Has two pigs in it, maybe more;
We've never seen them, but we know
That that's where all the leavings go.

. . . .

The goat's a pleasant animal,
Who eats most anything at all;
He steals the cookies and the string
And always smells like everything.

. . . .

I'm glad I do not like to fight,
    It's nasty to shed blood
And march all night without a light,
    Especially if there's mud.

. . . .

It's very wrong to be about
    At 9 o'clock when sergeant looks

To see whose blankets are not out
And finds someone to help the cooks.

. . . .

In drill time it is very nice
To whip the cream and chop the ice,
To fetch the water and the wood,
And help the cooks prepare the food.
116TH AMMUNITION TRAIN.

DRINKIN' ON THE RHINE

A soldier from Milwaukee lay dying in the rear,
There was lack of vinous comfort, there was lack of even beer.
He had fought the fight of absence—fifteen days he'd been away;
As he gasped his last a comrade bent to hear what he might say:
"Tell the boys I'll soon be pushing up the daisies here in France,
While the Allied hosts in Germany are holding their advance,
That I'll never live to realize this one fond dream of mine—
Of drinking beer in Bingen, dear Bingen on the Rhine.

"Ah comrade, it shall never be! I'm done, and that's no lie,
But, oh, for one good schooner or a stein before I die!
I'm sick, so sick of pinard and the wines they serve you here
That the signing of the peace pact makes me think of frothy beer
Served in some old quaint bierlokal reeking of the smell of kraut,
Not by some coquettish mam'selle, but by Gretchen fat and stout;
And I'd forget about the days of cognac and of wine
With a pail of suds before me, there in Bingen on the Rhine."
DAVID DARRAH, Mallet Reserve.

THE M. P.'s WILL GIT YOU
(Begging Mr. Riley's Pardon)

Uncle Sammy's Army has come to France to stay,
To sweep the streets and alleys up and keep the Huns away;
But now the war is over and the fighting all is done,
We want to go to Paris just to have a little fun.

But one thing keeps us here in camp; it is the brave M. P.;
He's always got an eagle eye to ketch you on a spree;
So don't you try to take a trip, and don't you chase about,
Or the M. P.'s will git you if you don't watch out!

Once there was a doughboy who thought he'd try to stall,
And when he went to bed at night—he didn't go at all!
The sergeant thought he saw him leave his bunk there by the wall,
And when they turned the covers down he wasn't there at all.
They called his name at reveille, he didn't answer "Here";
They seeked him all through England, France and everywhere, I fear;
But finally they found him locked in walls with bars so stout. . . .
Well, the M. P.'s will git you if you don't watch out.

                                                    H. C. C.

Elegy Written in a Barracks
(Thanking Mr. Gray)

The bugler blows first call of coming day,
    The drizzling rains upon the barracks sweep,
The doughboys stir but in their bunks they stay
    And lazily fall back to pleasant sleep.

Now comes a distant call of reveille,
    And all the world is silent, chill and damp,
Save where the doughboys wrapped in blankets stay,
    And echoed snores resound throughout the camp.

Save that from yonder nicely furnished room,
    The hard-boiled top does to the clerk complain
That doughboys there prefer to sleep till noon,
    And vows he'll chase them out into the rain.

Beneath the time worn shack the top appears,
    Where flows the rain in many a steady stream,
Each in a narrow bunk but naught he fears
    The raving they will substitute for dream.

A call upon his whistle, breathing scorn,
   Is followed by the top's gruff voice to bawl—
"Get up, you lazy dogs, d'you know it's morn,
   You fellers sure have got a lot of gall."

EDGAR BEATTY.

Even the shock of prohibition was not too numbing to anesthetize the lyrical impulse. In proof thereof our own Sergeant Carroll offered up "Drink to Me Only", and no one seemed to notice at the time his remarkably inexact use of the word oasis:

Drink to me only with thine eyes
   (Though God made them to wink with);
It's "Taps" at last for Scotch and ryes
   And things we used to drink with.
O Land, thou once were Paradise
   Of liquoring and wat'ring places;
What made the Councils of the Wise
   Transform you into an oasis?

Drink to me only with thine eyes
   (Though they were made for flashing);
The corpse of Johnnie Walker lies
   With others just as dashing
Beneath the faded Edelweiss.
   O Land, we ask, don't thusly shame us,
Bring back the schooners—largest size—
   Of that which made Milwaukee famous!

Drink to me only with thine eyes
   (Though they were made for sleeping);
Deep in the dusk are longing sighs
   Of kindred spirits vigil keeping.
O Land, revoke that law which tries,
   Without appropriate explanations,
To let your Councils of the Wise
   Put Carrie in the League of Nations!

Earlier in this comment appeared the statement that Private Abian A. Wallgren's metier was the comic strip, the posturing of the eternal predicament of being a soldier, and that as a serious cartoonist, a torch-bearer in one of the grand contro-versies of history, he sometimes left something (such as a Baldridge) to be desired.

"MY, HOW SHE HAS CHANGED!"—WALLGREN'S REACTION TO THE ADOPTION OF THE
EIGHTEENTH AMENDMENT

The enactment of prohibition was not one of those times. Putting his heart and his soul into his pen, Wallgren achieved a masterpiece of ironic caricature which I am very much afraid typified an all but unanimous A. E. F. opinion. There were one or two objectors, but their protests were drowned in an overwhelming chorus of fervent approval.

The staff devised a symposium labelled "Prohibition: Some A. E. F. Views" which was made up of alleged dispatches from various centers of dissatisfaction in the A. E. F. and elsewhere. It is conceivable that the allusion to Nebraska in the final dispatch may fall something short of intelligibility. Let it be recalled, then, that it was the voice of the Nebraska State Legislature which made the Eighteenth Amendment come true. Thirty-two affirmative votes were needed, and Nebraska's was the thirty-second.

"America has gone dry," said the cables. Forthwith this office was swamped with dispatches from all over the A. E. F. describing the effect of the announcement in various scattered military circles. In some of these circles the radii were completely dislocated. The swamp continues, the only portion of the A. E. F. which has not yet been heard from being Russia, land of the six-months long Arctic night. The reason for this is the fact that the news has not yet reached there. When it does the night will be a lot nightier than it ever was before, it is said.

The only group on whom the news has had no effect to date is a battery of Maine artillerymen, who, when informed of the event, merely asked: "What is prohibition? What has it to do with the licker question?"

TRIPOLI, Jan. 23.—Several troop transports have landed on the North African coast, having gone astray at sea. It is alleged that the captains became confused and made for the Sahara desert. The troops were all singing:

> It's home, boys, home
> It's home we should-a been,
> Home, boys, home,
> In the land of Liberty (prolonged laughter).

TOURS, Jan. 23.—Applications for transfers to the Department of Rents, Requisitions and Claims, billed (by no one who knows anything about it) as "the last bunch to go," have swamped the local post office.

PAUILLAC, Jan. 23.—The U. S. A. has nothing on this place. Pauillac went dry 24 hours after the news was received from the States. More has been ordered by wire.

LIVERPOOL, Jan. 23.—Seventeen hundred American soldiers will reach America 27 hours later than was intended as the result of an episode preceding their departure here today. As they marched to their vessel, the Megalomania, they sang:

Sing a song of sixpence,
Pocket full o' rye.

An alert embarkation official, catching the words, insisted that every man be searched again before boarding the transport. Results of the inquiry have been kept secret.

ST. AIGNAN, Jan. 23.—Sgt. Iva Weigh, once of Atlanta, was engaged in extricating his other foot from a mud puddle when the news of prohibition reached this town.

"My experience with prohibition," he said, "is that it greatly increased the cost of licker in Georgia."

HOCKBELSCHUNDGESUNDHEITSTEIN, Ger., Jan. 23.—When the news of prohibition reached here, Sgt. James Geharty Gee fainted. He was able to sit up the next day, and could be heard singing in a weak voice:

Glorious, glorious!
One glass of strawberry ice cream soda for the four of us!

GIEVRES, Jan. 23.—The Baggage Service here has received many letters similar to the following:

From: Corporal Archibald K. Thirsty.
To: The Baggage Service.
Subject: Packages.
1. How much baggage can a fellow take home who carries no equipment?
2. What is the exact weight of a keg of vin rouge?

BORDEAUX, Jan. 23.—Colonel Whozzis was reading his morning G. O.'s when interviewed about prohibition here this morning. He said, "Damn."

ORLY, Jan. 23.—Consternation greeted the announcement in this town of the impending dryness of the United States. A delegation was immediately formed at the Air Field and proceeded to Mme. Bussard's café to hold an indignation meeting.

Mme. Bussard, always anxious to sympathize with these rigolo Americans, tried hard to grasp the situation. Sgt. Jones did his best to explain.

"Les Etats Unis have gone dry—sont allé sec. Compree?"

It was obvious that Madame did not.

"Here, you," and the sergeant clutched at a French soldier who was sipping his drink in the corner and who knew a few words of English, such as "Avez-vous une cigarette?" "Tell Madame here there won't be any buvettes back home when we get there. Tell her that while we was all over here fighting, the prohibitionists stole a march on us and that now we won't be able to get anything to drink except citronade."

This was turned into French and poured into Madame's bewildered ear. She laughed heartily.

"Mais, c'est incroyable," she protested. "Est-ce que c'est possible que tout le monde est malade la-bas? Alors, vous devez avoir honte, vous autres."

"Mais non, mais non. They don't have to give up drinking. They just decided to do it anyway."

"Then," said Mme. Bussard, with conviction, "they must all be crazy."

"You said a mouthful, Madame," replied the sergeant.

"And Madame says," the interpreter went on, "that she understands it all now quite perfectly except for one little thing. I have translated for her this cry of yours, 'Down with Nebraska!' She has never sold any of Nebraska here. Does it come in bottles and could she procure some from your co-operative?"

"Oh, it's no use," said the sergeant. "I can never explain. America's in a terrible state, and I guess it's Nebraska."

"Ah," said Madame, as she dusted the cobwebs from the thirty-second bottle of Pommard. "Je ne comprends pas."

"Well, Madame," said the sergeant, "you've got nothing on the A. E. F."

Prohibition had not come early enough to ruin the A. E. F.'s Christmas. It was the second Christmas in France for the old-timers on *The Stars and Stripes* staff, and we felt uppity enough about it to reminisce in public:

They were five soldiers, and they were seated about a table—a round table —in an attractive little restaurant in an equally attractive little French city. It was Christmas Day, 1918. Good things had been set before them, including turkey with real stuffing, and there was a prospect, along toward the dim and distant end of the meal, of coffee with real sugar in it.

The first of the five sighed pleasurably and let his eyes linger on the white tablecloth.

"A year ago today," he said, "things weren't exactly like this. And yet it was one of the most pleasant Christmases I ever had. I had been in Tours for five weeks—my first five weeks in France—where it had been so mild that we used to go around the barracks grounds without our blouses. Then, two days before Christmas, they sent us up to a high hill near Chaumont. It was like changing from Florida to Minnesota. For Haute-Marne was a single sheet of snow; the air was beautifully crisp and cold, and it made you want to go out of doors and stand up straight and fill your lungs with it.

"The first day up there I was picked for K. P. When I went into the kitchen, the cook, a real old-timer, told me that K. P. tricks up thataway lasted a week. So I resigned myself to seven days of it—including Christmas.

"I didn't like the prospect at first. But when, on Christmas Eve, I saw the cook laying out I don't know how many apple pies, with real apples in them, and heard him say that he had been making tarts for soldiers for the last five Christmas Eves, I began to grow more enthusiastic.

"Christmas came, and I was still K.P. At noon the boys began to flock in —we were only about a hundred—and sat down to turkey, and I've forgotten how many kinds of vegetables, and apple pie—a piece to a man. Before they began a young aviator offered prayer. I guess he wasn't used to praying, for his prayer was a familiar, offhand kind of thing, but it was so genuinely sincere that if ever a prayer was listened to, that prayer was.

"That was my Christmas. Oh, yes, and I forgot to tell you that, being K. P., I knocked down four pieces of that apple pie—the best I ever tasted."

"A year ago today," said the second man, "I was aboard the good ship Tuscania, lying in the harbor at Liverpool. For a Christmas gift, I found in my sock a piece of hard, dry bread that a rat had feasted upon, a bone—no meat on it—from the leg of a chicken, and an empty can of sardines. For Christmas dinner I had a piece of corned willie for turkey, and for cranberries I had tripe.

"And then, for entertainment, a second lieutenant came along and bawled me out for not having cleaned up the mess by my bunk that I had made two nights before when one of those sickly little waves got funny with the ship and skidded up a couple of miles out of our course.

"Now that was a year ago, mind you, and many things have happened since then. The Tuscania, as you know, went down. But the second lieutenant who bawled me out went up. He's a major now."

"A year ago today," said the third man, "I thought I was the luckiest guy in the world, because three of my Christmas packages—we got man size ones in those days, you know—came on Christmas Eve, and when I got up for a delightfully late 7:30 reveille—postponed an hour in honor of the day—there they all were, smokes and eats and socks and all the things I had been hankering for ever since my arrival in France two months back. Right there I decided to pass up Cook Louie's breakfast, and beat it back to the billet with the rest of the squad just as soon as we were dismissed, there to dejeuner on cocoanut cakes and all the other well-known indigestibles. It was some breakfast.

"All this happened in the little town of Mont-le-Neufchâteau, in the department of Vosges, just above the well-known Yank town of Neufchâteau. Some of the gang went down there in the afternoon, after Christmas dinner in the mess shack, but I didn't. Reason? I was confined to the limits of Montey for having gone A W O L up to Nancy with a bunch of Y. M. C. A. men.

"Well, like every other outfit that was well quartered, we had a tree up in the square, and presents for all the French youngsters, and those of us who were godly went to mass in the little cold stone church and tried to keep warm by helping the wavering choir out on its 'Venite, adoremus.' And after that the battalion had a great get-together party, in the course of which the major —he's a loot-colonel now and a D. S. C.—read a speech in French, to which the mayor, who was my landlord, responded in much better French. In the course of the proceedings I made a speech, too, in which I took a slam at the major (he had confined me personally)."

"A year ago today," said the fourth man, "I was in a training camp at Langres with the snow a foot from the ground and the mercury trying to get out through the bottom of the thermometer to meet it. The features of the previous three or four weeks had been squads right, cold, candlelight, beans, slum and sore feet in generous overdoses. The afternoon before, until 8 o'clock at night, we had chased an imaginary enemy several kilometers across plowed fields and through woods, with the snow dropping from the trees down our backs—and melting.

"I answered reveille at 6 a. m. and went back to bed because the stove wouldn't burn. The Q. M. fell down and for Christmas dinner we had beans, for which there wasn't room after we had swallowed our indignation.

"In the afternoon a friend and I decided we ought to mitigate the bean atrocity with champagne. We went into town and found the places where champagne might be bought greatly outnumbered by M. P.'s, but we finally got a bottle with the understanding that we couldn't drink it on the premises.

"For two hours we hunted for a place to down it comfortably, eventually consuming it standing in the snow behind the Army Staff College, drinking out of one mess cup by turns. After eating deux oeufs—omelette—et pommes frites—oui, oui—oui, oui—I went back to the barracks. The stove was as cold and the room as dismal as the rest of the day had been. The whole room—20 men—went to bed at 8 o'clock to keep warm."

The fifth man was silent.

"Well," they said, turning to him, "how about you?"

"I haven't anything to tell," said the fifth man. "Nothing extraordinary happened in my young life last Christmas. But if you must know ——

"A year ago today," said the fifth man, "I was home."

Christmas of 1918, too, inspired some of our poets, none of them more effectively than Corporal Howard A. Herty, whose "The Christmas Call" will always be remembered (by me at any rate) as one of the loveliest bits we printed:

Far above the crash of conflict, ere the star shells flecked the morning,
    And we answered with defiance for the cause we love and know,
In our memory crept a picture of a day long since forgotten.
    And we thought of Grandma's turkey, and the Christmas tree, and snow.

We have slogged along the highways, we have heard adventure calling;
    We have banished dreams of comfort as we toyed with Fate each day;
Still across the red horizon, as the cold, gray dusk is falling,
    Stalks a vision of our kid days, and of Santa and his sleigh.

Perhaps we were still in our kid days. We were, of course, old men by comparison with the hosts of Grant and Lee—very old men by comparison with some of the beardless German drafts of 1918, very young men alongside the grizzled Landsturmers who now stood without hitching in the P. W. cages and wondered just how much of a mess things were in at home. President Wilson could call us boys without imparting thereto an air of "There, there, my good fellows." But we would be boys to nobody else—except, perhaps, in the privacy of our self-communings (which was about the only privacy the A. E. F. got), to ourselves.

CHAPTER FOURTEEN

BUT NOT FOREVER

BY THE beginning of April there were considerable areas in France where for hours on end one would not hear a word of English. A third of the A. E. F. had gone home. The War Department and G. H. Q. were doing even better than they had promised. But even though we were reduced to a skeleton force of 1,300,000, there were still enough of us to make it worth while to continue to get out a newspaper.

And there was still plenty of news to put in it. The older generation may recall a peace conference which produced a peace that was everybody's except ours. Third

"A. E. F. SCHOOLDAYS," BY WALLGREN

(later Second) Lieutenant Hilmar J. Baukhage was selected to handle the assignment and nobly upheld the traditions of his calling save for the regrettable occasion on which he fell asleep during the discussion of the Schleswig plebiscite.

Captain Joseph Mills Hanson, whom readers of the earlier portions of these notes will recall as a stalwart among the Army's Poets, began soon after the Armistice a series of narratives of the activities of the combat divisions which remains, to my mind, the best summary of the A. E. F.'s battle participation that has yet been written. Captain Hanson was especially loaned by the Historical Section of G. H. Q. for this task and had, of course, full access to all the necessary documents in the preparation of his narratives.

In the issue for March 14th had been initiated a series of articles by Sergeant J. W. Rixey Smith on the work of the major special and technical services that go to make up a modern army. In these eight articles due recognition was paid to the efforts of the 29,000 officers and men of the Engineers (Railway), the 26,000 in the Motor Transport Corps, the 78,000 in the Air Service, the 33,000 in the Signal Corps, the 14,000 in the Ordnance Department, the 147,000 in the Medical Department, the 100,000 in the Quartermaster Corps, and the 174,000 in the Engineers. The following extract is from Smith's account of the activities of the Signal Corps:

The most interesting and spectacular modes of signaling in combat were employed only in emergencies. Generally, if the lines were cut, the Very pistol with its star shell cartridges or the 15-centimeter French projector could be used. Many times pigeons supplied the only means of communication, as in the case of the Lost Battalion in the Argonne. Runners, of course, played a large part in the relaying of messages after the fighting became continuously open last summer.

The Signal Corps men at the front, both in stationary trench warfare and in the open advances, did their work in the face of the same dangers and hardships that faced the doughboy, suffered heavily in losses, and gained richly in thrilling experiences worth while remembering. They went over the top with their comrades and oftentimes had to go ahead of the Infantry.

When the town of Vaux was captured, June 30, 1918, because of a turning movement, a Signal Corps detachment reached the objective before the Infantry. A man was sent out to install a telephone. He found a likely looking dugout and went in, telephone in hand. He found nine Germans hurriedly packing up to move. He told them he wanted to put in a telephone. They objected and he insisted.

A fight ensued, and the lone American was decidedly underneath, when one of the German soldiers spoke in Polish. Once again the cosmopolitan character of the American Army saved the day. The telephone man was a native-born Pole himself, and in a few minutes he had re-enforcements, with the result that shortly after he emerged from the dugout with a broken telephone and nine prisoners, five of whom were Poles.

There was one kind of work done by the Signal Corps at the front which for interest and daring vies with anything the records of the war hold. This was the task performed by 12 officers and 402 men of the Radio Section, who maintained six different kinds of stations for keeping tabs on the enemy and policing our own lines to see that the enemy did not keep any tabs on us.

They had Intelligence intercept stations which copied messages in code from German ground-radio stations; airplane intercept stations which intercepted messages between enemy planes and ground stations; airplane goniometric stations which located enemy observation planes; control stations which supervised and policed the work of the American radio stations; goniometric stations which got bearings on enemy radio stations; and last but not least, the listening stations which copied telephone and T. P. S. messages of the enemy.

The story of how the Germans devised a new code for use at the front and of how the Allies got on to it before the Germans themselves illustrates the finesse

GERMAN PRISONERS FILLING IN OLD TRENCH LINES, VAUX, SPRING, 1919, AS
SKETCHED BY BALDRIDGE

of our Signal Corps in this kind of work. The new code was supposed to have gone into effect March 11, 1918. On March 13 an American Intelligence intercept station caught a message from a German station which had just received a message in the new code, asking that the message be repeated in the old.

From the call letters given in the message it was possible to find both the original message in the new code and the repetition in the old. This assured the solution of the new code before the Germans themselves were familiar with it.

As a contrast, and as a curious commentary on the much talked of German efficiency and American unpreparedness, when a code book was stolen from us by the Germans, not only was another code ready but our operators were actually prepared to use it when the order went out to put it in immediate effect.

There is no more thrilling page in the romance of the war than the little history of the American listening stations of the Signal Corps. They were always to the front and sometimes in No Man's Land itself, but wherever they might chance to be located, they were, as one of the men described them, "very near Heaven." Their business was eavesdropping, and if they didn't hear any good of themselves, they managed to do the doughboy lots of good.

Loops of wires were constructed out in No Man's Land parallel to the enemy's lines, and the tiny electric currents induced in them were magnified by means of an amplifier. Copper mesh mats or metallic rods were buried as near the enemy wires as possible and from them wires led to the amplifier. By this means ground currents and leaks from the enemy wires were magnified to audibility.

The planting of these "grounds" near the enemy's lines called out some of the most heroic instances of personal bravery and resourcefulness at the front. Time after time these men were caught by the spotlight of a star shell as they crawled out in the night toward the German lines and were seen no more. Often they were caught between a double barrage probably started by their own sentry. More often, however, they wiggled their way through barbed wire and shell holes, planted their wires, and returned to reap the benefit of their daring.

The devotion of the A. E. F. to its newspaper was well attested by the activities of the Soldiers' Service Department, a creation born of its own necessity and nourished to lusty adulthood by the ministrations of Army Field Clerk George W. B. Britt and a busy staff of assistants. Britt, then serving as assistant to the officer in charge, was mildly startled one morning early in his *Stars and Stripes* career when, after opening a lumpy envelope, he extracted therefrom two fragments of bridgework accompanied by a letter asking if somebody on the paper could please have them made into one. Britt obliged. Other and more routine requests began coming in unbidden. Eventually the total ran into the thousands, and Britt and his staff became purveyors of information regarding allotments, allowances, insurance, Liberty Bonds, the location of graves, the securing of marriage licenses, the proper lead from king-jack-ten, and the pennant winner in the Three-I League in 1911.

The Sporting Page had been restored in the final issue of 1918, and Sergeant Nat Worley found it not too difficult a task to fill it with real sports news and at the same time to live up to the paper's earlier promise to omit all reference to stars who had declined to shine in the uniformed firmament. In the issue for January 1st appeared a brief account of the opening of a new Knights of Columbus boxing pavilion in Paris, whereof the last two sentences read: "Gene Tunney, the Marine, had the best of Bob Martin, the 83rd Division giant, and won a popular victory. Martin

"ANOTHER SCRAP OF PAPER? NO!"—A CARTOON MADE IN GERMANY
BY CAPTAIN HERBERT MORTON STOOPS

tried to land a K.O. with his right but the Marine was too clever for him and jabbed the Ohioan's face for a faretheewell." A few weeks later the S. O. S. staged a series of boxing championships at Tours, and the story which featured the lightweight event contained, well toward the end, this paragraph: "Pvt. Gene Tunney, 11th Marines, knocked out Pvt. Dare Lewis, 319th Engineers, with a right to the jaw in the third round of their 175-pound match. Lewis proved inferior in skill, but was game." Tunney won his way through to the A. E. F. championship bouts in Paris on April 26th, in which, fighting as a light heavyweight, he defeated Wagoner Ted Jamison of the Third Army. That same evening his former opponent, Bob Martin, won the A. E. F. heavyweight title by defeating Sergeant Fay Kayser. Back in the States again, Martin was looked upon as the veterans' hope, but it was not to be. The war would be ancient history before the A. E. F. would produce a world's heavy-weight champion.

The close of Private Ross's orphan-adoption campaign a month after the Armistice, with 3,444 war-bereft French children assured of a year's security thanks to A. E. F. generosity—a generosity that approached the two-million franc mark in a less-than-six-francs-to-the-dollar day—by no means checked the influx of contributions. The campaign had gained too much momentum to settle down to small change on short notice. Ross and the Red Cross estimated that at least 450,000 members of the A. E. F. had already contributed to it, which figure, divided into two million francs, gave a per capita contribution of Fr. 4.444 plus.

The idea of the campaign now became to provide a continuation fund to care for the A. E. F.'s little charges (who before the end grew to be 3,567 strong) beyond the original year, and to give them such a start in life as would have been theirs if their fathers had lived. Not unmindful of its own, the staff dispatched Sergeant Woollcott as its envoy most extraordinary to the high court of Marie-Louise Patriarche, and he reported publicly as follows:

> The staff of *The Stars and Stripes* is in disgrace with its own orphan depart-ment. At a time when all the parrains in the A. E. F. are supposed to be plan-ning seriously for the future of the French youngsters they have adopted, the staff forgot all about the future of its own mascot, and on January 2 blew in all its francs on a lot of preposterous inessentials like dolls and mechanicals toys and candy.
>
> However, when Marie-Louise Patriarche finally fell asleep that night—her lips still a bit smeary with chocolate, one arm embracing the new doll, whose fair curls match her own, the other reaching out to protect its go-cart from any burglars that might covet it—when, exhausted from the bewildering excitement

of a most wonderful day, she fell asleep at last, she was probably not worrying much about her future. And as long as your parrains live, you need not worry, Marie-Louise!

When, on New Year's Day, the heap of gifts were amassed, there was need of some one to journey all the way to Pommard, the little village of good wine which nestles among the golden hills of Burgundy. For Marie-Louise lives in Pommard with her grandmother and her mother—her frail, gentle mother who, in these days of homecoming soldiers, seems always to be listening, listening for the step of one who has been missing since the fight in the Vosges in the first black month of the war.

The task of making the pilgrimage was assigned to the most rotund sergeant on the staff because of his superb command of the French language. When, after a night spent in the fragrant and somewhat crowded couloir of a third-class compartment in a train six hours late, he emerged all bedecked with lumpy packages and his own personal traveling library, he may have looked like Santa Claus, but he felt like the devil. Yet he would make the same journey every night of his life if, at the end, he could see such a wide-eyed, welcoming smile as irradiated dismal and dingy Pommard when he encountered Marie-Louise.

For word that one of Marie-Louise's parrains had come to town soon reached the little patronage behind the church where the young Pommardiennes spend their Thursdays. (In France they have a silly way of closing the schools on Thursday instead of on Saturday.) Escorted by her affectionate but somewhat boisterous aunt, Marie-Louise raced to meet the visitor, and in the front room of her grandmother's little café the bundles were opened amid such gusts and cries and explosions of excitement as made both Mme. Patriarche and the fat sergeant so absurdly choky they could not talk at all for a while.

Marie-Louise's Aunt Henriette also shrieked and roared a good deal and immediately assumed that an even half of the windfall was for her. To which Marie-Louise assented as a matter of course.

For it must be admitted that half of every good and every ill that comes to Marie-Louise comes also to her aunt. Marie-Louise is five years old. Aunt Henriette is not quite four. Together they play and eat and sleep.

If Marie-Louise wins a "Bon Point" for inexplicably good behavior at the patronage, so does Henriette. If (as happens sometimes) Marie-Louise is sent to bed in the middle of the afternoon, her aunt shakes her curly head solemnly and regretfully retires at the same hour. So, when Marie-Louise kissed her gratified parrain, she did not have to kiss the other cheek, French fashion. The enchanting Henriette attended to the other cheek.

After the first outbursts, the sergeant sat down to a bit of coffee and quelque-chose in the kitchen. Marie-Louise, with a look of new responsibility weighting her down, set out to take her doll (named Mascotte) for a long, long ride around and around the room. She could join in the conversation only in passing as she rounded the billiard table.

"And what do you think of President Wilson?" she was asked on one of these occasions.

"Who is President Wilson?"

There was a roar at that, and somewhat offended, she was not to be caught like that the next time she passed by.

"What do you think of the League of Nations?"

"I think," said Marie-Louise vaguely, "that it will be very nice."

Marie-Louise is no longer afraid of Americans as she was of the first olive drab detachments that passed through Pommard. Indeed, her own affiliation with the A. E. F. has given her a place on the fringe at the occasional dinner parties the Yanks from Beaune are wont to hold in Pommard of a Sunday night. Moreover, an empty Lowney's can was only one of several pieces of evidence that the Beaune crowd are trying to take our place in her affections. The big stiffs!

Just before it came time for the burly sergeant to tear himself away, there was a great tumult and shouting without, and in came trooping many children of the village, escorting a small and extremely solemn poilu of four who, with the look of one about to mount the scaffold, saluted the sergeant and sent a "gros baiser" to his dear parrains. For Marcel Meney is the mascot of 1st Platoon, Co. F, 166th Inf. If he were feeling any better, he couldn't stand it.

If any member of Company F can slip away for a flying visit to Pommard, he will remember it always. Certainly the weighty sergeant will carry with him all his days the memory of Marie-Louise's arm around his neck and the sight of the two of them—the little girl and her gentle mother—as they stood in the doorway and waved him down the road to Beaune.

So far as concerns Marie-Louise, who happens to be No. 1 in the A. E. F.'s family of French War Orphans, her welfare for the next few years is assured. The personnel of *The Stars and Stripes* has already pledged 1,800 francs for the War Orphan Continuation Fund to be devoted to her education.

With the rapid dissolution of the A. E. F. and the imminence of the discontinuance of *The Stars and Stripes*, the whole enterprise was turned over to the Red Cross for administration when there should be no more Americans in France. The fund totalled, by now, some two and a half million francs, to which some 600,000 members of the A. E. F. had contributed, and it was not going to total much more. Unless—

"AFTER US, THE TOURISTS," BY BALDRIDGE

There was the possibility of an enormous ace in the hole. *The Stars and Stripes* had made money—something like three and a half million francs. It would be just a grand day for the 3,567 if all those francs could be tossed into the continuation fund. Accordingly a petition was drawn up by a group of the editorial staff praying that the profits be so assigned, and the petition was embodied in a bill which was duly introduced in Congress. But Congress was too busy about the larger arithmetic of the war, or fighting President Wilson, or wondering who would be nominated for President in 1920, or telling the country what a terrible thing Article Ten of the League of Nations Covenant was, and nothing happened—nothing except that the three and a half million francs turned into dollars and slid into the United States Treasury, thereby losing their identity as effectively as a glass of water flung into the ocean.

Altogether *The Stars and Stripes* did very well by the United States Treasury. The March 14th issue announced that a book of Wally's cartoons was available, price six francs, the profits to be turned into the continuation fund. Two weeks later the announcement was reprinted—with a difference. The books could still be had, but the Judge Advocate had ruled that the profits from their sale could not go into the continuation fund. They must be turned into the United States Treasury. Who won the war?

A few weeks later we announced that Sergeant Seth T. Bailey's doughboy letters, "Henry's Pal to Henry," with illustrations by Wally, could be had in book form at three francs. This time we did not say where the profits were going. Some months later, when everybody was home again, G. P. Putnam's Sons issued an American edition of "Yanks: A. E. F. Verse" the foreword to which said, among other things: "The royalties accruing from the sale of this book will be devoted to *The Stars and Stripes* Fund for French War Orphans." The royalties were not sensational (it was the forget-the-war era), but such as they were, they did not go into the United States Treasury, and I hope the Judge Advocate is still biting his nails about it.

The Wally cartoon books had other than purely fiscal adventures. Intending purchasers were urged to place their orders with the nearest available field agent of *The Stars and Stripes* rather than to risk the dispatch of single copies. The money came in and the requested quotas were sent out. Cries of acute distress thereupon arose from the field agents. One had ordered two hundred copies and received fifteen, another fifty and received five. It was not an incident for a Sunday-school superintendent to take as a text but it was a heartening tribute to the esteem in which the A. E. F. held Wally.

The original suggestion for a society of American World War veterans was probably made on April 6, 1917. There was an occasional intimation of the inevitability of such an organization in *The Stars and Stripes* of war days, but nothing more than that—the only organizations for which there was room at the moment were the

United States Army and the United States Navy. A few weeks after the Armistice a thoroughly well-intentioned program was set in motion for the establishment of a veterans' association to be called Comrades in Service. Perhaps the chief defect of the plan was the name it chose, but that was enough.

On the front page of the issue for March 7th was printed a story headed "Veterans of A. E. F. in Liberty League." It announced that a caucus would be held in Paris on March 15th, 16th and 17th at which "definite steps for the organization of a veterans' association were to be taken." The whole business was pretty vague; in fact, the one important positive assertion about the organization in the story was this: "It will be known as the Liberty League." That much, obviously, was certain. As it turned out, virtually all the conjectures in the story became fact, and the one element which was not conjecture but affirmation was never heard of more.

Another advance story on the projected meeting, now but a day distant, appeared in the issue for March 14th. On the editorial page of the same issue was printed this comment, entitled "Veterans All":

> The air these days is crowded with suggestions for the forming of a veterans' association to preserve the American comradeship of the war, to inherit the task and the glory of the G. A. R. Tomorrow a caucus will open in Paris to plan, tentatively, an organization to perpetuate "the relationships formed in the military service."
>
> If such an organization is to thrive and serve America, it will be tied to no creed or party. It will grind no axes. It will forget the distinctions of rank which the Army happened to require for its job in hand; for, of course, times have greatly changed since the days when the society of the Cincinnati and the Loyal Legion were formed for officers only and the descendants of officers.
>
> Rather will it try to carry back into civilian life something of the shoulder-to-shoulder spirit of a citizen army, drawn from all social classes, all geographical sections of the people that sent it forth—a citizen army in which the scholar divided corned willy with the unlettered, in which the millionaire buttoned shelter-halves with the laborer, in which the descendants of the Mayflower company buddied with the later immigrants.
>
> Naturally, it will, for a time, look back through the softening mists of memory on these days of camp and bivouac, and yet, if its chief stock in trade is reminiscence, if it looks only backward, then will the germ of death be in its fiber at its very birth, and its days will be short in the land.
>
> The only veterans' association worth forming will be one that speaks to all the millions of America's youth that were enlisted to fight once more the age-

long fight for freedom and, as they melt back into the body of American citizenship, calls on them to fight that fight all the days of their lives. For—

There's nigh two million fellows from the country of the blest
Who know the cause for which their comrades died,

"THE PROMISED LAND," BY BALDRIDGE

Who have crossed the sluggish shallows where their little life streams ran
And broadened just a trifle, you will find;
And their vision's cleaner, clearer, and they hold just that much dearer
The great and glorious land they left behind!

(The poem by Sergeant Albert J. Cook from which these lines were quoted has been printed entire in Chapter Five.)

The success of the caucus can be measured from the fact that *The Stars and Stripes* led the paper with it in the issue for March 21st—which date was just one year removed from the devastating German offensive in the north that had all but ended the war. The story carried a two-column head: "American Legion, to Unite Wars' Veterans, on Way to Formation." A Signal Corps photograph of the meeting exhibits Sergeant Tyler H. Bliss of the staff occupying a prominent place at the press table opposite Army Field Clerk Dan Sowers, *The Stars and Stripes*' first newsboy, who had come down from Chaumont for the meeting.

The occasion produced, in addition to the lead story, the usual allotment of brief notes that trailed almost every important happening in the chronicle of the A. E. F.:

The first interim of laughter in the caucus—and there were several after it—came in the opening minutes Saturday when a member of the 79th Division, responding to requests from the chair for a suggested method of parliamentary procedure, clutched the balcony rail in front of him and said, without a trace of stage fright:

"I move we adopt the rules of the House of Representatives, with one amendment: that the one hour rule be changed to a five minute rule."

And it was so.

When one speaker pointed dramatically to the painted notice under which the delegates from a certain division would have sat if they had been there and asked who was going to represent that outfit, a captain who, had he been a top sergeant, would have merited the description hard-boiled, arose and said:

"My outfit's gone home, so I suppose all I can represent is the AWOL's and venereals."

The S. O. S. made a reputation for rapid action. Just before the caucus took a ten-minute recess Saturday a delegate observed that if the S. O. S. wished to get a vote for each of its base sections and other subdivisions it should have painted signs, similar to those used by the various combat divisions, G. H. Q., the Paris Command and other delegations. He also suggested that if the S. O. S. wanted such signs it was up to the S. O. S. to furnish them itself. When the caucus reconvened, the S. O. S. had the signs.

"Think of me being a veteran of anything at all," mused one of the enlisted delegates. "And when I left home I wasn't even old enough to buy a drink—legally."

Action may have been expedited by the reminder given a colonel shortly after the opening of the first day's session. "We must remember that we have only three days here," he said, "and Paris is well equipped with eagle eyes."

Lieut. Col. F. T. Pusey, from the 28th Division, has evidently learned much about the value of compactness in pack making. During recess it was noted that he was carrying his Paris baggage inside the lining of his cap. Item: One extra collar.

The road to the caucus was not a path of primroses for all the enlisted delegates. When Col. Carl E. Ristine of the 35th Division and his orderly, also a delegate, arrived at a certain station on the way to Paris, an unfeeling M. P. entered the train and commanded that the soldier vacate, evacuate and otherwise get out, it being an officers' train. The colonel's pleadings were of no avail. The orderly finally arrived at the caucus hall on Monday afternoon.

The Navy was not represented until late on the afternoon of the last day, when a lone sailor drifted in. He was asked whom he represented.

"Hell," he replied, "I don't represent anybody. I thought there was a show going on here."

A captain of the Paris Command got up to speak and in doing so knocked down the Paris Command sign. A colonel gathered up the sign and held it high while the captain spoke. "Thanks," said the captain when he had finished; "that's what I call true democracy."

That the word "legion" in the American Legion "smacked slightly of the silk stocking" was an objection raised by a sergeant in the Medical Department during the discussion on names. The word quickly found a defender in a colonel from the 1st Division, who said that his men had never felt more honored than when they were fighting shoulder to shoulder with the men of the French Foreign Legion. A quietus was put on the discussion when a delegate mentioned that he personally had no grievance against a silk stocking or even a pair of them.

Captain Joseph Mills Hanson of G. H. Q. wanted to adopt the name American Legion of the Great War, the letters A. L. G. W. comprising the initials of Abraham Lincoln and George Washington. One of the members of the committee on names had waxed poetic enough to demand American Crusaders.

The 35th Division claims the distinction of having been the first to appoint its members for the executive committee. Shortly after the chair had directed this action, "Kansas Post No. 1" was formed, with Col. W. McD. Rowan as chairman and Maj. J. F. Gordon as secretary.

The good old method of passing the hat was employed to raise the money to meet the 4,000-franc expenses of the caucus. It was moved that every delegate then present contribute 20 francs, but enlisted men with lively memories of allotments, insurance premiums and other deductions breathed easier when this was amended to apply only to officers.

The significance of the birth and christening of The American Legion was further emphasized in an editorial, "In Being," which appeared in the same issue:

The three-day caucus which closed Monday in Paris marks the inception, so far as the A. E. F. is concerned, of the first authentic, all-embracing association of land and sea veterans that has come out of America's participation in the war.

A score of organizations, in France and in America, have already made localized, misdirected or otherwise unfortunate attempts at a similar coalition of America's fighting men—a term which honorably includes those American soldiers who did not get to France, but who, as the great reserve, were clearly in the minds of the German armistice delegates.

These other attempts have failed, in every instance, either because they did not have their roots in, or gain their initial impulse from, the whole American Army.

The impetus that has already established the new association on the road to actual organization has come directly from the Army, and the whole Army. More than that, it has come spontaneously. It is something for which no one person, or group of persons, can in all honesty claim individual credit.

There had to be a veterans' association as surely as there had to be victory. That it actually started at a representative meeting of members of the A. E. F. in Paris on March 16, 1919, is simply to single out the peg on which history will hang it. It might have been done somewhere else at some other time. But the happy fact is that it has been done, that it has started, and that every man in the A. E. F. is a member of it unless—which privilege he owns—he chooses not to be.

Nine divisions were keeping the watch on the Yankee Rhine. Six of these—the First, Second, Third, Fourth, Thirty-second and Forty-second—had moved in soon after the Armistice, to be followed by the Fifth, Sixth, Eighty-ninth and Ninetieth, elements of the last-named, I regret to announce, occupying the village of Winterich. Each unit, small or great, had simply taken possession of whatever district had been assigned it without fanfares and hullabaloos and was now minding its own business with as little interference as might be with the civil activities of the community.

It was the life. For most of this conquering host there were roofs overhead, kitchens between four walls, mess-halls ditto, even beds o' nights. There was, to be sure, a rigid rule against fraternization, but this rigidity had taken on an increasing flexibility and finally went by the board, and anti-fraternization met its supreme antithesis in scores of German-American weddings—nothing like the total of Franco-American weddings, but enough to indicate that in the spring a young man's fancy was apt to turn to good account wherever G. H. Q. might happen to set him.

The American capital of occupied Germany was the comely city at the junction of the Rhine and the Moselle. *The Stars and Stripes* at first adopted the French rendering, Coblence, but soon went over to Coblenz, on the theory that although the Germans had lost about everything else, they might at least be allowed to keep their own spelling. In the quotations that follow I am adhering to whichever rendering was used in the original copy.

Woollcott had marched into Germany with the first troops—that is, Woollcott had moved up into Germany with the first troops and watched America cross the Rhine. The whole truth might as well be told. Woollcott rode into Germany in a floorless Ford piloted by Seth Bailey, the staff Sunbeam, which had gone through the war under the skilful tendance of First Sergeant Lloyd J. Ruble having collapsed like the one-hoss shay at the signing of the Armistice. Woollcott's account of the historic passage of the Rhine was printed in the issue for December 20th:

> On Friday the Thirteenth, in the fifth week of the armistice, the troops of the Allied Armies crossed the Rhine and so entered upon the last phase of the occupation. Today, the sentries who guard its bridges and pace their posts within the shadow of the ancient castles are not German soldiers. Poilus and Tom-

"PUT HER THERE, JACK," FROM THE DRAWING BY SERGEANT HAL BURROWS COMMEMORATING
THE ARRIVAL OF NEWLY-ENLISTED REGULARS TO RELIEVE THE VETERANS ALONG THE RHINE

mies and Yanks, these three—and it is their Christmas present to a tired, thankful world—these three are keeping the watch on the Rhine.

It was just at dawn that the close-massed forces of the Third American Army moved forward in the dismal December rain to take and hold the bridgehead that is theirs today. By four bridges and four ferries, they moved quietly across the river, which is more beautiful than any our own country can show and which means more to Germany than any American river can ever mean to us. The Rhine, for all its castle-crowned steeps, for all its massive and impotent fortresses, is more than a mere moat to guard the Fatherland.

To the Germans, it is a river of proud memories, the silver thread on which their history is strung, the link of lore and legend, the inspiration of their songs for which through countless generations its lisping waters have crooned a soft accompaniment. And then, in the gray of a December morning, an American army moved across the German Rhine.

For this great hour in the history of the United States, many Americans were up and abroad an hour in advance of the sun, though reveille meant nothing in their lives. Gray-haired staff officers, Salvation Army lassies, cooks from neighboring messes, couriers, artists, war correspondents, they were all there waiting at the Coblence pontoon—the Bridge of Boats—for the electric moment when the Rhine bridges should give forth the music, the ever-recognizable, ever-stirring music of American infantry on the march.

Yet they knew in their hearts it would be what the French would regard as an indifferent show. They knew from long and gloomy experience that the American Army simply refuses to be dramatic. They were right. There was no fuss and feathers, no flourish of trumpets. There never is.

On the stroke of seven, the first mounted men clattered forward over the cobbles of the quay and the order "Forward March" sounded from post to post along the river front. It was raining and there was scarcely enough light in the heavens to rival as yet the winking street lamps. Faintly silhouetted against the gray sky were visible the great ramparts of Ehrenbreitstein and not far below, where the Moselle swings into the Rhine, could be seen in sharp relief the stupendous statue of the first Wilhelm.

This bridge—it was at the point where, according to Rhineland legend, the lovely Riza walked upon the waters from shore to shore a thousand years ago —this bridge was set aside for the First Brigade. It was the same brigade which, less than a year before, had, to the intense and audible amusement of the German Army, modestly settled down in the American old home sector "northwest of Toul."

First came Major Paul Daly of New York. He was on horseback and two mounted men followed close behind. Then, if history must have the prosaic order of march, came Brigadier General Frank Parker and some officers of his staff. Then some French officers. Then a Y. M. C. A. girl in a fur coat carrying a bunch of cookies and—bless her for a kind lady—three boxes of cigars.

Then the correspondent of the Chicago Daily News, accompanied by his dog Vesle, a plump and celebrated poodle who waddled across the Rhine ahead of the troops, wearing an intent look and bent, as it afterwards developed, on searching for the first lamp-post on the right bank.

But the procession grew impressive enough as the doughboys tramped across, an endless column that thumped ahead, deliberately oblivious to the beauties of the Rhine or the significance of the occasion, listening indignantly to the patter of the rain on their helmets and wondering if the Quartermaster had enough shoes. Close to the further shore, the swaying, scarce-distinguishable column of olive drab melted into the all-enshrouding mist. Not so the flag and the standards, when their turn came to cross the Rhine. Always they shone bravely from shore to shore.

It was the one touch of color in all that drab and cheerless morning, from the moment when, midstream, the river wind caught and flung them wide, till, dwindling, dwindling, they became only a point of scarlet in a curtain of mist, like a poppy blooming in the cranny of a gray wall. And always, faintly from the other shore, came the music of the band playing in the rain.

While the First Brigade, with ponderous trucks and smoking kitchens, moved over the pontoon, the Second Brigade was crossing by the beautiful three-span Pfaffendorf bridge near by. Below, the famous Thirty-second was crossing and below them the Second, while above, the Third had edged up-stream a bit toward Bingen.

For this crossing, the troops had been massing on the left bank since the preceding Sunday, when the first cavalry trotted into Remagen and the first infantry—a whole trainload of affable doughboys—arrived in Coblence.

In their sector of the Rhine, certainly, the Yankees feel quite at home. They were sternly forbidden to wander out of it, for the various bridgeheads were kept as severely separate as water-tight compartments, but the outposts could not help meeting occasionally, and on Thursday of last week, when troops that looked hauntingly like our own marched into Bonn, the Yanks discovered, to their great delight, that their neighbors below stream were the Canadians.

The exchange of courtesies would run something like this:

"Cheer-o Kennida, what division?"

"The Second."

"Is 'at so? So's this."

"The Second American? Some division, from what they tell us."

"We'll say it is. Where's the British?"

"The Imperials? Oh, down stream somewhere."

"What's your main town?"

"Bonn."

"What kind of a place?"

"Ditto."

"How are things going?"

"Lovely. Just lovely. Couldn't be better if we were home in the States."

"*Home* in the States? Where do you get that stuff?"

"Oh, well, I'm from Ioway myself. Half of us are Americans."

"The hell you say. Then, why didn't you come over in our Army?"

"Because it didn't come over soon enough."

A thoughtful silence for a while. Then:

"Well, see you in Ioway, Kennida."

"Right-o."

Thus it befell that Canada and America crossed the Rhine shoulder to shoulder.

Now the Stars and Stripes float from the skyline flagpole of Ehrenbreitstein. Ehrenbreitstein sounds rather like the name of some cloak and suit house in New York, but it is really a fortress so formidable that it is called the Gibraltar of the Rhine. If, when they began to fashion it just after Waterloo, any prophetic soul had told the powers that were that a century later its garrison would echo to the tread of soldiers from the absurd little sapling republic across the Atlantic, they would have flung him into its lowest keep as a dangerous lunatic.

The fortress, which copies the old hilltop castles of which the weather-battered ruins still frown down on the Rhine, was reared on the site of just such a stronghold as had stood for centuries there at the junction of the Rhine and Moselle. It is hollowed out from just such a sheer riverside rock as the Lorelei itself. Its vast underground chambers will billet a hundred thousand men. By spiral paths that lead through tunnels and over drawbridges, you reach at last its battlements, which rise full 385 feet above the river bed. From them you can see triangular Coblence laid out like a relief map at the base of the fortress and survey the historic countryside from Stolzenfels to Andernach.

Baedeker's account of Ehrenbreitstein is accurate, though vague. It contains what today is a serious error. It says: "Foreign officers are not admitted." Correct this to read "German officers," and the sentence may stand.

From Ehrenbreitstein itself, which is a small town opposite Coblence, the bridgehead reaches for 30 kilometers into Germany.

The staff delegation along the Rhine sent an abundance of copy that did not get crowded out by the red-hot news of actual troop departures or the redder and hotter news of impending troop departures—data absorbed quite as eagerly in Trier or Cochem or Andernach as in Nevers or Romorantin or Bordeaux. Robert I. Snajdr of the staff even contrived to reach Berlin, which, under as jealous a guard after the Armistice as it had been during the previous four years, remained to the end the European metropolis most difficult of attainment to an alert and inquisitive A. E. F. From the bridgehead came to Paris throughout the winter and spring of farewell a steady stream of footnotes to history, these among them:

Little did the doughboy think, when first he encountered the French language, that before many months had passed he would be searching through German villages for some one who could compree French and so would understand him. Yet, so it is these days along the Rhine. A handy lexicon is being prepared which turns all the doughboy's French into German. With these phrases he will find his every legitimate need met. Here is a sample page.

C'est la guerre	Es ist der Krieg
Finee la guerre	Der Krieg ist aus
Deux bières	Zwei Bier
Un cognac	Ein Kognac
Toute droit	Immer gerade aus
Encore	Noch eins
A droite	Rechts
A gauche	Links
Pah bonn	Nicht gut
Sale boche	Edel Deutscher*
Allez	Heraus
Zig-zag	Getrunken
Merci, Mamzelle	Danke, Fräulein
Trois francs	Fünfzig Mark

*This is not a literal translation, but it facilitates conversation for beginners to use it on the Rhine.

When the first American Infantry reached Coblence they found waiting for them a discharged German soldier who had come down to meet them, because, long ago, he had lived in Kansas City and had served in the Missouri National Guard. He was looking for his old captain. He was too late. His old captain was killed on the edge of the Forest of Argonne.

The first man in the Army of Occupation to cross the Rhine died the following day. He was an Engineer who, two weeks before, was struck and injured by a train in the newly established railroad at Coblence. Across the river was a Red Cross hospital, packed with German wounded, and there he was carried. When he died, the next day, he was buried in the little village churchyard. The wounded enemy soldiers in the hospital chipped together and bought the wreath that lies now on his grave.

It isn't the well-stocked American kitchens which make the Rhinelanders as green as a prisoner uniform. They yearn for our white bread, it is true, and for our real coffee, but it is our soap they will sell their souls for and our rubber that astonishes them.

It is interesting to see a curb full of Germans staring wide-eyed at a passing American company, each member of which is clumping luxuriously through the December mud in high, swashbuckling rubber boots.

The Rhine has an unusual interest for the Americans, both officers and enlisted men. Even a grizzled top kick was caught gazing reflectively over its waters recently. Perhaps the fact that it was running with a particularly swift current and rising slowly had something to do with it.

Or perhaps his statement clears it up:

"Got a home in the good old Arkansas bottoms, boys. Wife and kids there —two of 'em. And if the old Father of Waters is kickin' up like this bird, I ought to be there, that's all."

Snow in the bridgehead has brought out the sleds and skates of the children living in the hills. The sleds are crude, and so are the skates, but they work. And many a fond memory do they bring to the mind of the boy in khaki as he watches the young ones romping and yelling—and beseeching him to try it.

He often does, but usually only to the extent of helping them pull their sleds to the top of the slopes or aiding them with a refractory strap.

And the M. P. at the foot of the hill is especially careful in warning passing traffic of the merrymakers' impending descent.

America is likely to find many more opera devotees when the boys come home. There is grand opera in Coblenz, with very good music, and the theater has become popular with both officers and enlisted men. The highest priced seat is five and one-half marks (about 65 cents in real money—opera producers in the States please copy), and from there it grades down to about a dime, or maybe a little more, so that the music is within reach of every soldier.

The men cannot understand, however, the peculiar system of choice places. The Germans consider their balcony seats the best, then the orchestra, then the standing room, and then the gallery.

There may be a food shortage in some parts of Germany, or in all the rest of it, but the little farm towns in the area in which the Americans are quartered are far from the starvation point. Walk into the little inns of these villages and you may get the tenderest of pork or mutton, hare or fowl or beef, with potatoes and real butter.

The bread, of course, is bad, and the landlord will not put it on the table, and the coffee is unspeakable. Eggs are as scarce as good weather, some that were seen miles out in the country being snapped up at a mark apiece.

The delicatessen stores continue to do a roaring business. The pastry is the nearest approach to the real stuff many members of the Third Army have had since they landed, and they're taking advantage of it. And the photographic galleries—you can scarcely get into them. Everybody wants to have his picture taken in Coblenz, it seems, in order to prove to the folks at home that he has gazed upon the Rhine.

The K. P. is coming into his own in these days of stability.

He's around a warm kitchen all day, generally in a place where kitchens are very comfortable. He doesn't have to wash dishes with mud over his shoe tops, nor does he have to rustle grub a quarter of a mile through woods and wire entanglements. And he sees to it that he gets plenty of between-meal extras.

In fact, in these days of interminable drill, he has a cinch—and perhaps it may not be believed, but there is more than one top sergeant who has had it borne in upon him that when he sentences some transgressor to the kitchen he is merely giving him a nice little boost to a perch on the top of the world.

The rising generation of Germany is not so much addicted to cigarettes as are the youth of France, but are in a fair way to become chewing gum fiends, judging from the requests which are heaped upon the Third Army. The soldier's answer is not now "No compree," but "No fraternize," thereby at the same time getting out of a dilemma and impressing upon the children the majesty of American military law.

Incidentally, the exact interpretation to be put upon the regulation against "fraternizing" is causing a lot of worriment in enlisted circles. A decision recently handed down from a high non-commissioned authority is that buying a glass of beer is not fraternizing, but that tipping the waiter is that evil in its most virulent form.

Castle Stolzenfels, the battlemented old pile on the Rhine above Coblenz, which used to be the property of the ex-kaiser, continues to be a very popular Mecca for O. D. tourists on leave in the bridgehead city.

The top of the tower, all that is left of an ancient castle which occupied the site in the 13th century, rises about 500 feet above the Rhine. And the Yanks take great pleasure in the view from the turrets and in promenading through the beautifully furnished rooms. The floors are of polished and waxed hardwood, the design being different in each room.

Do the hobs mar the floors? Not on your life; for just outside the castle there is a huge heap of felt sandals, a pair of which each man must don before he enters.

There is always a waiting list about a kilometer long of Germans who are frenziedly eager to grab off a job of some sort in the Third Army salvage plant at Coblenz-Lützel. Why? Rations.

Under provisions of the ruling which permits the rationing of Germans working on the railroads for Americans, Germans employed in the salvage factory—of whom there are about 400—are also entitled to draw a specific ration for each eight hours of labor. They get sugar, coffee, flour, goldfish, corned beef and fresh roast beef—and if any one is late for work in the morning he or she loses that day's ration. The beneficiaries are mostly women whose husbands or other dependents were killed in the war. No one is ever late.

Three-day permissionnaires returning from Paris to the Rhine last week met train after train of 42nd Division troops en route to Brest, hommes 40 style.

"How will you trade?" was the greeting from the comparatively comfortable passenger trains to the Yanks peering out of the box cars.

"Nothing doing," was always the answer. For once they were satisfied to be riding in box cars.

A general was busted in the 32nd Division just before it started for the coast —General Gloom. He was placed in command of the 158th Field Artillery Brigade, comprising the 322nd, 323rd and 324th Regiments, which had come over originally with the 83rd Division, and had been transferred to the 32nd in the Argonne. Someone spread the report that the brigade was not going home with the rest of the division. Funeral services were held over the red arrow, the divisional insignia, and the regimental band played dirges as members of the regiments buried their shoulder ornaments. There was some talk, indeed, of adopting "LB" as the new insignia—the "Lost Brigade."

Then the band was hustled out again, for the men heard they were to return, after all. The band played gleeful airs, and the insignia was resurrected. General Joy took command.

There is one solemn moment in the brisk and business-like life of the Third Army in Coblenz. That is when Old Glory, flying proudly over the topmost fortifications of Ehrenbreitstein, is lowered in the evening, while the clear bugle notes of retreat echo across the Rhine valley.

All Yanks snap to attention and stand at salute. On the bridge of boats, on the promenades along the Rhine, in front of American headquarters, outside the old imperial palace, beside the colossal statue of the first William, they stand rigid, their eyes fixed on the old fortress across the river.

In the club rooms of the Knights of Columbus at Coblenz and in the main lobby of the Fest Hall are two bulletin boards, both of them as characteristically American as the genuine Yankee twang and the doughboy's desire to call it a war and go home. The K. C. board contains sketches, bits of poetry, cartoons, take-offs on various personages in the Third Army and announcements. There is always a crowd in front, reading and smiling. And here, picked at random, are some of the things on the Fest Hall board.

Program for the coming week's entertainment at the Fest Hall; an ad seeking a watch, lost by a leave man when he was taking an excursion on the Rhine; a card from the States, bearing a young soldier's picture, describing him in detail, and asking that anyone knowing his whereabouts notify a St. Louis family; an announcement of new educational courses, including a course in the theory of music; a dozen or more inquiries concerning comrades; a notice to all Chicago men to get in touch with a certain corporal for the purpose of forming a veterans' association; a call for some officer to report at the desk, and an appeal to all soldiers to go to church.

American buck privates and officers take orders from a German every day at Neuenahr. The Boche is a German professor hired to teach at the Fourth Corps School. Speaking English in his class is strictly verboten.

White armbands on their sleeves, small Third Army details daily patrol the roads of the neutral zone, the ten-kilometer No Man's Land between American Germany and Germany proper. The patrols take a swing over the roads to see that doughboys do not stray into the zone.

The routine of the office was pleasantly upset one morning by the bestowal of the Croix de Guerre on Sergeant Major Kenneth C. Adams and Sergeant Kendall K. Kay for gallantry in action—not, alas, as members of the staff of *The Stars and Stripes* but as alumni of the 363d Infantry of the Ninety-first Division. There was no kissing. The bestowal was made by Major Mark S. Watson, temporarily representing the French War Office, with Hawley as cheer leader. Simple justice demands at this point the disclosure that Private Hawley had sold his birthright for a messkit and had permitted himself to be elevated to a sergeancy.

The millionth American soldier to go home boarded the transport May 11th. *The Stars and Stripes* was losing its circulation by leaps and bounds up gangplanks, and nobody was happier than the circulation department, with the exception of Sergeant Major Cliff Sterrett's treasury staff and everybody else. A benevolent G. H. Q.

"FOR THE SAKE OF AULD LANG SYNE," DRAWN BY HERBERT MORTON STOOPS FOR THE FINAL
ISSUE OF THE STARS AND STRIPES (JUNE 13, 1919)

determined that the final issue of the paper should appear on Friday, June 13th, and the most superstitious member of the outfit saw only good in the omen. By that time only about a fourth of the A. E. F. would still be in France and Germany. The Third Army, along the Rhine, itself gladly depleted, now had its own daily, *The Amaroc News*. The First Division, soon to be the last, would leave the bridgehead for home in August, and the occupying remnant would be turned into a small holding company known as the American Forces in Germany which, as things worked out, would not set out for home until the beginning of 1923.

Woollcott arranged for a group of us that included Ross, Baldridge, Winterich and himself to be hired by the Paris office of the *New York Times* and fired as soon as our discharges came through. (Getting out in France was not easy. Sergeant, ultimately Second-Lieutenant, John Palmer Cumming of the staff got a perfectly legitimate job in Constantinople and had to proceed thither by way of New York.) We became former soldiers at the St. Aignan discharge camp on May 1st and rode back to Paris wearing red chevrons on our sleeves, the official token of our release. On the 15th we sailed for home like the civilians we were—civilians all except Woollcott, hermaphroditic in fawn cap, blue shirt, orange tie, mustard tweed coat and issue trousers and leggins. The editorial destinies of *The Stars and Stripes* were left in the hands of Sergeant Major Philip Von Blon, under whose direction the flag was hauled down and Thirty written below the final batch of copy (something of Sergeant Hawley's, I warrant) for the issue of June 13th—which issue was supplemented by the only rotogravure section which *The Stars and Stripes* ever got out.

The story of those final days is Von's to tell, as is the story of the trip to Brest and the return across the Atlantic on board the transport *Pretoria*. It will include, inevitably, an account of the adventures of Corporal Kenyon and his roulette wheel and of the court martial on the high seas that failed to take.

For our anniversary banquet the preceding February one of us had fashioned an official anthem to be sung to the trio of Sousa's best-known march. Woollcott objected to the word whinny as a sacrifice of sense to the exigencies of rhyme, but the defense was put forward that whinny was a tribute to Lieutenant Ochs, our only cavalryman, who never rode a horse to the office:

> We're glad that we came, just the same,
>   And we'll stay till the day that it's finee;
> We'd like for to hike down to Brest,
>   For we need a—little—rest,
> But here we are stuck out of luck,

And we never shall bellow or whinny—
Home we long for but still we are strong for
The Stars and Stripes,
The Stars and Stripes—

(*Two full seconds' pause, then, lentissimo and fortissimo*)

But Not Forever!

No disrespect to the Flag was intended. At any rate Major General James G. Harbord and Brigadier General Charles G. Dawes were present and they didn't object. They wanted to go home too.

CHAPTER FIFTEEN

ROLLCALL

IN THE last of the seventy-one issues of *The Stars and Stripes*—Number 19 of Volume II—was published a roster, as complete as service records could make it, of the men who had put a hand to the halyards. It is given here as it originally appeared, and any errors in it, in good old army fashion, can be laid at the door of whole platoons of forgotten company clerks who have long since put aside their O. D. triplicating machines. The list was introduced with this explanatory note:

The men of the A. E. F., who at one time or another have worked on *The Stars and Stripes* and have contributed to its success are listed below in alphabetical order, together with their rank, as last reported, their original units, the department in which they did most of their work while with us, the date on which they reported for duty with the paper, and—as far as it has been possible to get them—their home addresses.

These men were obtained for service on the paper after a canvass of the whole A. E. F., a process in which the qualification cards filled out at replacement depots and reclassification camps played an important part. Some were recommended by their C. O.'s for service with us and some applied.

A good portion of them had no previous experience.

These lists are printed not only to give due credit in future years to the men who helped make possible one of the most interesting experiments in American journalism—and who for the most part stayed here voluntarily to finish the job after their original units had gone home—but to show the A. E. F., for whom they worked first and last, how representative was the outfit, both as regards the Army units and the States from which its numbers hailed, that got out the A. E. F.'s own particular paper during the sixteen and a half months of its existence.

The roster:

Name and Rank.	Former Organization.	Dept., S. & S.	Began Work.	Home Address.
ACKERMAN, Henry H. Pvt.	Q. M. C.	Field Agent	——	Philadelphia, Pa.
ADAMS, Franklin P. Capt.	National Army	Editorial	3-6-18	The New York Tribune, N. Y. C.
ADAMS, Kenneth C. Sgt. Maj.	Co. C, 363rd Inf.	Editorial	12-4-18	2727 M St., Sacramento, Cal.
AGEN, Meyer Pvt. 1st Cl.	Med. Dept.	Personnel	10-6-18	437 Hopkinson Ave., Brooklyn, N. Y.
AYERS, Milton J. 1st Lt., Inf.	R.O.T.C., Plattsburg	Circulation	4-1-18	Care Bernard Scholle & Co., 14 Wall St., N. Y.
BABBITT, Donald G. 1st Lt., Inf.	Co. E, 59th Inf.	Circulation	2-13-19	Bellows Falls, Vt.
BACHELOR, Louis R. Cpl.	C. O. T. S.	Field Agent	3-10-19	120 W. Lincoln Ave., Goshen, Ind.
BAILEY, Seth T. Sgt.	Co. L, 162nd Inf.	Editorial	8-5-18	332 W. Sherman St., Portland, Ore.
BALABAN, Sydney Pvt.	Motor School	Circulation	2-14-19	335 S. Central Park Ave., Chicago, Ill.
BALDRIDGE, C. LeRoy Pvt.	Infantry	Art	6-1-18	2400 A St., San Diego, Cal.
BARRY, Arthur W. Pvt. 1st Cl.	Troop D, N. G. Cav.	Transportation	3-1-19	441 S. Comstock Ave., Whittier, Cal.
BARTON, Frank W. Sgt.	Co. F, 18th Engrs.	Field Agent	5-11-18	Morning Oregonian, Portland, Ore.
BASSETT, Horace Y. Pvt. 1st Cl.	Repl. Troops	Circulation	2-14-19	586 Main St., Coatesville, Pa.
BAUKHAGE, Hilmar R. 2nd Lt., F. A.	32nd Co., C. A.	Editorial	12-27-18	13 W. 12th St., N. Y. C.
BEATTY, Edgar Pvt. 1st Cl.	B. H. No. 13.	Soldiers' Serv.	2-15-18	Chicago Athletic Association, Chicago, Ill.
BECKMAN, Edward J. Cpl.	112th Train Hq.	Field Agent	9-16-18	Ottawa, Ohio
BEDDOR, Frank Pvt.	Ord. Det.	Field Agent	9-4-18	Minneapolis, Minn.
BEER, Harold C. Sgt.	Co. K, 101st Inf.	Field Agent	6-2-18	300 Greeley St., Clinton, Mass.
BERGH, Sigurd U. Pvt. 1st Cl.	29th Engrs.	Editorial	2-7-18	1383 Grantham Ave., St. Paul, Minn.
BERNARD, August L. Sgt.	30th Engrs.	Field Agent	9-17-18	641 W. 10th St., Erie, Pa.
BESER, Nicholas R. S. M.	305th Supply Co.	Personnel	11-11-18	709 E. McMillan St., Cincinnati, Ohio
BLACK, John Cpl.	Med. Dept.	Circulation	5-3-18	Brooklyn Daily Eagle, Brooklyn, N. Y.
BLISS, D. L. Sgt.	319th Engrs.	Treasury	5-12-19	Milvia St., Berkeley, Cal.
BLISS, Tyler H. Sgt.	161st Inf.	Editorial	5-11-19	13 S. Highland St., Hartford, Conn.

Name and Rank.	Former Organization.	Dept., S. & S.	Began Work.	Home Address.
BOETJER, William C. Pvt.	16th Engrs.	Field Agent	9-4-18	501 Section St., Hannibal, Mo.
BONDY, Edward W. Pvt.	U. S. M. C.	Circulation	5-29-18	Baltimore, Md.
BONNET, Fred J. Cpl.	1st Army Supply Tr.	Field Agent	9-27-18	716 1st St., Hoboken, N. J.
BORCHERS, Harold Pvt.	Infantry	Personnel	5-18-18	San Francisco, Cal.
BORN, Nestor J. Sgt.	Co. B, 335th Inf.	Circulation	3-15-18	1228 Edgar St., Evansville, Ind.
BOTTORFF, Donald Cpl.	Hq. Det., 63rd F. A. Brig.	Circulation	2-14-19	Charlestown, Ind.
BRADY, Richard V. Cpl.	14th Engrs.	Circulation	8-7-18	461 E. 140th St., N. Y. C.
BRENTON, Donald R. 2nd Lt., Inf.	343rd Inf.	Personnel	1-25-19	1217 S. Dearborn St., Chicago, Ill.
BRISTOL, Claude M. Sgt.	Ordnance	Field Agent	11-12-18	254 Chapman St., Portland, Ore.
BRITT, George W. B. A. F. C.	A. G. O.	Soldiers' Serv.	3-20-18	New Bedford, Mass.
BRYSON, George T. 2nd Lt., A. S.	Signal Corps	Treasury	3-3-19	303 W. Grace St., Richmond, Va.
BUCHER, John M. A. F. C.	A. G. O.	Asst. to O.-in-C.	2-27-19	Y. M. C. A., Washington, D. C.
BURCHILL, Arthur E. Cpl.	Bat. C, 6th Regt., F. A.	Soldiers' Serv.	2-15-18	7067 Hilldale Ave., Chicago, Ill.
BURKE, Walter J. Pvt.	11th Engrs.	Field Agent	5-29-18	New York City.
BURNETT, Verne E. Sgt.	Ordnance	Field Agent	——	Homer, Mich.
BURROWS, Harold L. Sgt.	2nd A. A. M. G. Bn.	Art	2-6-19	26 Main St., Salt Lake City, Utah.
BURTON, Elon R. Pvt. 1st Cl.	330th Baking Co.	Field Agent	8-7-18	Americus, Ga.
BUSSIUS, Charles J. Sgt.	M. G. Co., 3rd D. C. N. G.	Field Agent	7-22-18	15 H St., N. W., Washington, D. C.
BYRON, Daniel E. Cpl.	103rd F. A.	Field Agent	9-27-18	65 Cottage Ave., Providence, R. I.
CALLIS, Richard M. Cpl.	Repl. Troops	Circulation	1-9-19	Dundas, Va.
CANNON, Percy F. Pvt.	7th Regt.,F. A. R. D.	Circulation	2-15-19	2210 Prairie Ave., Chicago, Ill.
CARROLL, Joseph W. Pvt.	M. T. Co. 415	Transportation	11-2-18	536 Oak St., San Francisco, Cal.
CARROLL, Leonard M. Sgt.	Supply Co. 301	Field Agent	7-20-18	3117 Flora Ave., Kansas City, Mo.
CARROLL, Stuart H. Q. M. Sgt., S. G.	Q. M. C.	Circulation	2-28-18	3117 Flora Ave., Kansas City, Mo.

Name and Rank.	Former Organization.	Dept., S. & S.	Began Work.	Home Address.
Cashen, John L. Sgt.	Co. A, 303rd Inf.	Circulation	1-9-19	88 Heart Ave., Cohoes, N. Y.
Charman, Elbert B. Cpl.	Co. E, 18th Engrs.	Field Agent	5-22-18	Box 12, Oregon City, Ore.
Claiborne, Richard S. Sgt.	29th Engrs.	Mechanical	2-10-18	Rusk, Tex.
Clary, Thomas M. R. S. Maj.	Evac. Hosp. No. 6	Circulation	6-17-18	136 W. 103rd St., N. Y. C.
Clower, Clarence E. Pvt.	Q. M. C.	Circulation	3-22-18	New York City
Coleman, Nelson B. Cpl.	15th Engrs.	Personnel	——	Pittsburgh, Pa.
Conerin, Clarence C. Cpl.	11th Engrs.	Field Agent	5-29-18	New York City
Conlee, C. S. Pvt.	1106th Aero Repl. Sqn.	Transportation	4-17-19	Bryan, Tex.
Connolly, Jack S. Cpl.	78th F. A.	Editorial	10-14-18	Newton Lower Falls, Mass.
Corcoran, Paul B. Sgt.	S. S. U. 642	Field Agent	5-1-18	New York City
Critchlow, Harry B. Sgt. 1st Cl.	316th San. Tr.	Field Agent	11-2-18	
Cumming, J. P. 2nd Lt.	Arty. Repl.	Circulation	2-15-19	Frankfort, Ind.
Cue, Merl K. Pvt.	305th Inf.	Editorial	3-31-19	Florence, Ala.
Cushing, Charles P. 1st Lt.	U. S. M. C.	Editorial	1-25-18	New York City
Cuthbertson, A. J. Pvt.	11th Engrs.	Field Agent	——	Denver, Colo.
Daley, Richard D. Cpl.	58th Inf.	Field Agent	——	Seattle, Wash.
Daly, Joseph G. Sgt. 1st Cl., G. M. C.	Q. M. Det., G. H. Q.	Transportation	5-11-18	526 W. 130th St., N. Y. C.
Darling, Chester A. Cpl.	Hq. Co., 352nd Inf.	Field Agent	8-7-18	1914 E. 26th St., Minneapolis, Minn.
Davies, L. L. Pvt.	Med. Dept.	Editorial	3-31-19	Portland, Ore.
Davis, Harold L. 1st Sgt.	305th M. P. C.	Editorial	5-7-19	2037 Harvard Blvd., Los Angeles, Cal.
Dayton, Logan M. Cpl.	Bat. C, 107th F. A.	Soldiers' Serv.	2-15-19	109 Rochelle Ave., Philadelphia, Pa.
Dee, Joseph P. Cpl.	Evac. Hosp. No. 6	Field Agent	11-11-18	320 West 120th St., N.Y.C.
De Grange, Joseph 2nd Lt., F. A.	141st F. A.	Circulation	2-15-19	1636 Gen. Pershing St., New Orleans, La.
Di Carlo, Charles Pvt.	327th Inf.	Circulation	9-4-18	2301 Crotona Ave., N.Y.C.

Name and Rank.	Former Organization.	Dept., S. & S.	Began Work.	Home Address.
DICKEY, Willis T. B. S. M.	1st M. G. Bn.	Treasury	11-19-18	Mulvane, Kan.
DILLY, Robert S. Pvt.	French Army	Interpreter	6-4-18	94 Blvd., Flandrin, Paris
DOLAN, Louis F. Pvt.	F. A. Repl.	Personnel	2-14-19	27 Hancock St., Dorchester, Mass.
DOSTAL, Eben J. Cpl.	18th F. A.	Circulation	2-15-19	6816 Cornell Ave., Chicago, Ill.
DOWD, Frank A. Cpl.	Co. C, 116th Inf.	Circulation	11-11-18	345 Pulaski St., Brooklyn, N. Y.
DOYLE, Lloyd L. Cpl.	Military Spec Co., Dept. Div., 1st Corps	Personnel	8-7-18	Utica, N. Y.
DUNN, Walter F. Cpl.	Med. Dept.	Editorial	2-26-19	Public Ledger, Philadelphia, Pa.
EARLY, Stephen T. Capt., Inf.	317th Inf.	Asst. O.-in-C.	12-12-18	1228 N. Carolina Ave., N. E., Washington, D. C.
EASINGWOOD, A. H. Pvt. 1st Cl.	Co. C, 10th Engrs.	Treasury	8-1-18	Clinton, N. Y.
EMMONS, Riley H. Cpl.	Air Service	Field Agent	8-7-18	Hill City, Kan.
EPSTEIN, Emmanuel Pvt.	320th Inf.	Circulation	8-7-18	322 Ophelia St., Pittsburgh, Pa.
FEENEY, Joseph E. Cpl.	200th Aero Sqn.	Field Agent	5-13-18	87 St. Lawrence St., Portland, Me.
FEHRENBACH, A. J. Cpl.	2nd Depot Bn., S. C.	Field Agent	11-11-18	Marshfield, Wis.
FENDRICK, R. S. 2nd Lt., A. S.	N. G. Cav. D. C.	Advertising	2-6-19	Mercersburg, Pa.
FITCH, Roy Cpl.	D Troop, 1st Cav.	Editorial	5-3-19	Los Angeles, Cal.
FLOOD, Patrick J. Pvt. 1st Cl.	Med. Dept.	Circulation	9-27-18	Brooklyn, N. Y.
FORBES, John P. Pvt. 1st Cl.	Med. Dept.	Field Agent	8-7-18	513 Washington St., Huntingdon, Pa.
FORSHAY, Stanley W. Pvt.	Signal Corps	Circulation	8-7-18	Paterson, N. J.
FRANTZ, John C. Sgt.	Co. B, 148th M. G. Bn.	Field Agent	5-11-18	640 Kerckhoff Bldg., Los Angeles, Cal.
FROWNFELTER, E. L. Sgt.	24th Engrs.	Transportation	5-10-19	Whittier, Cal.
FRUGONE, Lewis F. Pvt.	105th F. A.	Circulation	9-4-18	3302 Ave. D, Brooklyn, N. Y.
FULTON, Robert E. Cpl.	157th Aero Sqn.	Field Agent	8-23-18	Dallas, Tex.
GALLAGHER, Leo E. Pvt.	Bat. C, 6th Regt., F. A. R. D.	Circulation	2-15-19	424 Washington St., Freeland, Pa.
GARDYNE, Robert E. Cpl.	101st Amb. Co.	Field Agent	9-4-18	Montgomery Center, Vt.

Name and Rank.	Former Organization.	Dept., S. & S.	Began Work.	Home Address.
GAYLORD, Donald D. Cpl.	10th Engrs.	Field Agent	6-19-18	93 S. Main St., Branford, Conn.
GEESEY, Chester L. Sgt.	17th Engrs.	Field Agent	8-7-18	6341 Ingleside Ave., Chicago, Ill.
GELL, W. C. Pvt.	339th M. G. Bn.	Mechanical	5-5-19	Journal, Minneapolis, Minn.
GERBER, Albion T. Sgt.	4th Engrs.	Field Agent	8-19-18	847 E. 82nd St., N. Portland, Ore.
GERMAIN, William F. Sgt.	320th M. G. Bn.	Soldiers' Serv.	8-1-18	1140 Fox St., N. Y. C.
GESCHARDT, George A. Cpl.	Co. F, 308th Inf.	Circulation	8-7-18	505 E. 88th St., N. Y. C.
GIAUQUE, James R. Sgt.	201st Aero Sqn.	Treasury	11-14-18	90 Saratoga Ave., Yonkers, N. Y.
GIEGENGACK, Aug. E. R. S. M.	1st Pro. Recruit Bn.	Circulation	7-17-18	1146 54th St., Brooklyn, N. Y.
GILBERT, Leland R. Sgt.	Bat. A, 147th F. A.	Field Agent	7-5-18	1008 Ferry St., Albany, Ore.
GLENN, Edward H. Pvt.	167th Inf.	Circulation	——	
GLENNY, James A. F. Cpl.	R. T. C.	Treasury	8-28-18	625 E. 9th St., Chester, Pa.
GLICKMAN, Rudolph Pvt. 1st Cl.	469th Aero Sqn.	Circulation	11-2-18	Newark, N. J.
GOLBERG, Saul Cpl.	C. A. C.	Field Agent	5-1-18	944 Florida Ave., N. W., Washington, D. C.
GOLDEY, Louis Pvt. 1st Cl.	Base Hosp. No. 3	Soldiers' Serv.	11-2-18	167 E. 95th St., N. Y. C.
GOOD, Arthur J. Pvt. 1st Cl.	302nd F. A.	Editorial	11-24-18	23 Dorr St., Boston, Mass.
GOULD, George D. Sgt.	302nd Supply Tr.	Circulation	10-1-18	New York City
GOZA, Henslee D. 1st Sgt.	Co. B, 508th Engrs.	Field Agent	——	536 Thompson St., Ann Arbor, Mich.
GREELEY, Edwin Sgt. 1st Cl.	102nd Engrs.	Circulation	10-4-18	349 41st St., Brooklyn, N.Y.
GREEN, George D. Sgt.	104th Aero Repl.Sqn.	Treasury	11-2-18	San Francisco, Cal.
GREENSHAW, DeW. T. Sgt.	835th Aero Sqn.	Mailing	9-1-18	Phoenix, Ariz.
GRINSTEAD, Hugh G. Sgt. 1st Cl.	Q. M. C.	Field Agent	7-17-18	Kerrville, Tex.
HAGGERTY, John P. Sgt.	11th Engrs.	Field Agent	8-7-18	403 W. 21st St., N. Y. C.
HALE, William Sgt.	Co. L, 2nd Idaho Inf.	Field Agent	5-24-18	Weiser, Ida.
HALL, Nelson R. Sgt.	Co. M, 2nd Idaho Inf.	Circulation	3-19-18	Cardiff, Glenwood Springs, Colo.

Name and Rank.	Former Organization.	Dept., S. & S.	Began Work.	Home Address.
HALL, Norman D. Cpl.	Field Artillery	Circulation	2-14-19	132 DuBoise St., Newburg, N. Y.
HAMMER, Frank J. Pvt.	29th Engrs.	Mechanical	2-1-18	Minneapolis Journal, Minneapolis, Minn.
HANDBERG, C. L. Pvt. 1st Cl.	M. S. T. 409	Transportation	5-8-19	Viborg, Denmark
HANLEY, William L. Pvt. 1st Cl.	Base Hosp. No. 9	Editorial	1-27 19	Brooklyn, N. Y.
HANSON, Joseph M. Capt., F. A.	G. H. Q.	Historical	10-20-18	Yankton, S. D.
HARING, D. S. Sgt.	Ordnance	Field Agent	9-27-18	Port Jervis, N. Y.
HARMON, Harold H. Sgt.	Co. F, 117th Am. Tr.	Field Agent	7-24-18	Clyde, Kan.
HARRINGTON, G. L. Sgt.	301st Inf.	Circulation	5-9-19	726 Hyde Park Ave., Boston, Mass.
HAWLEY, Hudson Sgt.	Co. C, 101st M. G. Bn.	Editorial	1-20-18	Bristol, Conn.
HEALY, Thomas R. Sgt.	Co. D, 102nd M. G. Bn.	Circulation	9-17-18	397 Crown St., New Haven, Conn.
HEFFERNAN, Joseph L. Sgt. 1st Cl.	Base Hosp. No. 31	Field Agent	9-16-18	219 Lincoln Ave., Youngstown, Ohio
HELBIG, Louis W. Sgt.	Co. G, 2nd Wash. Inf.	Field Agent	6-24-18	Seattle, Wash.
HELD, Rene F. Cpl.	Infantry	Field Agent	8-20-18	2843 Prince St., Berkeley, Cal.
HENDERSON, A. E. R. S. M.	S. S. U. 575	Circulation	9-7-18	392 N. Village Ave., Rockville Center, N. Y.
HENNING, L. A. Cpl.	Co. D, 18th Engrs.	Field Agent	5-29-18	949 Vieau Place, Milwaukee, Wis.
HENRICHSEN, A. V. Cpl.	Hq. Co., 148th F. A.	Personnel	5-27-18	876 So. 4th East St., Salt Lake City, Utah
HERITAGE, W. H. Cpl.	Troop B, 1st Wash. Cav.	Field Agent	9-27-18	Seattle, Wash.
HERLIHY, John K. Cpl.	Casual	Circulation	2-14-19	24 Swan St., Everett, Mass.
HERSON, Edward J. Pvt., 1st Cl.	85th Aero Sqn.	Circulation	7-17-18	St. Louis, Mo.
HERTY, Howard A. B. S. M.	27th Div.	Editorial	5-2-19	121 DeMott Ave., Clifton, N. J.
HIBBS, Russell E. Pvt. 1st Cl.	Co. C, 1st Bn., 20th Engrs.	Treasury	7-17-18	260 44th St., Pittsburgh, Pa.
HICKMAN, George W. Sgt.	163rd Inf.	Field Agent	5-29-18	Logan, Utah
HIPP, Edward S. Cpl.	Hq. Co., 312th Inf.	Field Agent	9-27-18	131 Norwood St., Newark, N. J.
HOLLENWEGER, F. W. Sgt.	Ord. Dept. Co, No. 5	Field Agent	6-1-18	Cincinnati, Ohio

Name and Rank.	Former Organization.	Dept., S. & S.	Began Work.	Home Address.
HOLT, Felix C. Sgt.	115th Fld. Sig. Bn.	Editorial	1-28-19	San Diego, Cal.
HOLWAY, Harvard E. Pvt.	1st Repl. Dept.	Circulation	2-15-19	407 S. 9th St., La Crosse, Wis.
HOOKES, William L. B. S. M.	War Risk Ins. Det.	Field Agent	5-11-18	283 Bainbridge St., Brooklyn, N. Y.
HORN, Christopher J. Sgt.	Troop B, R. I. Cav.	Field Agent	8-12-18	318 Northup St., Edgewood, R. I.
HOUSER, Roy C. Sgt.	M. G. Co., 126th Inf.	Field Agent	8-17-18	60 Ridge St., S.W., Grand Rapids, Mich.
HOUSTON, Sid Cpl.	Co. B, 128th M.G.Bn.	Circulation	11-11-18	Mexico, Mo.
HOWARD, Charles M. Cpl.	S. S. U. 628	Circulation	9-4-18	12 E. River St., Waterloo, N. Y.
HOWARD, James G. Sgt. 1st Cl.	Q. M. C.	Field Agent	8-7-18	866 Walnut St., Alameda, Cal.
HOWELL, Stanley A. Pvt.	304th M. G. Bn.	Transportation	5-29-18	Riverhead, Long Island, N. Y.
HUCK, George C. Sgt.	327th Inf.	Personnel	4-28-19	Grand Forks, N. D.
HUFF, Norman D. Sgt.	Co. C, 112th Am.Tr.	Field Agent	11-2-18	Y. M. C. A., Dayton, Ohio
HUFSTEDLER, Stanley Cpl.	36th Div.	Personnel	4-17-19	Teague, Tex.
HUGGINS, Ernest W. Cpl.	416th R. R. Tel. Bn.	Field Agent	11-11-18	936 Le Claire Ave., Chicago, Ill.
HUMPHREYS, James P. Sgt.	Co. D, 304th Inf.	Soldiers' Serv.	1-8-19	Eagle Rock Ave., West Orange, N. J.
HUNSEHE, Raymond W. Sgt. 1st Cl.	486th Aero Sqn.	Field Agent	10-1-18	336 E. Delevan Ave., Buffalo, N. Y.
HUNT, Dwight G. Sgt.	Hq., 77th Div.	Treasury	7-12-18	108 W. 103rd St., N. Y. C.
ISACKSON, Louis O. Cpl.	333rd F. A.	Circulation	2-15-19	Albert Lea, Minn.
ISEMINGER, Lester D. A. F. C.	A. G. O.	Circulation	——	Hagerstown, Md.
JACOBS, Millard F. Sgt.	Q. M. C.	Field Agent	8- -18	45 Delancey St., N. Y. C.
JENKINS, J. Edwin A. F. C.	A. G. O.	Circulation	4-1-18	Labor Dept., Washington, D. C.
JENTZEN, Herbert Cpl.	M. T. Co. 371	Transportation	5-8-19	Milwaukee, Wis.
JOHNSON, Curtis O. Sgt.	112th Am. Tr.	Field Agent	9-27-18	5828 Goliad St., Dallas, Tex.
JONES, Richard S. R. S. M.	Co. D, 18th Engrs. (Ry.)	Circulation	5-1-18	1216 Harvard Ave. N., Seattle, Wash.
KANE, Charles J. Sgt.	Co. B, 1st Engrs.	Treasury	7-17-18	4804 Baum Blvd., Pittsburgh, Pa.

Name and Rank.	Former Organization.	Dept., S. & S.	Began Work	Home Address.
KATZ, Harry L. Sgt.	Baty. E, 306th F. A.	Mailing	8-2-18	100 Brunswick St., Roxbury, Mass.
KAY, Kendall K. Sgt.	Co. E, 363rd Inf.	Editorial	12-15-18	1140 L St., Eureka, Cal.
KEENAN, William P. Cpl.	76th Div.	Circulation	1-9-19	7 Sackett St., Westfield, Mass.
KELLY, Edward M. Pvt. 1st Cl.	347th F. A.	Circulation	8- -18	516 Capitol St., Valleio, Cal.
KELLY, Frank J. Hosp. Sgt.	Med. Dept.	Circulation	8-7-18	Milwaukee, Wis.
KELLY, J. J. Cpl.	309th Inf.	Treasury	11-2-18	New York City
KENYON, Alden H. Pvt.	12th F. A.	Field Agent	5-1-18	Box 60, R. F. D., S. Westport, Mass.

THE FINAL WALLY STRIP. THE MODELS EMPLOYED, FROM LEFT TO RIGHT (AND, IN SEVERAL INSTANCES, FROM START TO FINISH) ARE RAGS (PROPERTY OF SERGEANT BLISS), PRIVATE ABIAN ANDERS WALLGREN, SERGEANT TYLER H. BLISS, SERGEANT (NÉ PRIVATE) HUDSON HAWLEY, ARMY FIELD CLERK GEORGE W. B. BRITT, SERGEANT SETH T. BAILEY, SECOND LIEUTENANT HILMAR J. BAUKHAGE, SERGEANT WILLIAM F. GERMAIN, SERGEANT ALEXANDER WOOLLCOTT, PRIVATE H. W. ROSS

KETTERMAN, Harry A. Sgt.	90th Aero Sqn.	Treasury	7-17-18	Standard Oil Co., Portland, Ore.
KLEFBECK, Victor B. Sgt.	38th Inf.	Treasury	3-11-18	
KLING, Robert E. Cpl.	1st Depot Div.	Field Agent	7-22-18	Philadelphia, Pa.
KRACKENBERGER, H. W., 2nd Lt., F. A.	140th F. A.	Treasury	2-15-19	W. Terre Haute, Ind.
KRAEBEL, Charles J. 2nd Lt.	18th Engrs.	Field Agent	5-11-18	Portland, Ore.
KRAEMER, George D. Sgt.	165th Inf.	Treasury	7-21-18	Brooklyn, N. Y.
LAMM, Marvin A. Sgt. 1st Cl.	1st Repl. Depot	Transportation	1-20-19	Amarillo, Tex.
LAMMERS, Henry E. Sgt.	Fld. Hosp. No. 161	Transportation	7-26-18	822 Michigan Ave., Sidney, Ohio

Name and Rank.	Former Organization.	Dept., S. & S.	Began Work.	Home Address.
LAMPMAN, Rex H. Pvt.	78th Co., 6th Regt., U. S. M. C.	Editorial	4-7-19	Courier News, Fargo, N. D.
LAVINE, Harry Sgt. 1st Cl.	469th Aero Sqn.	Field Agent	9-4-18	
LAWRENCE, Joseph J. Sgt.	78th Div.	Field Agent	8-12-18	39 3rd St., Newark, N. J.
LEE, John F. Cpl.	16th Engrs.	Circulation	10-15-18	Detroit, Mich.
LEE, Robert E. Pvt.	308th Inf.	Mechanical	7-17-18	419 S. Salisbury St., Raleigh, N. C.
LEEFELDT, Leroy W. Sgt.	Ord. Dept.	Field Agent	8-7-18	617 S. Blvd., Oak Park, Ill.
LEVINE, Max Pvt.	305th F. A.	Field Agent	5-29-18	New York City
LEVY, Max Sgt.	Casual	Treasury	2-14-19	2013 Bryant Ave., The Bronx, N. Y. C.
LICHTENSTEIN, J. H. Sgt.	Q. M. C.	Field Agent	9-27-18	Los Angeles, Cal.
LISTER, P. B. Sgt.	Troop C, 2nd Colo. Cav.	Field Agent	5-11-18	Greeley, Colo.
LONG, Don M. Sgt.	Co. C, 18th Engrs.	Personnel	11-19-18	2536 Bellair St., Denver, Colo.
LUCKETT, Jack G. Sgt.	Co. C, 117th Sup. Tr.	Field Agent	——	Morning Journal, Albuquerque, N. M.
McCOLLUM, W. L. Pvt. 1st Cl.	145th M. G. Bn.	Circulation	5-9-19	Springfield, S. D.
McCOSKRIE, Frank U. 1st Lt.	——	Circulation	4-16-19	Spokane, Wash.
McDERMOTT, Hugh J. Cpl.	11th F. A.	Circulation	10-15-18	103 W. Center St., Butte, Mont.
McDONNELL, John A. Cpl.	Infantry	Circulation	12-1-18	P. O. B. 220, Manette, Wash.
MACK, Willard Capt.	A. G. O.	Circulation	——	Cincinnati, Ohio
MacNICHOL, K. H. Sgt.	Base Hosp. No. 5	Field Agent	5-30-18	6 Beacon St., Boston, Mass.
MAGILL, W. F. Pvt.	113th Engrs.	Editorial	5-7-19	Indianapolis, Ind.
MAHONEY, William H. Pvt. 1st Cl.	504th Engrs.	Circulation	——	New York City
MANSON, Emanuel Cpl.	318th Engrs.	Field Agent	11-2-18	21 Martin St., Rochester, N. Y.
MARSHALL, John L. Pvt. 1st Cl.	23rd Engrs.	Circulation	11-2-18	Rosedale, Kan.
MARTEL, Alfred J. Pvt.	Am. Peace Comm.	Personnel	12-29-18	506 W. 42nd St., N. Y. C.
MARTIN, James D. Cpl.	305th Fld. Hosp.	Field Agent	8-15-18	7 Charles St., Poughkeepsie, N. Y.

Name and Rank.	Former Organization.	Dept., S. & S.	Began Work.	Home Address.
MASON, Carman R. Pvt. 1st Cl.	Med. Dept.	Field Agent	7-17-18	
MATHIS, Frank H. Cpl.	Co. D, 311th Inf.	Editorial	9-10-18	W. Main St., Tuckerton, N. J.
MATTICE, Robert E. Sgt.	102nd Engr. Tr.	Field Agent	8-7-18	532 Broadway, Schenectady, N. Y.
MATURNA, Frank J. Pvt.	Ordnance	Field Agent	9-4-18	
MEDCALFE, Willis T. Cpl.	Base Hosp. No. 36	Field Agent	8-7-18	366 Belvidere Ave., Detroit, Mich.
MERRILL, Frank C. Sgt. 1st Cl.	Med. Dept.	Field Agent	11-17-18	162 College St., Middletown, Conn.
MERRIMAN, Lloyd C. Sgt.	Base Hosp. No. 36	Field Agent	11-14-18	Kenton, Ohio
MICHAEL, William K. 1st Lt., Inf.	101st M. G. Bn.	Advertising	1-20-18	Kansas City, Mo.
MILLER, Craig Sgt.	Co. K, 2nd Tenn. Regt.	Circulation	12-23-18	707 Church Ave., Dyersburg, Tenn.
MILLER, Daniel L. Sgt.	659th Aero Sqn.	Field Agent	11-4-18	305 W. Hamilton Ave., Baltimore, Md.
MILLER, Herman J. Pvt.	29th Engrs.	Mechanical	2-8-18	3367 Couler Ave., Dubuque, Iowa
MILLER, Jacob E. Cpl.	Ry. Tr. Corps	Mailing	10-4-18	2230 W. Estaugh St., Philadelphia, Pa.
MILLER, Joseph A. Cpl.	Co. G, 307th Inf.	Field Agent	——	246 Rugby Rd., Brooklyn, N. Y.
MILLER, Peter Cpl.	151st F. A.	Transportation	2-14-19	Comstock, Minn.
MILLER, William T. A. F. C.	A. G. O.	Circulation	3-1-18	Forest Glen, Md.
MOFFITT, William C. Sgt.	304th M. G. Co.	Treasury	1-9-19	Columbus, Ga.
MORAN, Bruce Cpl.	11th Engrs.	Field Agent	11-12-18	518 W. 182nd St., N. Y. C.
MULVANEY, George E. Sgt.	Ordnance	Advertising	5-1-18	Cincinnati, Ohio
MUMFORD, Philip G. Maj., Q. M. C.	G-2, G. H. Q.	Inspector	3-1-19	New York City
MURPHY, William C. Sgt.	91st Div.	Field Agent	7-14-18	1153 Lewisohn St., Butte, Mont.
MYERS, Alex. J. Sgt.	Co. C, 303rd Inf.	Treasury	10-22-18	72 W. 88th St., N. Y. C.
NICHOLS, A. Hayden Cpl.	Co. A, 356th Inf.	Field Agent	9-14-18	711 N. Rubey St., Macon, Mo.
NICOL, Lawrence Cpl.	1st Repl. Depot	Personnel	1-9-19	San Francisco, Cal.
NORRIS, Lewis M. Pvt.	Baty. A, 1st Kans. F. A.	Field Agent	2-12-19	Raymond, Kan.

Name and Rank.	Former Organization.	Dept., S. & S.	Began Work.	Home Address.
Ochs, Adolph S., II., 1st Lt.	Cavalry	Treasury	2-20-18	Chattanooga, Tenn.
O'Malley, Neil R. Sgt.	Co. A, 2nd Inf.	Circulation	12-22-18	3311 N. Monticello Ave., Chicago, Ill.
Omansky, Jacob Sgt.	5th Inf. Repl.	Field Agent	10-4-18	162 Bowery St., Akron, Ohio
Painter, James W. Pvt.	Hq. Co., 139th F. A.	Field Agent	2-13-19	502 6th St., Bristol, Tenn.
Painton, Frederick Sgt.	496th Aero Sqn.	Field Agent	11-2-18	Elmira, N. Y.
Palmer, Thomas W. Cpl.	18th Engrs. (Ry.)	Circulation	3-4-18	2638 35th Ave., Oakland, Cal.
Parker, Harry L. Capt., A. S. C.	2nd A. A. C., M. G. Bn.	Personnel	1-9-19	200 Irwin Ave., Spartan- burg, S. C.
Parr, John E. Cpl.	Med. Dept.	Circulation	9-11-18	Baltimore, Md.
Parry, Duke N. Cpl.	Base Hosp. No. 28	Field Agent	11-2-18	4009 Harrison St., Kansas City, Mo.
Patrey, Harry B. Sgt.	Base Hosp. No. 9	Circulation	7-27-18	311 Dennis St., Adrian, Mich.
Pendland, William E. Cpl.	485th Aero Sqn.	Field Agent	7-17-18	S. Wayne St., Auburn, Ind.
Penny, George A. Sgt.	Co. B, 309th Inf.	Treasury	11-10-18	20 Gorham St., Buffalo, N. Y.
Pfanner, Robert R. Pvt. 1st Cl.	331st Inf.	Circulation	——	Chicago, Ill.
Phillips, David L. Cpl.	Baty. F, F. A. R. R.	Soldiers' Serv.	2-14-19	N. College St., Yellow Springs, Ohio
Pierson, Jacob Cpl.	Co. L, 330th Inf.	Field Agent	10-4-18	13601 Emily St., Cleveland, Ohio
Plant, Marlowe H. Cpl.	165th Inf.	Transportation	4-11-19	New York City
Post, Levi A. Sgt.	Co. B, 2nd Pioneer Inf.	Soldiers' Serv.	1-8-19	Stanfordville, N. Y.
Prendergast, J. S. Cpl.	Q. M. C.	Field Agent	7-17-18	542 Madison Ave., York, Pa.
Printz, Arthur Sgt.	506th Engrs.	Field Agent	6-19-18	1351 E. Blvd., Cleveland, Ohio
Prosser, Alfred L. R. S. M.	W. R. I. Dept.	Field Agent	5-1-18	314 McDonough St., Brook- lyn, N. Y.
Raddant, George T. Sgt.	Co. C, 110th Engrs.	Field Agent	10-6-18	Shawano, Wis.
Rappaport, Louis A. F. C.	A. G. O.	Personnel	5-1-18	New York City
Rhodes, Wallace W. Sgt.	Amb. Co. 20	Circulation	5-29-18	16 Simpson St., Atlanta, Ga.
Rice, Grantland 1st Lt.	115th F. A.	Editorial	7-5-18	New York Tribune, N.Y.C.

Name and Rank.	Former Organization.	Dept., S. & S.	Began Work.	Home Address.
RICHARD, Jesse L. Sgt.	Infantry	Personnel	7-23-18	Waco, Tex.
RIGNEY, Frank P. Cpl.	103rd F. A.	Circulation	9-4-18	Providence, R. I.
RILEY, Earl E. Sgt.	9th Inf.	Circulation	5-29-18	829 L St., Lincoln, Nebr.
RILEY, James F. Pvt.	——	Circulation	——	
ROCK, Dallas Pvt.	61st Inf.	Circulation	4-7-19	Morrisonville, N. Y.
RODD, Harry C. Sgt.	102nd M. G. Bn.	Field Agent	——	
ROGERS, Wilson B. S. M.	5th Bn., F. A. R. R.	Editorial	12-18-18	Baltimore Sun, Baltimore, Md.
ROSS, Harold W. Pvt.	18th Engrs. (Ry.)	Editorial	2-15-18	622 Elizabeth St., Salt Lake City, Utah
ROWE, Walter S. R. S. M.	136th F. A.	Personnel	10-30-18	Hamilton Club, Hamilton, Ohio
RUBLE, Lloyd J. 1st Sgt.	502nd Engrs.	Transportation	5-29-18	Amity, Ore.
RYAN, Patrick J. Pvt.	168th Inf.	Circulation	7-17-18	New York City
RYDER, Clayton M. Sgt.	22nd Fld. Sig. Bn.	Field Agent	8-10-18	201 Walnut St., Minneapolis, Minn.
RYDER, Melvin R. S. M.	Hist. Sect., S. O. S.	Field Agent	5-24-18	538 N. 5th St., Steubenville, Ohio
SANGSTER, George M. Sgt.	Co. F, 305th Inf.	Field Agent	9-4-18	321 Jefferson Ave., Brooklyn, N. Y.
SCHALLENBERGER, Geo. Sgt.	M. T. C.	Transportation	8—-18	Miami, Fla.
SCHENECK, Ferdinand Sgt.	306th Inf.	Treasury	11-2-18	
SCHIEBLE, Raymond M. Cpl.	149th F. A.	Field Agent	2-15-19	4157 N. Leamington Ave., Chicago, Ill.
SCHNEIDER, Harry Cpl.	Infantry	Field Agent	5-1-18	San Francisco, Cal.
SCHNEIDER, M. H. Pvt.	A. S. C.	Transportation	5-8-18	
SCHWARTZ, Fred Pvt. 1st Cl.	463rd Motorcycle Co.	Field Agent	8-7-18	New York City
SCHWARTZKOPF, Otto Pvt.	A. S. C.	Circulation	5-10-19	Lyndhurst, Wis.
SCOTT, J. John Sgt.	303rd Inf.	Personnel	1-8-19	164 Division St., Amsterdam, N. Y.
SHEPARD, Herbert O. Cpl.	302nd Inf.	Mailing	1-9-19	Wrentham, Mass.
SIGMUND, Harold Sgt.	328th Inf.	Advertising	8-16-18	361 W. 56th St., N. Y. C.

Name and Rank.	Former Organization.	Dept., S. & S.	Began Work.	Home Address.
SIGWALT, Harold P. Sgt.	Q. M. C.	Field Agent	8-7-18	3326 Sycamore St., Milwaukee, Wis.
SLAGHT, Arthur J. Cpl.	363rd Inf.	Field Agent	9-27-18	2512 E. 15th St., Oakland, Cal.
SLATOR, William J. Sgt. 1st Cl.	Med. Dept.	Field Agent	9-27-18	New Haven, Conn.
SMALLEY, F. J. Sgt.	Q. M. C.	Treasury	5-13-19	153 S. Normandie Ave., Los Angeles, Cal.
SMITH, Harley A. 2nd Lt.	59th Inf.	Circulation	4-5-19	Hamilton, Ala.
SMITH, Homer S. A. F. C.	A. G. O.	Soldiers' Serv.	3-1-18	Pawnee City, Nebr.
SMITH, J. W. Rixey Sgt.	Med. Dept.	Editorial	1-13-19	Basic City, Va.
SMITH, Leslie H. Cpl.	164th Inf.	Circulation	11-2-18	
SNAJDR, Robert I. Sgt.	308th Am. Tr.	Editorial	11-11-18	7505 Lawnview Ave. N. E., Cleveland, Ohio
SNEVILY, Henry N. 1st Lt.	1st A. A. M. G. Co.	Personnel	——	New York City
SPAHR, Clarence E. Pvt.	344th M. G. Bn.	Field Agent	9-4-18	San Diego, Cal.
SPIERO, Gerald B. Cpl.	52nd Pion. Inf.	Field Agent	11-20-18	654 W. 161st St., N. Y. C.
STACK, Robert M. Pvt.	23rd Engrs.	Circulation	12-16-18	
STANLEY, Harold B. Sgt.	148th F. A.	Field Agent	7-17-18	Rocky Ford, Colo.
STEPPE, Joseph H. Cpl.	155th Inf.	Personnel	5-10-19	St. Louis, Mo.
STERRETT, David R. R. S. M.	163rd Inf.	Treasury	6-18-18	915 Manhattan St., Pittsburgh, Pa.
STONER, Harry Pvt.	16th Engrs.	Soldiers' Serv.	——	414 Fairview Ave., Gallion, Ohio
STOUT, Thomas W. Cpl.	18th Inf.	Circulation	5-29-18	720 S. Douglas Ave., Springfield, Ill.
STUARDI, Norman E. Sgt.	60th C. A. C.	Field Agent	10-1-18	Springhill and College Sts., Mobile, Ala.
STURR, Thomas W. Pvt.	23rd Engrs.	Mechanical	9-4-18	1578 Oakland Ave., Springfield, Ohio
SULLIVAN, David F. Cpl.	Q. M. C.	Field Agent	8-11-18	4 Hale St., Worcester, Mass.
SUNDIN, Hjalmar Pvt.	102nd F. A.	Personnel	9-5-18	New Bedford, Mass.
SWEENEY, Arthur V. Sgt.	103rd F. A.	Field Agent	3-14-18	103 America St., Providence, R. I.
THOMAS, A. R. Sgt.	649th Aero Sqn.	Circulation	5-6-19	

Name and Rank.	Former Organization.	Dept., S. & S.	Began Work.	Home Address.
Tostevin, Earle H. Pvt. 1st Cl.	164th Inf.	Circulation	7-25-18	Mandan, N. D.
Truslow, Harold M. Sgt.	49th Inf.	Field Agent	10-1-18	391 Bainbridge St., Brooklyn, N. Y.
Tuck, William Cpl.	304th Inf.	Mailing	1-18-19	432 W. Main St., Waterbury, Conn.
Tyler, S. L. 2nd Lt.	Infantry	Circulation	——	Memphis, Tenn.
Van Hoose, Hershell Sgt.	1st Repl. Depot	Field Agent	5- -18	Atlanta, Ga.
Van Horn, Archie M. 2nd Lt.	129th Inf.	Circulation	2-20-19	417 Garfield Ave., Aurora, Ill.
Vance, George K. Cpl.	Ord. Dept.	Field Agent	5-19-18	Kokomo, Ind.
Vieau, Erne Sgt.	320th Sup. Co., Q. M. C.	Field Agent	11-2-18	The Bulletin, San Francisco, Cal.
Viehman, Carl E. Cpl.	319th Inf.	Circulation	12-23-18	113 Park Way, Garrick, Pa.
Viskniskki, Guy T. Maj. Inf.	320th Inf.	Officer in Charge	1-10-18	Montclair, N. J.
Von Blon, Philip R. S. M.	Base Hosp. No. 4	Editorial	7-25-18	Upper Sandusky, Ohio
Vroom, Clifford H. R. S. M.	Fld. Hosp. No. 104	Treasury	7-29-18	8 Center St., Exeter, N. H.
Waldo, Richard H. Capt.	W. R. I.	Circulation	4-1-18	City Club, 55 W. 44th St., N. Y. C.
Walker, Raymond E. Pvt.	116th Engrs.	Mechanical	7-23-18	1636 E. Hattie St., Fort Worth, Tex.
Wallace, H. H. Cpl.	Q. M. Det., 89th Div.	Personnel	4-30-19	Brockport, N. Y.
Wallgren, Abian A. Pvt.	Sup. Co., 5th Rgt., U. S. M. C.	Art	1-20-18	1208 S. 52nd St., Philadelphia, Pa.
Walsh, David J. Cpl.	102nd F. A.	Mechanical	9-18-19	94 Franklin St., Arlington, Mass.
Walsh, Peter C. Sgt.	S. S. U. 552	Field Agent	——	735 S. Orange Ave., Newark, N. J.
Waltman, William C. 2nd Lt.	Ord. Dept.	Treasury	3-8-19	634 N. 16th St., Philadelphia, Pa.
Walty, Francis J. R. S. M.	A. S. C.	Circulation	5-11-18	Dorranceton, Pa.
Warren, Charles J. Cpl.	18th F. A.	Circulation	6-1-18	Washington, D. C.
Warlick, Bernie C. Cpl.	359th Inf.	Field Agent	10-1-18	911 W. 10th St., Dallas, Tex.
Warner, Clifford T. Sgt.	S. S. U. 38	Field Agent	9-19-18	Danville, Ind.
Watson, Joseph H. Cpl.	Casual	Treasury	2-17-19	Lamar, S. C.

Name and Rank.	Former Organization.	Dept., S. & S.	Began Work.	Home Address.
WATSON, Mark S. Maj. F. A.	340th F. A.	Off'r in Charge	11-29-18	1223 E. 50th St., Chicago, Ill.
WEESNER, Edward J. Sgt.	1st Ind. F. A.	Field Agent	9-12-18	Clayton, Ind.
WEINSTEIN, Jacob Sgt.	29th Engrs.	Personnel	2-10-18	596 Schenck Ave., Brooklyn, N. Y.
WESSELLS, G. W., Jr. Sgt. 1st Cl.	57th Aero Sqn.	Treasury	10-1-18	125 Magnolia Ave., Jersey City, N. J.
WHITE, Egbert G. R. S. M.	Signal R. C.	Treasury	8-1-18	6135 Jackson St., Pittsburgh, Pa.
WHITE, Ernest F. Cpl.	465th Aero Sqn.	Field Agent	9-4-18	Atlanta, Ga.
WHITTLE, William E. R. S. M.	Hq., 82nd Div.	Treasury	12-15-18	Chattanooga, Tenn.
WIENER, Robert Cpl.	S. S. U. 510	Circulation	8-7-18	6 Sacramento St., Cambridge, Mass.
WILLIAMS, Oscar G. Sgt.	Co. C, 9th Sig. Bn.	Mechanical	9-25-18	Temple Telegram, Temple, Tex.
WILLOUGHBY, Geoffrey Pvt. 1st Cl.	107th Fld. Sig. Bn.	Circulation	11-2-18	
WILSON, Albert C. R. S. M.	18th Engrs. (Ry.)	Field Agent	5-11-18	1015 Doris St., Los Angeles, Cal.
WILSON, Howard M. 2nd Lt., Inf.	6th Div.	Personnel	10-1-18	Waco, Tex.
WILSON, Lee M. Pvt.	F. A. Repl.	Circulation	2-14-19	328 Fulton St., Chicago, Ill.
WINKEL, Raymond Cpl.	463rd Motorcycle Co.	Field Agent	8-15-18	5743 Oak Ave., Indianapolis, Ind.
WINSTON, Leo A. Sgt.	504th Engrs.	Circulation	4- -18	1515 2nd St., E. Menomonie, Wis.
WINTERICH, John T. Pvt.	496th Aero Sqn.	Editorial	2-17-18	467 Plainfield St., Providence, R. I.
WOOLLCOTT, Alexander Sgt.	Base Hosp. No. 8	Editorial	2-28-18	Phalanx, N. J.
WORLEY, Nathaniel T. Sgt.	11th Engrs.	Editorial	11-2-18	715 19th St., N. W., Washington, D. C.
WRENCH, George P. Cpl.	Signal Corps	International Courier	3-14-18	Thomasville, Ga.
YOUNG, King D. Pvt. 1st Cl.	1st Idaho Fld. Hosp.	Transportation	1-31-19	Filer, Idaho
ZIMMERMAN, Chas. W. Cpl.	Med. Dept.	Field Agent	——	Boston, Mass.

DISMISSED